Strengthening *Music Ministry*

in the Evangelical Church

CALVIN M. JOHANSSON

WESTBOW
PRESS®
A DIVISION OF THOMAS NELSON
& ZONDERVAN

WestBow Press books may be ordered through booksellers or by contacting:

WestBow Press
A Division of Thomas Nelson & Zondervan
1663 Liberty Drive
Bloomington, IN 47403
www.westbowpress.com
1 (866) 928-1240

ISBN: 978-1-9736-4301-2 (sc)
ISBN: 978-1-9736-4302-9 (hc)
ISBN: 978-1-9736-4300-5 (e)

Library of Congress Control Number: 2018912573

Print information available on the last page.

WestBow Press rev. date: 1/11/2019

Table of Contents

Prologue ix

Author's Note xi

PART I

Chapter 1   Visiting 1

Chapter 2   Evangelicals 20

Chapter 3   Strengthening Music Ministry in
             Evangelical Worship 33

Chapter 4   Furthering the Reach of the Church's
             Music Ministry 76

PART II

Chapter 5   Culture and Religious Popular Music 111

Chapter 6   Music 140

Chapter 7   Church Music and Aesthetics:
             Theological Insights 161

Chapter 8   Scriptural Discernment Extended 192

Epilogue 223

Subject Index 225

Prologue

T he fast-paced rate of societal change bidding the evangelical church to move with the times continues unabated. Church music, faced with the march of a culture largely out of step with the basic tenets of the Christian faith, needs frequent review and shoring up. Whatever style and format worship might take in the future, its music will need to be examined and discipled in the light of Scripture. This present work is offered as an aid in those endeavors.

Part I consists of four chapters: (1) Visiting (2) Evangelicals (3) Strengthening Music Ministry in Evangelical Worship and (4) Furthering the Reach of the Church's Music Ministry. This section, concerned with practics, chronicles my church visitations, defines the term *evangelical*, and makes specific suggestions for strengthening the music ministry of the evangelical church.

Part II hosts four chapters: (5) Culture and Religious Popular Music (6) Music (7) Church Music and Aesthetics: Theological Insights and (8) Scriptural Discernment Extended. This division examines Christian contemporary music in some depth. It delves into the aesthetics of music and digs deep into the Scriptures for guidance in carrying out music ministry.

Part II supplies the rationale for implementing Part I. Theological and philosophical, Part II makes a compelling case for building up the music ministry of the evangelical church along the lines of Part I. Ultimately it is God's Word that empowers church music to reach its full potential in any given place.

My writing of this book postulates accepting the present

reality of evangelical music-making with grace and respect. I offer to each musician and church leader these old/new thoughts with the hope and prayer that they will be valuable in helping to fulfill each leader's pastoral/musical calling. Expanding the kingdom, maturing the saints, and glorifying God are objectives worthy of our best efforts.

To that end these pages are dedicated.

Author's Note

Throughout this work the reader will find that key theological, philosophic, and aesthetic concepts, terms, and assumptions are very often restated from chapter to chapter, as well as within individual chapters. These commonalities, bringing their own specific contribution to each chapter's general topic, give a comprehensive unity to the book. I believe such redundancy will be of assistance in the overall assimilation of the central themes contained in the text.

Commonly repeated keywords and subject matter include the following:

Taste	Relativism
Value	Worldview
Muzak	Postmodern
Culture	Rock, CCM
Worship	Pop, popular
Nihilism	Post-Christian
Pluralism	Entertainment
Aesthetics	Subjective/objective
Relevancy	Judeo-Christian theism

PART I

1   Visiting

I t was Sunday morning. In the east a few faint rays of the morning sun managed to break through the cloudy, threatening, overcast sky. I was on my way to visit the morning service of a church unfamiliar to me. Months before, in talking with an acquaintance, I had gleaned from our conversation that this was his home church and, although he had not invited me to attend, my curiosity was piqued—not so much by what he said about it, but by what I knew of him. *Why would he choose to attend this particular church?* I mused. He was a man of learning and obvious intellectual attainment.

As I drove into the parking lot, I noted the carefully manicured islands that divided the lot into sections. Tall light poles were spaced evenly on each island, along with an attractive array of ornamental shrubbery. On each pole was mounted an outdoor loudspeaker from which emanated a not especially subtle species of muzak.[1] It was the first time I could recall arriving for a Sunday service to popular music—religious or not, I could not ascertain—broadcast to the incoming faithful. Somebody had set all of this up. A matter of careful foresight and planning, it obviously did not just happen by itself.

Leaving my car and making my way to the entrance of the church, I pondered what I was experiencing aurally. Was it a matter of being novel or of one-upmanship from the church down the road? Or perhaps the local supermarket's audio ambience had become so normal that such was thought to be

---

[1] Muzak, a registered trademark of MUZAK LLC, is a brand of background music. Its name has come into common usage and simply refers to both pre-recorded and live music used as background.

required here. Then again, was it just a sincere desire to put people in the mood for the coming service? It could, of course, be simply background music to fill the void of silence between car and church entrance. As a newcomer experiencing this audio welcome for the first time, I was not sure how to react. I wanted to be in a good frame of mind for the coming service. So in spite of a certain unease, I did my best to focus on the immediate future rather than the momentary present.

Entering the church foyer was a pleasant experience. At the door were two sets of enthusiastic greeters. As I shook hands with the couple immediately at hand, I was bombarded with questions: was I a newcomer; what was my name; where was I from; would I like a cup of coffee and a doughnut? I responded to each friendly query as best I could and then moved on into the foyer.

Another couple interrupted my walk across the floor and introduced me to the morning's coffee host. Shouting over the "background" music and the abundant good-natured bantering between friends, I again answered the obligatory questions and was offered a cup of coffee and a wonderfully tempting glazed doughnut of pure carbohydrate. Declining both, I accepted a small bottle of water, which I slipped into my pocket. I then followed a few worshipers on into the auditorium, where an usher supplied each of us with the paper handout of the day.

It would be normal to report that one's first impression upon entering a new place of worship would be visual. Mine was aural. The parking lot muzak had nothing over what was broadcast here. The sheer volume of sound was so overpowering that conversation was not possible unless a person resorted to shouting. Looking around, I noted a high side table to my right on which sat a number of items relating to the life of the church: papers of various sorts, sign-up sheets, a cup of coffee stirrers, sugar packets, and creamers. One thing especially caught my eye: a container of foam ear plugs. Taken somewhat aback, I helped myself to a package, found a seat toward the back of the room, and sat down.

Inserting the hearing protectors, I took my first real look around. The walls and ceiling were painted entirely in black. The ceiling lights had been dimmed, no doubt to aid in viewing the two wall screens on the right and left, plus a center screen high on the front wall. There were no windows. The room was very dark. There was an audiovisual booth at the back of the auditorium that took up about two-thirds the width of the room. Three technicians, eyes glued to their computer screens, appeared to be getting ready for the coming service. In the center of the back wall, another screen had been mounted as an aid to platform personnel as they ministered to the congregation. There were no visual evidences of the devotional purpose of the building—no cross, no altar, no communion table, no art of any sort.

The screens displayed an endless loop of congregational announcements interspersed with extended lengths of pastoral scenes from the natural world. The announcements, well written and precise, scrolled through fairly rapidly. I noted that not all the announcements on the screen were included in the handout given to me upon entering. The membership, which as I looked around seemed mostly middle-aged or younger, obviously had multiple opportunities to be active in the church on many levels and in many different ways.

Suddenly the screens became solidly, stunningly white. The background music ceased. Silence reigned. Nine musicians moved from behind the curtains and made their way onto the platform to their assigned microphones and music stands: four singers, four instrumentalists, and a percussionist whose drum set was positioned in an isolation cage at rear center stage.

While this was taking place, there appeared from behind the drapes on both the right and left side of the platform huge amounts of fog or smoke that rolled out onto the stage in great billowing clouds. This was new to me! Taken aback and not comprehending what was going on, I was further puzzled by the appearance of bright, multicolored, flashing lights. Some of these were muted, filtered through the swirling layers of fog.

Others with the direct intensity of strobe lights burst directly into the auditorium, setting it ablaze with blinding, scintillating spangles of colored incandescence.

The screens were showing a one-minute, second-by-second countdown. When zero had been reached, a huge, black bull's-eye exploded onto the screen simultaneously with an even greater explosive blast from the drummer—a shocking outburst obviously designed to get my attention. Joined by the instrumentalists, and eventually the vocalists with the lead singer getting the congregation on its feet, the group performed its morning repertoire for the next twenty-one minutes. We stood through it all.

The style of the music being performed would be appropriate for any popular music venue. It was loud to the point of being painful and, should the truth be known, textually unintelligible. Hence it was a good thing that the words of the songs were shown to the congregation line by line via the three projection screens. The room was dry acoustically, having no discernable reverberation.

The clear intent of the performing group was to have the congregation join them in their songs. In reality this did not happen. The ambient decibel level was so high that no one could possibly hear himself or his neighbor sing even if he had a mind to. I tried to follow, but failed. Not knowing any of the songs, I might have given it another try had I had access to the music.

As I looked around I noted that no one, with the exception of a few who appeared to move their lips (my not being able to hear them), was singing. As a worshiping community, this exercise was definitely not congregational. People just looked up and stared at the singers. Some watched the video screens; a few moved rhythmically to the music by clapping or bouncing from one foot to the other; some raised their hands. In a way, the congregation acted as if a show was taking place on a stage: they an audience, the band an assemblage of entertainers. Surprisingly, almost no one sat down before this part of the service was over. But I found that standing that long did require stamina.

The morning's musical offering was highly repetitious. Each song was sung over and over again until it eventually gave way to the next tune in one long, seamless string. The texts were varied, but the overall central theme was subjectively introspective, focusing on the self and on personal individuality in relationship to God. The melodies of the music being sung were highly syncopated and filled with an abundance of the current vocal ornaments now in vogue. The vocal quality was strident and harsh, quite in step with what one might expect to hear from a leading pop vocalist, rap singer, or rock and roll performer. The harmony was nonconventional, even simplistic at times. Rhythm was driving, continually pulsating, and invariably toe tapping. As an ensemble, they were well rehearsed, executing their arrangements with precision and professional flair. All told, their presentation was impressive. The music itself was wild.

Toward the end of the twenty-one-minute time slot, the band slowed down the pace of the music somewhat. They became quieter and a hairsbreadth more tranquil in preparation for the associate pastor's prayer. When he concluded praying, he gave the announcements, and the band played a number while the offering was being taken.

Now I was in for another surprise. As the last sounds of the band's offertory faded away a huge movie screen was lowered. *What, a video?* I thought. *All of this and we just get a canned visual? Surely not!* But as it turned out, it was not a recording. What we were looking at and listening to was the pastor sure enough. Larger than life, he was giving his sermon in real time at another location and broadcast our way via satellite technology.[2] It didn't take long to realize that we were being treated to a carefully crafted and professionally delivered sermon. He was eloquent and articulate without any sense of haughtiness or

---

[2] Three-dimensional holographic projection imagery, a newer technology, is also being used.

superiority. To my own discredit, I honestly cannot remember the subject. But I do remember my impression; he was smooth and easy to listen to. And he had the knack of making me think that he was talking directly to me in spite of the fact that he was not physically present.

When he finished, the large screen was retracted and the band returned for another number. As the concluding notes died away, the congregation was dismissed by the band leader with a shouted, "Have a good week." The service was over.

The muzak returned immediately, as loud and as intrusive as ever. The operators of the audio and visual equipment had not missed a cue all morning.

As I left the building, my mind was as cloudy as the overcast sky above. Had I been to church? I was not sure. During the service, dim shafts of sunlight had come through to me from time to time, but on the whole it was difficult to reconcile the incongruity of the show-biz entertainment I had experienced with the worship of almighty God. It was not that I didn't know my own mind. What I struggled with was trying to understand the rationale—especially from a biblical perspective—of those who advocate and practice such an approach to the Christian life and Christian worship.

The apparent success of large congregations such as this one is no doubt the result of many factors. But not inconsequential among them is the part that the worship service plays in attracting people. Professionally produced contemporary music complete with religious lyrics and popular style appear characteristic. At home with one another, "The distinctions between secular and sacred are often minimal at best. Such blurring is easily seen in the use of technology and pop cultural influences in the services. Recent movies are often used as examples in sermons; contemporary Christian music in the service could easily be heard on the radio or at a Grammy Awards show."[3] All in all,

---

[3] Scott Thumma and Dave Travis, *Beyond Megachurch Myths* (San Francisco: Wiley, 2007), 16.

worship presents itself as a kind of divertissement, entertaining and friendly.

The Wider Field

Visiting many different churches these last several years has deepened my knowledge of the current direction of the evangelical church-music movement. I was not unfamiliar with evangelicalism, having been a staunch adherent since my youth. But the churches with which I had been associated were never at the cutting edge of evangelical evolvement. What I wanted to ascertain was the present course of the movement as a whole. How was it changing and what effect did the changes have on congregational worship?

To that end I joined in the worship of many congregations over the span of about five years. Some were limited in size, the smallest being a church with a Sunday morning attendance of five, including the pastor. Some were megachurches of thousands with services on Saturday night and multiple services on Sunday morning. Most were congregations of average size from about one hundred to five hundred. Many congregations had a denominational connection; others were stand-alone independent works. There were also churches affiliated with organizational entities of the type that disavowed any semblance of traditional denominational structure. All were racially diverse and, as far as I could tell, socioeconomically mixed. Many churches had multiple staff, though I was not always able to tell whether or not all staff were paid. Most congregations still retained specific learning opportunities for children, and almost all offered a children's church program for ages five to twelve. Located north and south, east and west, some were urban, others rural. Several I found on TV and the internet.

In 2008 Beacon Press published a book by Suzanne Strempek Shea, *Sundays in America: A Yearlong Road Trip in Search of Christian Faith*, that chronicled the author's mission of surveying the broad diversity of American protestantism. One finding noted by the author concerned music in worship. She wrote, "I have been fascinated by the presence of electrified bands in most of the churches I've visited since Resurrection Sunday."[4] Her observation clearly underscores the change in attitude, decades in the making, toward the use of the organ, piano, and hymn singing in worship. Once staples, it is clear that other options are crowding the gallery. In addition, many mainline denominational churches are now offering a "contemporary service" to compete with the "traditional" service. Choosing one or the other is a matter of the worshipers' preference and taste.

Her trip then, not limited to evangelical houses of faith, shows contemporary music as a possible repertoire choice for the rank and file of protestant churches. Not confined to churches "on the other side of the tracks," Christian contemporary music (CCM) is fully ensconced to some degree in the very warp and woof of present-day protestantism.

So, mainline churches, historically bastions of tradition, presently furnish nontraditional music as an option in their various worship offerings—but only as an option. Evangelicals, on the other hand, have long used forms of popular music. Hence they have not needed to make an extraordinary, atypical place for religious contemporary musical fare (though for some individual evangelicals the actual move to CCM has been disquieting and distressing). The reason for this is telling.

Sixty years in the making, evangelical churches evolved from a gospel song and chorus structure accompanied by organ/ piano,[5] to a CCM[6] format accompanied by a pop band. The musical differences between the two appear enormous, though perhaps not as different as it might seem on the surface.

---

[4] Suzanne Strempek Shea, *Sundays in America: A Yearlong Road Trip in Search of Christian Faith* (Boston: Beacon Press, 2008), 271.

[5] In some places an instrumental group was added to the piano and/or organ accompaniment.

[6] Christian contemporary music (CCM) or contemporary Christian music. Other designations are Christian worship music (CWM), praise and worship (P&W), or just contemporary music.

Moving On

The gospel song was a 19th- and early 20th-century type of religious popular music not incompatible with the secular popular music of the day. These gospel melodies were for the most part light and bouncy, sprinkled throughout with couplets of dotted eighths and sixteenths or other pulse-stimulating combinations. They had a toe-tapping rhythm that encouraged enthusiastic hand clapping, particularly during the singing of the chorus, when the hymnal could be laid aside until the singing of the next stanza. These gospel tunes were not as musically weighty as those found in normative hymnody. Compare the music of Martin Luther's hymn "A Mighty Fortress Is Our God" to William Doane's gospel song "To God Be the Glory;" or Joachim Neander's "He Is Risen, He Is Risen!" to the waltz-like "He Lives" of Homer Rodeheaver. Set side by side, we can readily see (hear) that, musically speaking, the gospel song is considerably more airy and breezy than its hymnic counterpart. The gospel song was not incompatible with the era's popular music.

The die having been cast, evangelical religious music continued to follow secular pop trends. In the years immediately following World War II, secular popular music changed radically with the advent of rock and roll. And it was not long before religious versions of the new style were formulated and gradually absorbed by segments of the evangelical church. As the years passed, the rate of change increased as an avalanche of churches embraced the new music and made it their own. Having begun slowly in the 1960s, Christian contemporary music eventually became the predominant music of evangelical worshipers.

However, there are rumblings today that contemporary worship has run its course. Just as traditional evangelical worship gave way to contemporary worship, some believe contemporary worship must now move over in favor of an "experiential worship experience."[7] Exactly what the term "experiential worship experience" entails remains unclear. But one thing is certain: the words *experiential* and *experience* mean *participation*. Evangelical worshipers of tomorrow will need to become more active and less passive; more involved and less laid-back; more vocal and less closemouthed; more congregationally orientated and less stage orientated; and, as concerns singing, more wholeheartedly enthusiastic and less serenely dispassionate.

Over the last few years, my travels have unquestionably (with few exceptions) borne out the fact that present evangelical worship is characteristically contemporary. Hence, it is accurate to assert that the universal musical genre of evangelicalism is its identification with, and adoption of, contemporary Christian music. A *fait accompli*, the music of evangelicals is now CCM, period.

The change from gospel hymnody to 20th-century popular music was not accomplished without a sense of loss by many in the evangelical movement. Dozens of books railed against the evils of rock and roll, both secular and religious. Magazines were filled with articles pro and con, and letters to editors abounded. Eventually, at one point, I recall the editor of a prominent religious periodical stating that the topic had been explored thoroughly enough and that the subject was now closed. As a prophetic statement, that was indeed the case. Academics aside, CCM won the day.[8]

Two Transitions

Except for objections by traditional musicians, the move to CCM by individual churches was largely accomplished

[7] Chris Railey, "Is Experiential Becoming the New Contemporary?" *Influence*, no. 12 (June–July 2017): 8.
[8] From time to time there are expressed uncertainties about the CCM movement. For example, Donn LeVie Jr.'s decision to leave contemporary Christian music and embrace sacred, traditional music for worship is reasoned out in his penetrating book *It's All About Hymn: Essays on Reclaiming Sacred and Traditional Music for Worship* (Austin, TX: Kings Crown Publishing, 2011). Similarly, Dan Lucarini's *Why I Left the Contemporary Christian Music Movement* (Webster, NY: EP Books, 2002) explains the author's rationale behind his departure from the world of contemporary Christian music.

without major upheaval. Seeker-sensitive pastor Rick Warren of Saddleback Community Church in Mission Viejo, California, expressed the emerging viewpoint of most evangelical leaders and pastors when he wrote:

> When I first started Saddleback, we tried to appeal to all musical tastes. We'd go "from Bach to Rock." We'd use a hymn, then a praise chorus, then a classical number, then jazz, then easy listening, then rap. We ran the spectrum. We alienated everyone. Any radio station that tried to appeal to everyone would go broke.
>
> So I took a survey and asked, "What radio station do you listen to?" Ninety-seven percent listed a contemporary adult middle-of-the-road rock station. So we unapologetically use that style. We've driven off some potential members but have attracted many more who relate to that sound.
>
> I believe music style is the single greatest positioning factor in a local church, even more than preaching style. It determines whom you attract. Tell me your style of music, and I will tell you whom you're reaching and whom you will never reach. The moment you define your music, you position your church.[9]

The changeover in the church of my youth was typical of many established congregations. Newer congregations generally began with Christian contemporary music right from the very beginning. The assembly in which I had grown up had for some years employed an older pastor along with the services of his wife, a gifted and accomplished pianist and choir leader. She used well the church's fine grand piano for service music, solo work, and for accompanying the choir and congregation. The music of the church was traditional: evangelical in style with the usual complement of hymnals in the pew racks and a choir which graced worship with well-rehearsed praise.

When the minister retired, a younger man became the pastor. His predilection was to adopt contemporary music and discard traditional fare. And so, after a couple of years and without a congregational vote, CCM was installed as the music

---

[9] Rick Warren, "On a Niche Hunt," *Leadership, A Practical Journal for Church Leaders* XIV, no. 2 (Spring 1993).

of the church. The piano was given away, the hymnals removed, and a contemporary band established without so much as an ecclesiastical shot being fired.

Variety

Some congregations utilized what was termed convergence or blended worship in which traditional and contemporary musical genres were mingled. But my impression remains: blended worship has often been but a brief hiatus on the way to full CCM adoption.

Churches that use CCM often design their services utilizing a binary framework. I found that most of the evangelistic assemblages I attended used this form, their services containing (1) an extended time of singing (twenty minutes or so, congregation standing) followed by (2) the sermon.

One of the 2,000-member churches I observed utilized a variant of this model. This particular church employed the basic binary structure but embellished it by adding two components: a choir offertory and a pastoral prayer. The words of the congregational songs, two lines at a time, were flashed on the large screens at the front. Most of the contemporary songs seemed unfamiliar to the people and were not sung well. The one hymn fared marginally better.

The music director drew many instrumentalists from the sizeable congregation to play in what we might term an "orchestral band" of about forty players: one violin, two oboes, three clarinets, three flutes, one piccolo, six saxophones, multiple brass, an amplified grand piano, and an enormous drum set. The vocal praise ensemble of four women and two men was augmented by a good-sized choir, which sang special music for each service, usually during the offertory.

The contemporary music programmed was not a surprise. What was a surprise was the limited participation by the congregation. With a full complement of instruments and a large choir, I would have expected more of an effort by the

1,200 people present. As one song melded into the next, I found myself very much in league with them, for I too did not know the songs being rendered so energetically by the platform participants. Moreover, I could not discern the tune and, not having the music in front of me, was very much shut out from any participation at all.

I was in a frame of mindlessness, glazed eyes staring at the stage, when I heard the strains of a familiar hymn. Brought back to the present, I realized that we were about to embark upon the singing of a known entity. I took a deep breath and prepared to join in with the choir, praise team, and fellow believers in singing Edward Perronet's "All Hail the Power of Jesus' Name" (to the tune "Coronation").

People began to sing. I joined them and then faltered. The tune I knew had been altered rhythmically and melodically to make it more like CCM style. But those around me seemed OK with it. Obviously they had sung this version enough to make it familiar. I continued. With a pounding backbeat which gave a rather cheeky feel to this otherwise stately hymn, the percussionist led the pack. When we arrived at the last note of the first stanza, the musicians moved right on in forced-march style. We had no recourse but to follow. One, TWO, three, FOUR, and we were at the beginning of stanza two. Christian contemporary style had struck classic hymnody!

Throughout that morning most songs were unfamiliar to me. What was familiar, however, was the quest of the music leader to "play" the congregation, directing and altering at will their emotional state. Moving people toward a particular end has long been a customary *modus operandi* of evangelical music-making. Ecstasy to introspection, exuberant praise to sorrowful passion, rapture to reverence, exultation to earnestness and all emotions and frames of mind in between, are at the beck and call of the music director.

Choosing and putting the requisite songs in an order that achieves the desired end is one of the proficiencies every successful music leader must possess. In this particular service

we moved from snappy, upbeat, happy-go-lucky clapping music
to a more respectful, dignified, stately tone, then on to a more
introspective yet rhythmic beat, and finally we arrived at a
reverential mood, which morphed into a time of prayer led by
the pastor. As an evangelical, this methodology was familiar
to me. Music has always been used to direct and manage the
affective state of the people. Knowing what outcomes were
desired, musicians made every effort to bring about the desired
result. In his award-winning book, *Heaven Below: Early
Pentecostals and American Culture*, Grant Wacker shows that
singing was central to Pentecostal meetings and was used to
lead the congregation. He cites David Martin:

> Music offered leaders a ready means for managing the intensity
> of the service. They could ratchet up the tempo until worshipers
> broke into ecstatic praise, or tone it down when things seemed to
> be getting out of hand. Either way, music gave leaders a tool for
> regularizing the expression of emotion.[10]

Credit must be given the music director of the church I
visited that morning. To find music to achieve the desired
psychological progression of the song service, to recruit so many
musicians, and to coordinate rehearsals for the choir, praise
ensemble, and orchestra week after week would be an immense
task. And the groups performed well. Of course, a single violin
pitted against an entire brass section had little chance of being
heard. But in this case the director had found a remedy by
providing a microphone for the one lone stringed instrument.
The choir sang an anthem that was well within their grasp,
and their rendition of the CCM songs was compatible with the
performance of the razor-sharp praise team.

I found that the use of contemporary worship music,
widespread as it is, is nevertheless very much a matter of local
usage. The various styles of CCM, the varied instrumentation,
the physical demeanor of the worship team, the decibel level

---

[10] Grant Wacker, *Heaven Below: Early Pentecostals and American Culture* (Cambridge,
MA: Harvard University Press, 2001), 109.

of the group, its size, and its overall purpose, are matters that are fairly diverse. Whatever assertion may be made about evangelicals, as a disparate lot they are fiercely independent and autonomous. And there are still those—few in number to be sure—who are deeply committed to evangelicalism and who are persuaded that CCM does not musically embody their faith.

Two Non-CCM Churches

In my travels, two of the non-CCM churches I visited stand out in my memory. The first, in rural New England, was a typical white clapboard church building complete with dark green shutters and clear glass.[11] Visiting in the fall, the winter fund drive for heating oil was in full swing. Evidently the congregation was unable to fund the cost from the regular operating budget.

I entered twenty minutes before the morning service began, intruding on the adult Sunday school class being held in the sanctuary. The auditorium was clean with straight-back pews, varnished plank flooring, hymnals neatly arrayed in the pew racks. The pressed-tin ceiling featured multiplied repetitions of a typical 19th-century two-foot square decorative pattern. In the center of the ceiling, there hung a huge, ornate chandelier. At the front, a pulpit, located in the center of the raised platform, was flanked by the Christian flag on the far right and the flag of the United States on the far left. On the wall in back of the pulpit was an ornate reredos crafted out of pine upon which was imposed a large, artistically simple cross. The communion table sat on the main floor just below the pulpit. On it was placed a large open Bible (complete with Apocrypha) printed in 1872 by the A. J. Holman Co., Philadelphia. As I soon came to find out, this open Bible was a visual depiction of the place God's Word had in the theology of the church. Though attendance was low, the congregation's view of Scripture was high. God's Word was paramount.

---

[11] I returned the next year for the church's 150th anniversary.

As it turned out, the pianist (there was no organist) had suffered a debilitating injury, so that morning's two gospel songs and one hymn were accompanied by an MP3 player or sung a cappella when the batteries died. Fortunately, the building had wonderfully reverberant acoustics and the pastor a loud singing voice, so all in all the congregation sang as one voice. The songs were sung at a fairly fast clip and in strict time throughout, including the final note of the song. Moving on to the next stanza, I could hardly get my breath.

The church obviously retained its gospel-song heritage. Maintaining the popular music tradition of the 19th- and early 20th-century variety (distant though that might be), the hymnal contained mostly gospel songs. But there were some objective hymns, one of which was sung in the morning service. There was no Christian contemporary music.

The service was straightforward with an honest simplicity and directness that gave testimony to the unalloyed, earnest faith of pastor and people. Worshiping with them in the context of their conservative, fundamental theological heritage, I could see that the church clearly espoused an especially strong evangelical emphasis in its preaching and outreach. As part of the congregation, my spirit was reassured in the central truths that form the bedrock of evangelical belief.

A second non-CCM evangelical church I attended was an inner-city church with a membership of over 1,000 and Sunday attendance of about 2,000. Being early (my usual habit), I took time to observe the comings and goings of its congregants before entering the auditorium. I noticed the abundance of young people and many, many families with young children running to and fro. Though I could not be sure, I noted people from abroad and from all walks of life. There was no background music in the foyer.

The plain-looking building was constructed in the early 19th century. A distinctive feature of the auditorium was the high central pulpit at the front, flanked by two high-backed bishop's chairs upholstered in bright red, the identical color of the carpeting. I surmised that preaching was a featured and essential part of the life of the church. The organ console was located on the main floor, and the grand piano opposite on the right. The choir sang from the rear gallery. The pew racks contained hymnals and Bibles.

As I entered the sanctuary, I was struck by the peace that reigned as people found a place to sit. When families entered with small children, parents shepherded them appropriately. I found it a joy to be part of a going, "lively" congregation.

Just prior to the 11:00 service the organist commenced the prelude. The composition played was one of artistic integrity and creativity. Obviously meant to be actively listened to, this was not religious wallpaper music. Then the choir sang an introit and Psalm 34 was recited. The opening hymn, "Holy God, We Praise Your Name," was sung deliberately, thoughtfully, and with conviction. The organ supported but did not intrude upon the congregation's singing, thereby achieving in the vocal praise of the people a camaraderie and community rarely found in churches that still use the organ. The congregation then prayed together, after which they greeted one another. The choir sang an anthem (text printed in the bulletin), a lengthy Scripture lesson was read, children were dismissed to go to children's church, and the sermon was given. Another hymn (unfamiliar but able to be sung because of having the music in the hymnal) preceded a pastoral prayer, the offering was taken, and a final hymn, "Eternal Father, Strong to Save," was sung. After the choral benediction, the organist played the companion fugue to the prelude played at the beginning of the service. There was no throwaway organ music at any point in the service.

Many things were notable. The sermon was something one had to concentrate on. The pastor was not a particularly smooth communicator who used funny stories and jokes to establish rapport with the people. What he did was to systematically exegete the twenty-four verses from 2 Samuel that had been read prior to the sermon. It was a model of biblical exposition. The hymn singing lifted my heart. The congregationally unified voices, all singing God's praises together in one accord, was something rare and precious. The well-played organ accompaniment, restrained yet solidly foundational, inspired the congregation to raise their voices together in heartfelt praise. Also, I found the flow of the service not unlike the Isaiah passage in which the prophet is struck by the mighty awesomeness of God and in that frame of mind ends his encounter with the Almighty with, "Here am I; send me" (Isaiah 6:8, KJV).[12]

Questions

How different was my visitation in this urban setting than that described at the beginning of this chapter. Here I had to hunt for a parking spot and, finding one, then had to walk a fifth of a mile to the church. The sidewalk was filled with bustling humanity and the streets crowded with automobiles. When I finally arrived at the church, I found no polished greeting ministry at the door and no offering of glazed doughnuts and coffee. But people were friendly, with a kind of genuine everyday amicableness that was not pushy or presumptuous. In other words, I did not feel acted upon. I felt as if I was simply one of them on the way to celebrate a common Lord.

My experience in this evangelical enclave was uplifting and instructive. I was overflowing with wonder at the grace afforded me by this almighty God who sent His son to die for my sins. The worship service ministered to my heart in ways difficult to explain. Even now I realize that I had been with God and His people.

As I walked to the car through the falling leaves of autumn, I grappled with the reality I had found in this church versus that which I had tasted months before at the contemporary satellite church described earlier. What was the difference between them? To be sure they both professed to be ardently evangelical; they both had a heightened sense of the importance of preaching.

---

[12] The well-known anthem "In the Year that King Uzziah Died" by David McK. Williams is a particularly compelling and effective setting of Isaiah 6:1–8.

Yet here they were, vastly different in their worship. Were these differences just a matter of style, one style as good as another? Or were there deeper issues involved, fundamental issues that spoke to and perhaps determined the content of the worship of God? It was something to think about. After all, worship is the central activity of believers.

2   Evangelicals

With between 90 million and 100 million evangelical Christians in America,[13] evangelicals constitute a significant presence in the country's religious and national life. Their influence, consequential and far-reaching, is keenly felt on all fronts, not the least of which is in the field of church music.

For readers unfamiliar with contemporary evangelicalism as generally understood, or for whom the word "evangelical" is ambiguous, the words may be used in two basic ways: broad and narrow. The narrow understanding of the term is by far the more common. In fact, most people (including the media) invariably use the word in its more restrictive sense.

But it is not always possible to discern on the surface which of the two usages, broad or narrow, is applicable in any given case. For example, a church with a name such as "The Evangelical Lutheran Church of Our Savior's Atonement" sounds definitively evangelical. Although clearly stated in its name, it remains unclear whether or not the church belongs to the broad evangelical camp or whether it is evangelical in the more restricted and narrow sense. We would have to ascertain its evangelical position by investigating the parent denomination with which the church is affiliated and/or the church itself. If, as in this case, the church was part of the Evangelical Lutheran Church in America denomination, then knowing the belief

---

[13] The Institute for the Study of American Evangelicals, Gallup Inc., and the Pew Research Center all conclude there are too many variables to know the exact number of evangelicals in America. The 90 million to 100 million figure is based upon interpretation of the best data available.

system of this particular denomination would show it to be evangelical in the broader, more comprehensive sense, but not evangelical in the narrow, more circumscribed, and microcosmic meaning of the word.

Broad Evangelicalism

A look at the broad use of the term evangelical shows that it comes from the Latin root "evangelium" and from the Greek "euangelion" and simply means "good news." More specifically, "evangel" refers to the Christian "godspell" or gospel. It defines the good news found in Scripture, in particular the first four books of the New Testament: Matthew, Mark, Luke, and John. Here the Gospels proclaim the evangel, the good news that the long-awaited Savior, the Jewish Messiah, has come to save His people from their sins and offer everlasting life to all. Good news indeed! The root "evangel" yields many forms of the word: evangelization, evangelistic, evangelism, evangelist, evangelizer, evangelic, evangelicalism, evangelically, evangelical, evangelistically, evangelize. Most churches lay claim to being agents of the evangel, agents of the good news, agents charged with celebrating and spreading the evangel, the good news of God in Christ.

Hence the Roman Catholic Church, Anglicans and Episcopalians, Methodists of all stripes, Presbyterians, Pentecostals, all forms of Lutheranism, Congregational and independent churches, Baptists, Brethren, Nazarene churches, and on and on are, in the broad sense, evangelical. Catholic, Orthodox, and all variants of Protestantism[14] share this commonality: they are all macrocosmically evangelistic.

---

[14] Philip Gulley, *The Evolution of Faith* (HarperOne, 2011), 173. According to the author there are now 39,000 Christian denominations in the world.

Narrow Evangelicalism

However, as noted above, the word evangelical has another, more common, more colloquial use. This narrower and more restrictive understanding of the word is customarily reserved for churches with a closely held parochial theology assiduously and singularly faithful to a particularly defined understanding of the Christian faith as revealed in Scripture and Scripture alone.

It is this second, carefully defined and circumscribed understanding of the word "evangelical" that concerns us in this volume. In general parlance, the term describes perfectly the congregations that exercise a narrower, conservative evangelicalism quite out of step with liberal theology and large segments of 21st-century culture.

These churches, congregations, and fellowships adhere to a narrow evangelicalism with the following theological parameters:

A high view of Scripture. God's written word, divinely inspired and infallible, stands as the final authority on all matters touching the Christian faith.

Personal salvation. Transformation and regeneration are necessary and occur through the born-again experience of accepting the crucified and resurrected Christ as one's personal Savior.

Grace and works. An understanding of redemption founded on grace alone, coupled with the belief that following Christ is a work in progress.

Evangelization. Evangelicals exhibit an energetic, even all-consuming drive to fulfill the Great Commission by spreading both at home and abroad the news that all must come to repentance through the shed blood of Christ, the only remedy for sin and the only way to receive eternal life.

Such evangelical churches include all narrower classifications of evangelicals including so-called Fundamentalist, Holiness,

Charismatic, Reformed, Anabaptist, Baptist, and other groups. Many have a denominational affiliation; others are fiercely independent. A varied and diverse lot, some are affiliated with organizations such as the Alliance of Confessing Evangelicals and the Society of Evangelical Arminians that endeavor to establish fellowships within evangelicalism to promote a specific conservative, theological bent. Many evangelical denominations are members of the National Association of Evangelicals (NAE), as are unaffiliated churches that subscribe to its statement of faith. There are, however, many independent churches large and small that have no formal connection with the NAE, yet may be identified as evangelical as defined by the four theological criteria listed previously. For example, the Southern Baptists who, in general, are devoutly evangelical have no formal connection to the NAE. These theologically narrow fellowships are the focus of this text.

Narrow Evangelical Worship

Evangelicals have other characteristics by which they may be identified, all connectable in some way, directly or indirectly, substantially or superficially, explicitly or vaguely, to their doctrinal belief system. Though these characteristics may or may not be as centric or singularly defining as theological positions, they nevertheless are often used first and foremost—rightly or wrongly—to identify and set apart America's evangelicals. In other words, an immutable conservative theology is not the only distinguishing mark of evangelical churches in America. There are other features of contemporary evangelicalism that, to the average person and to the media, may be more telling than its often unknown (or misunderstood) theological position.

These features show evangelistic churches to be a diversified lot. Indeed, a basic operating premise is independence. A perusal across the broad evangelical landscape confirms the importance of evangelicalism's underlying postulate: the autonomy of each individual church. Such liberty results in a vast and wondrous array of practices and assumptions. "Many," "most," "in general," and "almost all" are words that are needed when describing evangelicals as a group. The enormous differences between one congregation and another in various areas of evangelical life, other than their commonly held most basic and defining theological assumptions, are not only to be expected but are the very essence of what it means to be an evangelical. Therefore, when people assert "evangelicals do this," or "the evangelical church claims that," or "characteristic of evangelicals," we must realize that exceptions to whatever is being asserted are fairly typical. This is especially true with church music, a subject invariably treated as a discretionary matter.

The "worship wars" that began in the late 1970s, which were largely about the use of Christian contemporary music in worship, are essentially a thing of the past. CCM emerged as the hands-down winner. However, some differing perspectives yet remain and are aired from time to time. This is not unexpected, given the independence within the evangelical movement. One present-day writer fervently believes that evangelical worship has deteriorated into sheer entertainment while another lauds its upbeat atmosphere. The former found the volume of the music to be so loud that participation was minimal and termed the dimmed house lights, flashing strobes, and lasers a "sound and light show." The latter found the thump of the worship team's bass in his chest, the laser lights darting around the sanctuary, and people jumping to the rhythmic music to be an exciting experience.[15] There yet remains a spectrum of evangelical thought on the worship of God, but it must be said that the latter's appreciation of contemporary worship is essentially the predominant view and practice today.

Evangelical churches accentuate, even make paramount, the convention of preaching. Services are focused and designed around the centrality of sermonizing. Not exactly a short, easygoing, laid-back homily, such discourse tends to be highly

---

[15] "Perspectives: Worship as Entertainment?" and "A Multisensory Worship Experience," *Influence* (June 2016): 28–29.

charged, content laden, expositional, and often emotional. That which precedes the proclamation of God's infallible Word is often referred to, or thought of, as preliminary (i.e. "The Preliminaries") to the main event: the sermon. The point of the preaching often, though not always, includes a salvation invitation to any in the congregation who are unbelievers. Coming to faith, a step referred to as being saved or born again, is a major component of the evangelization effort to spread the gospel. In addition, sermons also focus (through mind and emotion) on strengthening converts to live overcoming, transformed lives for the glory of God and the building up of His church.

Evangelicals are not sacramental. That is, their worship is not centered around the Eucharist, as in Catholic, Lutheran, and Episcopal churches. Not that the celebration of the Lord's Supper is unimportant, being commemorated routinely, perhaps once a month or once a quarter. But it is not paramount.[16] For evangelicals the Word is of utmost importance. It has the spotlight. Furthermore, the Word as printed or recited is less important than the Word as proclaimed from the pulpit in sermon format. While sacramental churches generally have as part of their worship a reading from the Old Testament, a Psalm, a reading from an epistle, and a reading from one of the Gospels for a total of four readings in all, evangelicals have considerably less Scripture *in toto*, generally reciting Scripture only in relationship to the sermon. And some evangelistic churches include no public reading of Scripture at all, utilizing it only as reference material during the sermon.

Eschewing formalized liturgy remains another evangelical distinctive. Liturgy, as prescribed in a prayer book or some other book of worship, remains alien to their worship methodology. Evangelicals practice "free" worship. Not answerable to any higher ecclesiastical authority and not bound by a prescribed

---

[16] It is noteworthy that for the first 1,500 years of Christianity there is no record of Sunday worship without the Lord's Supper. Tim Ralston, "Remember and Worship: The Mandate and the Means," *Reformation and Revival* 9, no. 3 (Summer 2000): 82.

form, they design worship according to the dictates of personal preference. To some evangelicals, liturgical worship seems like empty ritualism: boring, repetitive, wordy, and without spiritual weight. Not having a prescribed form, evangelicalism, going its own way, ends up with a variety of worship formats about equal to the number of evangelical churches in existence. While it is true that every evangelical church has two main sections to its worship service—(1) before the sermon and (2) the sermon itself—there are considerable differences in details. Music, prayer, Scripture reading, collection of the offering, announcements, videos, communion, fellowship, and other aspects of worship may be utilized in any order, more than once, or not at all.

The word "free," in describing evangelical worship, defines the praxis of every evangelical church. Free worship means that evangelicals are at liberty to choose that which they believe will best fulfill their mission. And the variety of differences between them appears endless.

Notwithstanding this broad expanse of free choice, the overall style of evangelical church music has remained (for the most part) in the popular camp. Finding music for a particular church fellowship became a matter of choosing from among the numerous subspecies of popular religious song. As a rule, not many evangelicals will be found using Psalm tones or singing Gregorian chant, metrical psalmody, Anglican chant, chorales, or a steady diet of traditional hymnody. Rather, choices tend toward folk song, spirituals, the gospel song and chorus genre, Jesus music, Charismatic scripture songs, praise and worship music, southern gospel, Christian contemporary music, rock, and rap. Though a broad-based concerted effort was advanced after World War II to integrate traditional hymnody into prevailing evangelistic repertoire, evangelicals eventually abandoned the initiative.[17] Reaffirming their allegiance to popular music forms, CCM and its derivatives took firm and persistent hold throughout the latter part of the 20th century as evangelicals strongly embraced secular culture's preference for new emerging styles of popular music.

Further Traits

Informality in dress and deportment, another characteristic of evangelicals in worship, enjoys widespread acceptance. Historically, the general practice of worshipers was to honor the Lord by dressing in one's best and treating the house of God with a certain reverence and respect. Over the years that attitude morphed into a certain nonchalance. Casual clothes (no coats and ties) and a *laissez-faire* attitude have become the order of the day. Occasionally coffee, doughnuts, and other breakfast items find their way into the morning service as people eat and drink during worship. Such practice produces a breezy, off-the-cuff approach to worship. Such a *modus operandi* has developed as a deliberate attempt to make people comfortable and relaxed. Church should not be something to be endured; it should be something to be enjoyed. Creature comforts compatible with

---

[17] As a case in point, in 1946 Gospel Publishing House (an arm of the Pentecostal denomination Assemblies of God) republished the 1931 Nazarene hymnbook *Glorious Gospel Hymns.* It was a forward-looking book of over 600 pages and included some traditional hymns along with a preponderance of gospel songs. Also included were responsive readings, the Apostles' Creed, and other readings for use in worship services. Introductory remarks noted the "need among many denominations for a hymnal having a combination of the most famous and widely used hymns and the strongest and best loved gospel songs obtainable." Haldor Lillenas was the editor, assisted by over 500 pastors. Gospel Publishing House followed its 1946 publication with other hymnals: *Melodies of Praise,* 1957 (which featured both round and shaped note editions); *Hymns of Glorious Praise,* 1969; and in 1991, *Sing His Praise,* which featured additional hymns complete with tune names, responsive Scripture readings, and an exhaustive series of indexes: Index of Scripture Readings, Index of Credits (authors, composers, sources and translators), Index of Tunes, Index of Meters (only those meters represented by more than one tune are listed), Index According to Key, Topical Index and General Index (titles are in regular type; familiar first lines of verses and choruses are in italics.) The opening hymn of this Pentecostal hymnal was "All Creatures of Our God and King" (set to "Lasst Uns Erfreuen, 8.8.8.8. with alleluias). This was the last hymnal GPH published and was not widely used.

worship "lite" has become the pattern for Sunday's Sabbath devotion.

An emerging concept from the late 1960s is the practice of using the word "worship" to indicate what used to be called the "song service." Having evolved, worship now generally refers to the music led by the stage musicians with people standing, usually for an extended period of time. The terminology used in the report on Southwestern Seminary's Youth Ministry Lab clarifies the point: "worship was led by the Sixteen Cities Band" and also "from the David Gentiles Band."[18] We can surmise that in the second decade of the 21st century it is common for "the worship" to simply mean "the music."

Evangelical worship depends heavily upon technology in its worship. Not particularly obvious, it nevertheless has become increasingly important with the use of computers, PowerPoint, multiple-wall screens, theater-size pull-down screens, satellite-video projection, holographic-projection imagery, image magnification, DVDs, film projection, and computer-projection systems. These are used for all manner of things (background imagery, sermon notes, biblical references, information loops, background music, etc.), as well as an often staggering array of high-fidelity speakers and amplifiers coupled with a host of microphone types. Such devices indicate the extent to which evangelicals rely on audiovisual mechanization. Larger churches employ professionals to staff this technological component of evangelical worship, while smaller churches use volunteers.

The cost of purchasing, installing, and maintaining audio and visual media hardware can be significant.[19] Such equipment appears mandatory because of the technical demands now required in the worship service. Visuals are necessary for congregational singing, as there are usually no hymnals; Bibles are generally not provided, hence the need for projecting Scripture on the front wall or screens; information

---

[18] Katie Coleman, "YML Equips Leaders for Christ-Centered Youth Ministry In a Changing Culture," *Southwestern News* (Summer 2016): 55.
[19] It is not unusual for a church to spend from 10 to 20 percent of the cost of a new building on electronics.

and announcements are broadcast visually, as are background tableaus. To help provide the best visual definition possible, the interior of the auditorium may have shuttered windows or no windows at all and be painted entirely in black to keep any ambient light from creeping into the worship space, which would degrade the clarity of screen imagery.

The ability to hear well in an often dead acoustical space depends upon the clarity of the sound system. The quality of the audio equipment directly affects not only the congregation's ability to hear speech but the vocal and instrumental ensembles' ability to project their musical offerings without distortion (sometimes at an ear-splitting level). Heavy-duty equipment gives the best service, thus justifying any additional expense.

A developing concept is that of the satellite or multisite church. Here the home church sponsors other congregations that may be many miles away and connected to the home church via a technological link.[20] The possibility then exists for there to be one main pastor whose sermons and other communiqué may be shared with all congregations simultaneously via satellite. At the appropriate time in the worship service, a king-sized theater screen drops down and the pastor, larger than life, preaches to all the gathered faithful at the same time, regardless of location. Such technology, via a recording, also has the advantage of allowing the scheduling of simultaneous services in multiple locations without the pastor having to be physically present for each service.[21]

In Summary

Understandably, evangelicals are lumped together as a group, for they hold much in common. They do have a primary, underlying, fundamental biblical belief system. But upon that frame we discover a multitude of theological shadings often

---

[20] Life.Church, the largest church in the United States, has twenty-six locations in eight states.

[21] In addition to video technology, holographic imaging is being developed for satellite church use.

quite diverse from one another. A fiercely independent streak runs through the entire evangelical movement.

Most evangelicals, not being liturgical or sacramental, commonly use a binary form to structure their services: (1) before the preaching/teaching and (2) the preaching/teaching itself. Within this structure there also exists large-scale generalized commonalities across the face of their worship: informality in dress and demeanor, popular religious music, a relaxed approach to worship. Yet here again, within these similarities, there are many, many variations in detail.

Fellowships that are manifestly in the evangelical camp have a penchant for relying heavily on audio and visual media technology. This is especially true for the large megachurches that dot the land and is absolutely mandatory for the satellite church concept. But it is not true across the board. There are congregations that cannot afford high-end systems and those who for one reason or another eschew all visual media technology, finding the like unnecessary at the least and at the most a hindrance to worship.

Being biblically based as they are, it is not surprising that evangelicals generally show a consensus on moral issues. Concerning sex, abortion, and marriage, there is little disagreement, at least in principle.[22]

To be sure evangelicals are a diverse lot. Yet there are things that hold them together, however loosely that may be. The adage "in essentials, unity; in non-essentials, liberty; in all things, charity" does not really describe the reality of evangelicalism because there is little unanimity on just what are essentials and what are nonessentials. It is this interplay between basics and preferences that is the reason for so much of the diversity found in the evangelical church.

Evangelical churches, distinguished from mainline

---

[22] The Biblical basis for the traditional evangelical view of human sexuality and related issues was reviewed by the *Council on Biblical Manhood and Womanhood* in August 2017. Known as the "Nashville Statement," the document's fourteen articles clearly delineate the teaching of scripture in contradistinction to post-Christian belief and practice concerning sexual matters.

protestantism by evangelicalism's adherence to theological fundamentals and manner of doing things,[23] utilize their liberty voraciously in shaping the specific characteristics of each individual church. Clearly distinguishable from most mainline churches, evangelical churches sometimes unknowingly diminish the very gospel being promulgated by adopting unsound worship practices. From congregations of only a few to megachurches of thousands, size is no indicator of such evangelical wandering. Though not theologically fundamental in relationship to the four core beliefs mentioned earlier, that which concerns us here does affect the church theologically in its worship, evangelism, and discipleship. Much in evangelicalism needs strengthening and shoring up, for the liberty evangelicalism has exercised in allowing societal standards to influence its course—including the content of its worship—is often immoderate, not to say grievous.[24]

Why be so concerned with the conduct and content of the worship service? Because worship is powerful and of paramount importance in the forming of faith and practice. The Latin axiom *Lex orandi, lex credendi, lex vivendi* ("As we worship, so we believe, so we live") points up the fact that worship is formative. It is not an exercise to get through, a thoughtless, unemotional, spiritless ceremonial; it is a corporate, dynamic meeting between God and us, a touching of and connection with the Almighty. Encountering the living God in worship fashions, forges, frames, and forms the worshiper. Worship, the

---

[23] In *The Triumph of the Praise Songs*, Michael S. Hamilton hypothesizes that Americans choose a church more by musical preferences than by denomination. He suggests that the new creeds are musical dogma; worship seminars the new seminaries; seminar directors the new theologians; and worship leaders the new ministers. *Reformation & Revival* 9, no. 3 (Summer 2000): 120.

[24] Ron Sider cites polls by Gallup and Barna which indicate that "evangelical Christians are as likely to embrace lifestyles every bit as hedonistic, materialistic, self-centered, and sexually immoral as the world in general." Such would indicate a pressing need for the evangelical church to pay remedial attention to its adoption of worldly culture, and as far as this volume is concerned, in making pop music normative as worship music. William H. Gross, synopsis of and comments on *The Scandal of the Evangelical Conscience*, by Ron Sider. http://www.onthewing.org/user/Ev_Scandal%20of%20the%20Evangelical%20Conscience.pdf

primary activity of the body of Christ, the church, merits careful attention and tender loving care. It makes us who we are. And it blesses the One worthy to receive honor, glory, and power for ever and ever—the slain Lamb who sits upon the throne of God.

3   Strengthening Music Ministry in Evangelical Worship

Worship[25] is essential to the life of the body of Christ, the Church. Admonished not to forsake the assembling of themselves together,[26] believers find in worship a corporate venture near to the heart of God. It is a work of the people that defines their very being. We do well to continually strengthen this primary undertaking of the people of God.

Evangelicalism's Passion

I am an evangelical. I am convinced that evangelicalism's emphasis on the need for personal salvation, with heaven as its outcome, and the consequence of rejecting such a gift—namely hell—is true.

As a child, listening to the big four-legged parlor radio on Sunday afternoons, the rallying cry of evangelicals then as now came through clearly and unambiguously:

"We have heard the joyful sound: Jesus saves! Jesus saves!
Spread the tidings all around: Jesus saves! Jesus saves!
Bear the news to every land, Climb the
steeps and cross the waves;
Onward—'tis our Lord's command; Jesus saves! Jesus saves!"[27]

---

[25] The word "worship" is used approximately 8,500 times in Scripture. See www .biblegateway.com.
[26] Hebrews 10:25 (NIV).
[27] Text: Priscilla J. Owens (1829–1907); music: William J. Kirkpatrick (1838–1921).

This song opened Charles E. Fuller's *Old Fashioned Revival Hour*, a staple of Christian radio broadcasting for over thirty years.[28] "Jesus saves" was what evangelicalism was all about; it said it all.

Today, evangelical churches continue their focus on Jesus as Savior. Whether in a service of worship on Sunday or as people share the good news during the week, evangelicals are fixed on the biblical teaching that unless a person is saved, that person remains lost. The question, "Are you saved?" may not sound politically correct, but the presentation of the question establishes the very *raison d'etre* of evangelicalism. Evangelicals are resolute about spreading the gospel. They are possessed by the Great Commission[29] and captivated and controlled by the fact that Jesus saves. Being born again remains the only key to eternal life.

Worship

The weekly Sunday gatherings of the congregation for worship may be referred to by using any one of the three following terms interchangeably: service, worship, and worship service. Though this may seem to be rather mechanistic in dealing with the prime activity of the church (its worship), these terms nevertheless succinctly and specifically simplify addressing matters concerning the content of the activity. It goes without saying, however, that for worship to have profound significance, it cannot be mechanical or robotic or perfunctory. Worship entails levels of meaning that go to the very heart of the relationship between God and His people. As subjects, we revere and venerate Him, the object of our praise. In point of

---

[28] After the choir's singing of the first stanza of "Jesus Saves," Brother Fuller would begin his opening: "The Gospel Broadcasting Association presents the *Old Fashioned Revival Hour*, an international broadcast of the gospel. This gospel hour comes to you from the Municipal Auditorium at Long Beach, California. This is Charles E. Fuller speaking." The *Old Fashioned Revival Hour* commenced in 1937 and concluded in 1969. It was a staple in the lives of thousands of evangelicals and remains a cherished memory of my growing-up years.

[29] Matthew 28:16–20; Mark 16:14–18; Acts 1:4–8.

fact, "The ultimate goal of worship is to display and proclaim and magnify the glory of God."[30]

The word "worship" comes from the old English *weorth* (worth) *scipe* (ship, meaning the quality of having), hence "worth-ship." We worship the One who is of ultimate worth, God, the beginning and the end of our worship. From our innermost being, from the heart and spirit of the believer, we ascribe respect, honor, adoration, and praise to God, the holy One, the sovereign King of Glory. He is worthy to be worshiped first, for who He is; second, for what He has done in Jesus Christ; and third, for the Spirit who dwells within. Worship, a stand-alone endeavor, requires no justification beyond itself. We worship God, who is deserving of worship. Moreover we "do not worship God on Sunday in order to live better lives on Monday: we give concentrated expression on Sunday to the worship which will also characterize our Monday."[31] It is the everyday life-mark of the believer. The Harold Friedell anthem "Draw Us in the Spirit's Tether" speaks to the comprehensive nature and scope of the believer's worship.

Draw us in the Spirit's tether; For when humbly, in thy name,
Two or three are met together, Thou art in the midst of them:
Alleluya! Alleluya! Touch we now thy garment's hem.

As the brethren used to gather In the name of Christ to sup,
Then with thanks to God the Father Break the bread and bless the cup,
Alleluya! Alleluya! So knit thou our friendship up.

All our meals and all our living Make as sacraments of thee,
That by caring, helping, giving, We may true disciples be.
Alleluya! Alleluya! We will serve thee faithfully.[32]

Worship, inspired by the Holy Spirit, is characterized by an attitude of awe and wonder toward God, the ultimate reality. It

---

[30] Ron Man, "Worship and the Word," *Reformation and Revival Journal* 9, no. 3 (Summer 2000): 145.

[31] Charles Cleall, *Music and Holiness* (London: The Epworth Press, 1964), 37.

[32] Text by Percy Dearmer; music by Harold Friedell. Used by permission.

flows from the soul and spirit of a believer in response to God, whose overwhelming and extravagant love is freely bestowed upon us, His creation. We use mind and emotion in worship. But they do not constitute the corpus of worship. The essence of worship is our responding to God's initiative through Jesus Christ in the power of the Holy Spirit, a trinity of persons with whom we have a special relationship, that of sons and daughters. And the music that the family of God uses to express its homage to the King of kings needs to reflect something of the character of Christ, the object of our worship.[33]

Some people make a distinction between praise and worship: God being praised for what He has done and worshiped for who He is. I make no such distinction; worship treated holistically encompasses prayer, praise (adoration, thanksgiving, obeisance, exaltation, veneration, devotion), preaching, listening, singing, reciting, meditation, and partaking of the Lord's Supper.

Corporate worship is an activity. Believers, as part of the temporal world, express their worship from deep within the human heart through material form: words, music, bodily actions, art, architecture, thought, and listening. "When you come together, everyone has a hymn, or a word of instruction, a revelation, a tongue, or an interpretation. All of these must be done for the strengthening of the church."[34] The material content of the worship service is a work—the work of the people. What is needful is that God's people be "zealous for good works,"[35] even good musical works in worship, not for our sake but for the sake of the gospel. It is this work, this activity, which constitutes the subject of the present text and more particularly the principal theme of this chapter on strengthening the ministry of music in evangelical worship.

---

[33] William G. MacDonald, "Drum-Free Worship of Christ" (unpublished paper), 17.

[34] 1 Corinthians 14:26 (NIV)

[35] John MacArthur, *The Gospel According to Paul* (Nelson Books, 2017), 127. See Titus 2:14 (NKJV).

Worship Style: Traditional vs. Contemporary

Often the word "style" is invoked when considering evangelical worship. Reflecting upon designations such as traditional and contemporary, common wisdom maintains that there exists no biblical support for one worship style over another. Style, it is said, stands as a neutral entity. Neither good nor bad, right or wrong, good, better, or best, all worship styles are thought equally valid, a matter of personal taste—like choosing vanilla over chocolate ice cream.

The rationale behind the acceptability of all worship styles remains the belief that worship is exclusively a matter of a worshiper's heart. John 4:24, "God *is* a Spirit: and they that worship him must worship *him* in spirit and in truth (KJV)," is often interpreted as evidence for deemphasizing worship's content and emphasizing the heart attitude of believers when worshiping.

I contend that all worship, traditional or contemporary, liturgical or free, sacramental or non-sacramental, liberal or conservative, must begin with the *a priori* assumption that worship is to be heartfelt. Without a warm and passionate attitude of the all-encompassing, all-embracing love of God and neighbor, any and every "style" of worship is dead as a doornail. But this does not indicate that all worship styles are coequal. Regardless of an individual's right relationship with the Almighty in worship, the worship of God does have parameters.

What defines a style is its musical content. And accepting a particular style means accepting its content. But accepting all content is short-sighted.

The Scripture is replete with teaching which codifies, determines, emphasizes, refines and defines worship content and hence worship's style. For example, to participate with a right heart in a worship context which harms the body, makes light of the holiness of God, redefines sin, or is fashioned and chosen to please the worshiper is worship which is unacceptable to God in spite of any warm, passionate, and loving disposition felt by the worshiper.

In this volume it is the content of worship which is addressed rather than the styles "traditional" vs. "contemporary." Such labeling merely serves to fracture the body of Christ further and continue the worship wars of yesteryear.

The real issue is to discover the scriptural stance on the individual content ingredients of worship so as to be able to choose well those that are in accord with Holy Writ.

Separate and Unequal

In general, evangelicals separate the words and the music of their songs into two distinct entities. Practicing a Gnostic dualism, they believe texts belong to the spiritual realm, music to the material world; texts enunciate truth, music cannot; words give voice to the gospel, music does not. Such belief in separating the spiritual from the musical, the eternal from the temporal, cuts music loose from the responsibility for conveying gospel witness. This allows evangelicals, on the one hand, to choose texts that they believe have theological truth and, on the other hand, to use music selected on the basis of likeability and personal taste. The fact that music has its own message seldom occurs to them or, if it does, it is generally dismissed as unimportant.

Evangelicals, then, often consider music itself to have no message as such. However, the fact remains that a song is primarily a musical form, and secondarily a poetic one; song selection is often made first on the basis of its music, and second on the basis of its text—though this may not be recognized by those making the selections. Specific musical choices are largely dependent upon finding that which will be enjoyable, pleasant, entertaining, or fun. Because evangelicals believe music itself incapable of conveying a worldview, such convention, shortsighted though it may be, is certainly understandable. Music, understood as a subjective entity dominated by individual personal taste, stands inert; it is believed to be a blank slate, worldview neutral, unable to communicate objective truth.

Therefore any music and musical style is entirely permissible. The music simply serves as a kind of word lubricator.

However, music has more of a role in gospel witness and worship than that of grease gun or oil can. Music is beyond that of being a disputable matter, a personal preference. Inextricably linked with worship and witness, music functions best when in tune with gospel principles. Nevertheless, evangelicals tend to treat music and musical standards as a discretionary matter. Those who do not are encouraged to do so.[36]

Customarily, evangelicals are dominated by words. That is to say, they are word-oriented, almost exclusively so. The truth of Scripture is contained in words, the implementation of the gospel a matter of word-speech. Verbal language is revered, the message of "Jesus saves" communicated via preaching, singing, or telling. For evangelicalism, then, words alone provide the means of fulfilling the Great Commission.

Music has been treated as quite secondary. Song texts are carefully evaluated for their biblical orthodoxy; musical scores get no such scrutiny. Music has had license to go its own way and to do its "own thing," especially since the 1950s. As a result, the present music of most evangelicals is rock-derived CCM, CWM (contemporary worship music) or some other type of rock spin-off, country, southern gospel, and/or other popular music styles that are commonplace in our culture. Since it is thought that the music is not responsible for gospel truth (that being the responsibility of the words), its less important role takes it off the hook, so to speak, allowing any type, kind, quality, quantity, or style to be used in ministry. When there has been significant congregational disagreement over musical issues (usually concerning stylistic taste preferences), some congregations have come to use what has been called blended

---

[36] Jonathan Schaeffer, "When Christians Disagree," *Alliance Life* (February 2007): 31. Interestingly, the same issue of *Alliance Life* contained an excerpt from A. W. Tozer's book *The Pursuit of God* (1948), "Following Hard After God," in which Tozer spoke out against shallowness of experience, hollowness in worship, and imitation of the world. For Tozer these preferences were not acceptable.

or convergence worship—a mix of contemporary and traditional musical styles.

The Present Music of Evangelicals

Presently, the evangelical church almost universally uses popular music styles of one sort or another for worship. From midcentury to the present time, there have appeared a declining number of books, articles, sermons, conferences, and informal discussions warning the church against making popular music normative in evangelical worship. The arguments were sound, but they were of no avail.[37] Like it or not, pop music and its derivatives became the music of the general evangelical movement. Today, one must look long and hard to find an evangelical church that has not embraced this type of music or has not subscribed to some form of religious popular music. It is endemic to our church culture. Approve or disapprove, CCM is today's evangelical music.

Making Progress

I believe it to be scriptural that evangelicals are to welcome any advance in their music ministries that will make them more effective. And that includes continual reassessment of what is sung, played, or listened to. We have not achieved perfection yet!

The current musical usage of the evangelical church needs shoring up. It is essential that music and worship be strengthened in such a manner that the church's witness is enhanced and congregational edification increased. The initial presentation of

---

[37] In addition to hundreds of examples, my own writings (still in print) may be added: *Music and Ministry: A Biblical Counterpoint*, 2nd ed. (Peabody, MA: Hendrickson Publishers, 1998); *Discipling Music Ministry: Twenty-first Century Directions* (Peabody, MA: Hendrickson Publishers, 1992); two chapters in Samuele Bacchiocchi's book *The Christian and Rock Music: A Study on Biblical Principles of Music* (Biblical Perspectives, 2000); a chapter in Eric Patterson's and Edmund Rybarczyk's book, *The Future of Pentecostalism in the United States* (Lanham, MD: Lexington Books, 2007); and numerous articles.

the gospel and the long-term working out of the faith in the life of every believer can be improved. The net result: an increase in souls saved, an enhanced worship for the glory of God, and better discipled believers.

Congregational Participation Fundamental to Evangelical Worship

When Martin Luther nailed his 95 theses to the door of the Wittenberg Church in 1517, and when John Calvin and other reformers subsequently contributed their theological constructs, each within his own sphere of influence, a large-scale spiritual renewal movement was born known as Protestantism. Noteworthy is the fact that wherever this new faith direction took hold, hearty congregational singing followed. Community song and Reformation worship went together like the proverbial hand in glove.

From the very beginning, ingrained into the very warp and woof of the Protestant movement was the imperative to make worship a communal activity—everyone taking part. Such was not the custom of churchgoers in the latter part of the 15th and early part of the 16th centuries. Of course, worshiper participation was but one factor among many on which the reformers placed their focus. But it was a crucial issue. The very nature of New Testament worship revolves around the priesthood of all believers and the consequent personal involvement of every individual believer. Worship was not something done for worshipers. It was something worshipers offered, with others of like precious faith, to God. This key imperative drove the music practices of the Reformation from its beginnings and is fundamental to evangelical worship today. The apostle Paul notes in 1 Corinthians 14:26, "What then shall we say, brothers? When you come together, everyone has a hymn, or a word of instruction, a revelation, a tongue or an interpretation. All of these must be done for the strengthening of the church."[38]

---

[38] NIV www.biblegateway.com

Participation Problems with CCM

One key problem with the use of CCM in worship is that its use mitigates against the participatory concept, the heart of Protestant evangelistic worship. The overall impact of reducing such a congregational role in church services has been a gradual erosion of the Reformation idea and, in a way, a hearkening back to medieval worship, where once again hearty congregational participation by everyone gives way to watching those at the front, be it chancel, altar, stage, or platform.

Primarily a performer's music, CCM does not lend itself to community singing. Its orientation is musician/listener. Regardless of what musicians believe rock, CCM, or CWM to be, the fact remains that the locus of this style of music is centered in those who generate it, namely the performers. Improvisation of melodic, harmonic, and rhythmic components is germane to the genre. It has a soloistic vocalization style that is unsuitable for congregations. The use of heavy amplification produces a dominance that calls attention to those generating the sounds. And the stage elevation, the spotlights, sometimes even the clothing and bodily movements[39] of the singers all call attention to the performers. Underlying it all is the fact that before anything else, rock's locus is performance,[40] not corporate participation.

When a CCM praise band plays and sings, the congregation generally just watches and listens. My personal experience when visiting evangelical churches of all sizes and stripes bears this out.[41] It is true that some congregations try to sing more than others. Standing, often for extended periods of time, they may close their eyes and raise their hands. The physical stimulation of the musical beat prompts some to clap their hands or dance in place; others move their lips, watching the prompts on a screen;

---

[39] These are distracting to say the least and are often better suited to a nightclub than to a worship service.

[40] Bruce Baugh, "Prolegomena to Any Aesthetics of Rock Music," *The Journal of Aesthetics and Art Criticism* 51, no. 1 (1993): 23–29.

[41] The chapter "Visiting" chronicles the details.

some just listen. Mostly they just stare at the stage and watch the performers.

As noted previously, we are, in one way, back to the church of the Middle Ages, where the action took place up front and worshipers were essentially bystanders. The evangelical church needs to guard against its worship becoming a weekly spectator event. Few pastors or worship leaders would endorse such a situation. But that does not alter the fact that some evangelical worship has regressed, more or less, into a nonparticipatory form of religious observance quite out of step with the Reformation and with New Testament Christianity.

Just as a reminder, there are about 400 references to singing in Scripture. One whole book, the longest book of the Bible, is a hymnal (specifically referred to as the Psalter[42]). There are many forthright directives to sing God's praises, such as the familiar passage, "In the midst of the church will I sing praise unto thee" (Hebrews 2:12, KJV). Also see Ephesians 5:19 and Colossians 3:16. Jesus and His disciples sang together at the Last Supper (Matthew 26:30), Paul and Silas sang praises together in prison, and Paul, in Romans 15:9 (NIV), wrote, "I will sing hymns to your name." We could go on. Singing is very much a part of how God has set up corporate praise. It constitutes an essential ingredient of worship and an imperative activity for all believers.

Strengthening Congregational Music-Making

If the music of contemporary evangelicalism is essentially a performer's music, steps should be taken to remedy the situation—and strengthening congregational singing in the worship service should have the very highest priority. With the advent of electrified bands and the use of popular music, full participation of the church in unified musical praise has dramatically fallen off. This abatement results from numerous

[42] An interesting study is to be found in Suzanne Haik-Vantoura's book, *The Music of the Bible Revealed* (Bibal Press, 1978), in which she lays claim to having found the original music of the Bible.

factors. But for whatever reasons, less participatory involvement weakens corporate worship. The elementary, even essential, nature of the Reformation's reawakening of the priesthood of all believers becomes dissipated when worship and praise lapses into fragmented, disunited, hit-or-miss participation. Worship requires the undiminished, enthusiastic, cooperative engagement of the whole body of Christ. We cannot afford to ignore the full power and potential of congregational singing in the worship of the Almighty.

In evangelicalism, singing has historically taken a greater share of service time than any other component, excluding the sermon. Songs have the ability to address the emotions and intellect simultaneously, centering on all aspects of the faith. The topical index of a hymnal reads like a veritable who's who of lived-out Christianity. From Genesis to Revelation, birth to death, Advent through Pentecost, invitation to salvation, it's all there. Music is a commanding presence in worship, preeminent over unadorned verbalization. "But even more powerful than the spoken word is the musical word. When our words of praise to God are set to music they can be more focused and thoughtful than in simple narration."[43] Music has the ability to express what is in the heart more directly and in greater measure than words alone. As mentioned earlier, the book of Psalms, the hymnal of Scripture, is a song book and the longest book in the Bible.[44]

Some Biblical References on Singing

"The Lord thy God in the midst of thee is mighty; he will save, he will rejoice over thee with joy; he will rest in his love, he will joy over thee with singing" (Zephaniah 3:17, KJV).

"And these are they whom David set over the service of song in the house of the Lord, after that the ark had rest. And they ministered before the dwelling place of the tabernacle of the congregation with singing" (1 Chronicles 6:31–32, KJV).

---

[43] Ronald B. Allen, "Worship in the Psalms," *Reformation & Revival* 9, no. 3: 113.
[44] Suzanne Haik-Vantoura's book, *Music of the Bible Revealed*, contains a compelling look into the sounds and aesthetic of scripture's music.

"Serve the Lord with gladness: come before his presence with singing" (Psalm 100:2, KJV).

"When they had sung an hymn, they went out unto the mount of olives" (Matthew 26:30, KJV).

"Speaking to yourselves in psalms and hymns and spiritual songs, singing and making melody in your hearts to the Lord" (Ephesians 5:19, KJV).

"And that the Gentiles might glorify God for his mercy; as it is written, 'For this cause I will confess to thee among the Gentiles, and sing unto thy name'" (Romans 15.9, KJV).

"I will declare thy name unto my brethren, in the midst of the church will I sing praise unto thee" (Hebrews 2:12, KJV).

"Let the word of Christ dwell in you richly in all wisdom; teaching and admonishing one another in psalms and hymns and spiritual songs, singing with grace in your hearts to the Lord" (Colossians 3:16, KJV).

"And at midnight Paul and Silas prayed, and sang praises unto God" (Acts 16:25, KJV).

"I will sing with the spirit and I will sing with the understanding also" (1Corinthians 14:15, KJV).

"Is any among you afflicted? Let him pray. Is any merry? let him sing psalms" (James 5:13, KJV).

"And they sing the song of Moses the servant of God, and the song of the Lamb, saying, Great and marvelous are thy works, Lord God Almighty; just and true are thy ways, thou King of saints" (Revelation 15:3, KJV).

Some Practical Helps

1. Familiarity

Choose familiar songs, those that the congregation knows well. Don't choose on the basis of your personal preference. If CCM has been the music of the church for many years, there probably will be a cadre of songs recognizable to the congregation. If the texts are theologically solid and the people able to participate commensurate with the technical difficulty of the music, it might be a good time to add new material from other genres of Christian song, particularly the hymnody connected with the larger evangelical reform and holiness movements. Such standbys as "O For a Thousand Tongues to Sing;" "Holy, Holy, Holy, Lord God Almighty;" and "All Hail the Power of Jesus' Name" are exemplary expressions of musical praise. Their inclusion, and hymns in a similar musical vein whose specific focus is God and God alone, give depth and breadth to corporate worship and will strengthen the ministry of music in the assembly.

2. Sing All of It

If the song or hymn is strophic, sing all the stanzas. The more times the tune is sung the more deeply embedded it and the text will become in the minds and hearts of worshipers. Furthermore, singing only some of the stanzas renders the poet's thought incomplete. For coherence, all the stanzas are needed.

3. Keys and Range

Keep in mind that the normal average range for congregational singing (using the treble clef) is one octave from middle C to third space C (with an occasional note up to D or down to B-flat). While experienced singers and some in the congregation will have a much greater range, it is incumbent upon the worship leader not to exclude anyone from singing because of the range requirements demanded by the music. Any key is suitable if the melodic compass stays within the above prescribed limits.

4. Texts

The words of a song used in worship should be theologically sound and spiritually profound. Find material that reflects the character of God and that is written in good poetic form. Reject that which is banal and trite. Quality music and texts should be the norm. But keep in mind that song texts used in congregational worship must not be so inscrutable or esoteric that their meaning is unclear and beyond the congregation's ability to comprehend.

5. Memorization of Texts

One of the prime helps in memorizing words is to put them to music. The mnemonic potential inherent in music is absolutely wondrous; its ability to link tune with text astonishing. When words, rhyme, meter, and melody are combined, the result is a memorization aid that is powerful and proven. Songs used as learning devices are widely used in educational circles. Deuteronomy 31 gives us the Song of Moses, written and taught to all the people as a means of recounting God's words. One of the best ways to hide the precepts of God deep in mind and heart is to memorize them in a song. The trinity, God's love, Jesus' birth, the church, the death and resurrection of our Lord, prayer, healing, worship, and on and on are examples that are replete with musical tunes. It is needful, however, that tunes be memorable, singable, and be sung by the participant in order for text and tunes to link up. But once they do, worshipers will be better able to retain words and music over the long haul.

6. Tempo

Of the many evangelical worship services I have visited over the years, almost all contained congregational song tempos that were much too fast. Text and music seem trivialized. Rather, choose moderate tempos. Sing with a deliberate pace so as to not gloss over significant, deeply moving, and thought-provoking content. Conscientious, earnest singing will draw the most out of a song. Fast-paced, thoughtless singing, bordering on amusement and fun, fosters a casual and jaunty attitude that reduces worship to an exercise in jocularity.

7. Be a Realist—Is the Congregation Really Singing?

Don't hide your head in the sand. Encourage, even require, people to sing. But you will never accurately know their level of involvement until you can actually hear them sufficiently to render a judgment. Singing and playing into a heavily amplified mike will not allow you to hear the congregation adequately enough to make an accurate analysis. From time to time, silence your own singing (and playing) to better hear the intensity of their vocal output. Encourage everyone to sing and join in. Make the activity truly communal. As Scripture reminds us, "Let the people praise thee, O God; let *all* the people praise thee" (Psalm 67:3 and 67:5, KJV). As necessary, comment (briefly) on this point from time to time.

John Wesley was adamant that worshipers sing heartily. He wrote, "Be no more afraid of your voice now, nor more ashamed of its being heard, than when you sang the songs of Satan."[45] In his *Select Hymns: with Tunes Annext* (1761), Wesley gives his "Directions for Singing":

1. Learn these tunes before you learn any others; afterwards learn as many as you please.

2. Sing them exactly as they are printed here, without altering or mending them at all; and if you have learned to sing them otherwise, unlearn it as soon as you can.

3. Sing All—see that you join the congregation as frequently as you can. Let not a slight degree of weakness or weariness hinder you. If it is a cross to you, take it up and you will find a blessing.

4. Sing Lustily—and with good courage. Beware of singing as if you were half-dead or half-asleep, but lift up your voice with strength. Be no more afraid of your voice now, nor more ashamed of its being heard, than when you sang the songs of Satan.

---

[45] John Wesley, *Sacred Melody or a Choice Collection of Psalm and Hymn Tunes, with a Short Introduction* (London, 1761; rpt. Gale ECCO, 2010), 1.

5. Sing Modestly—do not bawl so as to be heard above or distinct from the rest of the congregation that you may not destroy the harmony, but strive to unite your voices together so as to make one melodious sound.

6. Sing in time—whatever time is sung, be sure to keep with it. Do not run before and do not stay behind it, but attend closely to the leading voices and move therewith as exactly as you can and take care not to sing too slow. This drawling way naturally steals on all who are lazy; and it is high time to drive it out from among us and sing all our tunes just as quick as we did at first.

7. Sing spiritually—have an eye to God in every word you sing. Aim at pleasing Him more than yourself, or any other creature. In order to attend strictly to the sense of what you sing, and see that your heart is not carried away with the sound, but offered to God continually, so shall your singing be such as the Lord will approve here, and reward when He cometh in the clouds of heaven.

8. The Song Leader

Most evangelical congregations that utilize a CCM band are guided in their singing by the lead singer of the band. But there may be situations in which a separate song leader would be advantageous. Someone who has the responsibility of engendering musical praise from the people and who has no other responsibility (such as playing an instrument or directing an ensemble) is better able to focus on the task of leading the assembly in musical praise and worship. Influencing a congregation to sing with fervor and heartfelt worship by inspiring them through one's own devout praise; a brief motivating comment; a warm, loving, pastoral attitude toward the people; encouraging words; and, if used, reasonable conducting gestures that help the singing without calling undue attention to the director, are all useful in kindling and galvanizing passionate musical exaltation to God.

Spoken directives should be enunciated clearly and distinctly. Keep one's decorum commensurate with the task at hand. When leading people in the musical worship of a holy God, save the jokes and standup comedy for other occasions. Getting the congregation to chuckle and feel good may be amusing and entertaining, but worship it is not.

Unless the leader is knowledgeable as a music director, conducting gestures tend to be meaningless and distracting. I have witnessed too many song leaders waving their arms to no purpose. Beating a three pattern to a song in 4/4 time does not work.

Dress appropriately; i.e., follow the lead of the pastor and pastoral staff. Do nothing that calls attention to yourself.

If there are stories behind the texts of the songs being sung, it is rare that verbalizing them is an edifying addition to musical worship. Use wisdom here.

9. A Cappella

As an instrumentalist, I am increasingly attuned to the fact that the unaided human voice is the ultimate instrument. Think about it; everyone is born with a singing voice; you can't discard it—it goes with you wherever you go. If one can speak, one can sing—no further training is necessary.

It would be well to normalize unaccompanied singing in worship, as many churches have done through the centuries. It is highly unlikely (though we do not know for sure) that Jesus and His disciples sang an accompanied hymn at the Last Supper, or that Paul and Silas had an accompaniment instrument with them when they sang praises together in prison. They sang without accompaniment. For centuries chant was sung without accompaniment. And the Genevan reformer John Calvin strongly believed that congregational music should be sung in unison; no accompanying instruments and no harmony was countenanced. Today there are still some churches such as the Churches of Christ, some Presbyterian congregations, Old Regular Baptists, Primitive Baptists, Plymouth Brethren, Conservative Mennonites, and others that sing a cappella. And there is at least one current congregation, part of a nonevangelical denomination, that continues specifically as an assembly which utilizes only unaccompanied song.[46]

Most contemporary-music congregations tend to be laid back. They rely on the platform people to do the work. Often they just listen or mumble a song, relaxed and uninvolved. Unaccompanied singing tends to mitigate against such an attitude. It takes energy and vigorous engagement by the congregation.

There is something about singing with voice alone that gives intensity and corporate companionability to song. Not relying on outside support such as that provided by instruments causes us to look to one another, holding hands (figuratively speaking) as together the unified body of believers lifts its praise and worship to the One who is worthy of all praise.

Worship requires effort. It is an overt action. Watching "worship" unfold at the front is not worship. That is but a kind of observer diversion, having little to do with the worship of the Creator.

For this reason, give your congregation music that they are able to sing, including unaccompanied song, and then actually expect them to do so. Occasionally, take time to rehearse new music prior to the start of the service. If they do well, commend them. If they are able to do better, have them practice the song again.

Worship leaders will never have an accurate picture of their congregations' actual singing level unless they listen to them without the intrusion of backup instruments or amplified voices. The people need to become familiar with the context of congregationally made music. Put the congregation on notice: "The work of worship starts with you."

In considering unaccompanied song, look for music that is conducive to a cappella singing: hymns, gospel songs, praise

---

[46] Donald Schell, "Music That Makes Community: Renewing Unaccompanied Song and Oral-Tradition Music-Making," *The Journal of the Association of Anglican Musicians* 26, no. 1 (January 2017): 1.

and worship choruses. The CCM or CWM genre, however, generally requires amplified instruments and voices together as one integral unit. Such is endemic to the style. For this reason popular music of this type is not easily compliant with the a cappella mode of rendering congregational song.

10. Accompaniment—Lower the Volume

Most evangelical churches use a CCM band for accompanying congregational singing. Perhaps "accompanying" is not quite the descriptive word that explains the reality of what actually happens. In my experience, such groups far outplay and outsing the congregation. It is discouraging for the congregation to try and compete with such high decibel sound levels. When people cannot hear themselves sing, let alone their neighbor, they tend to remain silent.

Worship is not a rock and roll concert. If a band is what you have, tone down the volume to where you think it should be, then turn down the volume a couple of notches more. A good rule of thumb is: If you cannot hear the congregation's output clearly and at a reasonable level over that of the band, the band is too loud. The purpose of accompaniment is to support the congregation, not dominate it.

There is ample evidence that stentorian sound levels will damage hearing. A Norwegian clinical survey of relatively young rock musicians found that 37.8 percent had significant hearing loss while only 2.5 percent of the control group had a loss. Interestingly, 64.9 percent used ear protectors in practice and 47.7 percent used protection in performance.[47] Some evangelical churches offer ear protection at the door, a practice that speaks

---

[47] Carl Christian Lein Størmer, Einar Laukli, Erik Harry Høydal, and Niels Christian Stenklev, "Hearing Loss and Tinnitus in Rock Musicians: A Norwegian Survey," *Noise Health* 17, no. 79 (Nov.–Dec. 2015): 411–421. See also Frank Garlock and Kurt Woetzel, *Music in the Balance* (Greenville, SC: Majesty Music), 153. The authors noted that the amplification used by rock musicians may boost the sound level to 130–140 decibels, exponentially higher than a jet aircraft at about 120 decibels.

volumes about the deafening sound levels the congregation will be exposed to in the worship service.

11. Fermatas

If what is being sung is strophic, such as a hymn or other type of song comprised of several stanzas, be sure to give people ample time at the end of each strophe to do several things: they may need to swallow, perhaps cough or sneeze; mentally wrap-up the prevailing poetic thought and get ready for the next one; find the new place on the page or screen; take a relaxing moment or two to "gird up one's loins for the next go-round;" and take a breath.

Musically, singers need a break; they need time. For that reason treat the last note as a fermata, a cessation of rhythmic/beat activity. In other words, no drum beats at the fermata. If drums continue during the fermata we change the whole musical feel from rest to that of a forced march. The purpose of a fermata is then lost and the mechanization of continuation is inflicted on the participants. This same discipline of observing a hold at the end of each stanza also applies when organ or piano are used. Fermatas are almost always a necessary rhythmic respite.

12. Choosing Songs

Making choices of what and how to sing has always been a part of church worship decision making. Luther, gripped by the fact that worship was a people's participatory event, chose congregational songs that were accessible; essentially simple, they were singable, not melodically or rhythmically complicated, and had a suitable vocal range well-suited to the average person. The first book printed in the New England Colonies also indicates the care with which the assembly's music was chosen. *The Bay Psalm Book*, published in 1640, contained several matters for consideration:

1. Should song be limited to the Psalms and other scriptural songs or ought hymns of human composure be allowed?

2. If the Psalms are to be sung, ought they be sung verbatim as printed in Scripture or are metrical versions acceptable?

3. Should the entire congregation sing or should it be left to a single individual?

Similarly, one of the challenges facing a contemporary worship leader is the struggle to find suitable material for worship. If a CCM band is the accompaniment ensemble of choice, the leader needs arrangements for the instrumentation at hand. If commercial contemporary praise music is the music of choice, there is no dearth of instrumental accompaniment material available. On the other hand, if songs of the hymnic variety are chosen, there is a good chance that appropriate band accompaniments may be more difficult to find.

Hymn singing is much more within the technical capability of the average person than is the singing of religious popular music. In terms of range, melodic twists and turns, vocal ornamentation, rhythm, and general style, the hymnody of the church has much to recommend it. One caution, however; don't attempt to sing hymns in the pop style of CCM. Let the genuine, forthright simplicity of hymns be retained for the good of the assembly's vocal song and the furtherance of the full gospel husbanded in its texts.

It is tempting to choose CCM songs on the basis of one's favorite contemporary group and the music such a group popularizes. I have no statistics, but I would hazard a guess that many (if not most) of the songs chosen come from a cadre of contemporary hits or favorite former hits. Thus the basis of choice ends up as market-driven as any other commercial commodity.

A tried and true hymnal is still worth looking into. It is a compact compendium of possibilities at one's fingertips for pennies a song. So reexamine the possibilities of a hymnal; its enormous musical repertoire and depth of theological expression remain unparalleled. When choosing from its contents, find material that best fits and benefits your congregation. Most books contain songs with varying degrees of quality, so hunt for those having the musical and textual integrity commensurate with one's objectives. The hymn "O For a Thousand Tongues To Sing" may be a beginning point. Written to commemorate the first anniversary of Charles Wesley's conversion,[48] it is well known and worthy of being in the church's repertoire. The tune is simple, lies within one octave, and has a balance between similar rhythmic patterns and melody notes that are freely sequential. This makes the tune memorable and, if done in the key of F, performable by everyone in the congregation in terms of vocal range.

Another example of a different type, Pauline Mills' chorus "Thou Art Worthy" (1963), paraphrases Revelation 4:11. Its particular draw is the use of Scripture as text. For evangelicals nothing surpasses the Word, and Christians find that the singing of Bible passages aids in the memorization of Scripture following the injunction: "Thy word have I hid in mine heart, that I might not sin against thee."[49] This chorus addresses God directly. Being about the Creator, not about self or how I feel about God, it offers the highest form of praise. Consider it a candidate for the church's canon of songs.

If chosen, it should be sung in the key of A-flat. The lowest note will be B-flat (for two measures) and the highest the C above middle C. For the average congregation, I prefer A-flat over the key of B-flat because the tessitura hovers at the top end of the bass or baritone range. If done in B-flat, there are a dozen high Ds (including one held for six beats), which many male singers will not attempt. If, on the other hand, there were only an occasional high D, the song sung in B-flat would be possible.

---

[48] May 21, 1739.
[49] Psalm 119:11 (KJV).

13. Melody

The tune, made up of pitch and rhythmic components, is arguably the most important part of the musical texture. It is, after all, that to which the text is set.

But even more importantly, it is the melody that is performed by the congregation. As the explicit property of the people, the melody will largely determine whether or not the congregation finds a song agreeable both in its level of difficulty and in its general ambiance.

Wholehearted participation and involvement by the congregation embody the New Testament teaching of the priesthood of all believers. If there is any one thing that distinguishes and characterizes evangelical worship, it is the need for every person to individually engage with the body of Christ in collective praise and worship of our Lord.

Choosing tunes for congregations—that is, a group made up of men and women, young and old, from all walks of life and with varying degrees of musical ability and spiritual maturity—means finding material within the capability of all the people, not just a targeted few.

Meticulous searching for such suitable tunes so that everyone can sing does not represent the usual musical praxis. Yet the necessity for doing so becomes apparent when attempting certain types of popular music. For example, one particular week in February showed Reba McEntire's "Back to God" to be at the top of the chart of "Hot Christian Songs." Be that as it may, this song will not invite or encourage full congregational participation. From the standpoint of the melody alone, the song gives forth an uncertain sound. The song's soloistic nature requires too much vocal agility and, though repetitious, is not memorable.

To test a song's congregational potential, repeat the song over and over to a nonmusician (perhaps four or five times without accompaniment) and then ask a nonmusician to sing back the melody from memory; use a nonsense syllable if necessary. If such a test proves positive (generally accurate), be assured that, from the standpoint of melody, the song in question is indeed a candidate for the church's repertoire.

Often, people cannot find the melody in the music of CCM or CWM or other popular religious genres. This is not an uncommon observation and is one of a number of reasons why participation often falls short. What is needed are simpler tunes, tunes that people can actually sing, tunes that are memorable enough and ingrained enough in the mind and heart that they are able to be sung during the week by the individuals who have sung them on Sunday.

For the nonmusician, tunes that are mostly quarter notes and half notes (with a scattering of other rhythms), that are diatonic, and, for the most part, generally conjunct seem best. I am not implying that these are locked-in entities; rather, they provide a guideline. As mentioned before, the range should be about one octave from middle C to third space C (treble clef).

14. Arranging

Because one's church utilizes a band, eschewing piano and/or organ, there is no reason to limit the congregation's musical diet to only a popular genre of music. This is where the music director's creativity needs to come into play. In all likelihood the internet and other helps will not feature the exact arrangement of a particular song for every possible instrumental combination. But adaptations can be made. Time consuming? Perhaps. Worth the time? It depends on the material in relation to congregational need.

Harmony. In most cases use the harmony of the original version of the song. Don't omit secondary chords if they are part of the composer's harmonic scheme. Some tunes such as "A Mighty Fortress Is Our God," "All Hail the Power of Jesus' Name" (using the horn fifths in measure five), or "Praise God From Whom All Blessings Flow" depend on secondary chords for the warm variety of color they accord the song. Using only primary triads is possible, but doing so detracts from the richness inherent in the composed version and yields music with a relatively bland and pale harmonic complexion.

Bass. Leave the bass line intact. Opt for music with chord inversions as they give a melodic contour to what is often a dull line, melodically speaking.[50] There are folk-like tunes, however, that require just the primary notes in the bass line if the artless simplicity of the original is to be retained. "I Love Thee, I Love Thee" from Jeremiah Ingalls' *Christian Harmony* presents a case in point. Consider the bass part of "My Jesus, I Love Thee." It offers (within the genre) an example of some increase in bass line variety. The first, second, and fourth phrases of the song use only the tonic and dominant notes in the bass, giving an overall unity to the line. On the other hand, the third phrase (line three) is conceived almost melodically in the bass, giving variety to the song. The bass part parallels the melody line for two measures at the distance of a tenth, along with first inversion positions of tonic and supertonic chords in the first and third measures (of the third phrase) respectively.

The bass is the foundation of the harmonic design and as such should be altered sparingly from the composed version. It is a part that needs to be emphasized. Hopefully there will be some type of bass reinforcing instrument in the ensemble that can do this, be it string bass, cello, trombone, baritone, electric bass guitar, bassoon, or organ.

15. Drums

Though the use of the drum set in worship has been one of the thorniest issues in church music ministry, its current use among evangelicals is widespread, if not universal. The reason for this is simply that rock music and all spin-offs of one sort or another are dependent on drums for their essential

---

[50] A case in point is Russell K. Carter's "Standing on the Promises," which opens with a string of eleven consecutive tonic notes in the bass before a run of eight subdominant notes followed by another chain of sixteen consecutive tonic notes.

character. A drum set makes no tone and has no pitch. It makes only percussive resonance. They are, according to some, the musical equivalent of the discordant and rebellious nature of the pop culture in which rock arose. Loud, often disquieting, and generally raucous,[51] they are the characteristic sound of a stressed, driven society and are used in all rock-derived musical species. Some would say the drum set is the instrumental incarnation of contemporary living.

Drums emphasize the beat of the music. Though overlaid with cadenzas of intricate rhythmic patterns, its throbbing pulse tends to dominate the texture. It often manifests a degree of power that rides roughshod over the entire ensemble, regardless of instrumentation.[52]

The drum set is not mentioned in Scripture. Its development, begun only about a century and a half ago, reflects the age of mechanization and the developing early 20th-century popular music scene. The Bible does mention percussion instruments, but none resembling the modern drum set. The percussion instruments in Scripture were gentle by contrast and were stroked with the hand, generally not with sticks or mallet, let alone a bass drum pedal.

What alternative does a worship leader have, given the fact that the use of drums is currently an established practice of the evangelical church?

First, recognize that the voice of the congregation comes first. Do nothing that will inhibit their full participation. Therefore, soften the drums on your most exuberant songs to that of musical understatement. People will not sing when their contribution to the church's song gets drowned out or significantly diminished by an overwhelming drumbeat. They need to hear themselves sing and to hear one another. Singing communally is what congregational music-making is all about.

Second, eliminate the drum set on the softer, more

---

[51] Drum sets are often placed in a sound-isolation booth.
[52] William MacDonald makes the point that the drum set was not originally intended to be used to accompany singing. William G. MacDonald, "Drum-Free Worship of Christ" (unpublished paper), 1.

meditative songs. As a matter of fact, sing portions of such songs without accompaniment at all. Or, if necessary, use only an unamplified acoustic guitar. Encourage people in this form of congregational song. You should anticipate that people, used to being watchers, listeners, and passive participants, will initially find it strange, perhaps unsettling, to get involved and actually be expected to sing. Take courage, though; it can be done.

Third, for songs that might be classed as neither exuberant openers or introspective reflections, use a creative approach and treat some stanzas (if strophic) or repetitions in a variety of ways. One might utilize the drum set in the usual manner for a portion of the song. The next portion might include a scaled-down version of the drum set with cadenzas greatly simplified and rendered considerably less ornate. Another stanza or repetition might eliminate the heavy bass beat and concentrate on the lighter, more fluid and intricate sounds.

16. Instrumentation

Churches often contain people who are gifted enough musically to make a positive contribution to the worship ensemble or band. This means that an unusual variety of instrumentalists and/or vocalists could be available to the worship leader. So what does one do, for example, with two bassoons, one guitar, and a French horn? Much of that answer depends upon the expertise of each of the players and the skill of the leader as an arranger. Granted, such a grouping of instruments does not lend itself to the usual CCM band. But it is possible for the guitar to play the chords, one of the bassoons to play the bass part, the other bassoon to play the tenor, and the French horn to play the alto. The singers would take the melody. Or, the worship leader could find or write out obbligato parts for each instrument. It would be a big help if there were a keyboard player, freeing the instruments from carrying the total harmonic load.

17. The Human Voice

In Scripture, the human voice stands out as the primary worship instrument. It is the only instrument capable of all the nuances and breadth of expression fundamental to musical worship. And it is the most personal, hence the biblical instrument of choice. The singing of the congregation prevails as a priority; therefore, vocal music commensurate with their needs should be preferred over any other type of musical material.

Whether singing takes place standing or seated, there is a tendency for people to sing with little attention to body position. This commonly results in less than vibrant congregational song. When song sheets or hymnals are used, they are often held too low relative to body position, causing the head to be angled downward in order to read the music. This causes a restriction in the vocal mechanism resulting in a repressed, sometimes strangulated, vocal sound which is directed downward rather than out into the room. Conversely, when the head is elevated and tilted back in order to facilitate singing from a high screen, the voice box is stretched out of position; the sound becomes breathy and less robust and vibrant than it could be.

The most favorable singing position is with the head tilted slightly downward, both feet on the floor, one placed somewhat ahead of the other (or if seated, with legs uncrossed, body erect, and leaning slightly forward) with reading matter held just below the chin so the sound enters the room rather than into the musical score. If singing from a screen, the eyes—not head—should be tilted upward in order to read the song text.

18. Vocal Quality

Exemplary singing and singers are rare in our culture. Music directors face issues of vocal proficiency and, more importantly, vocal quality. In a culture that extols pop music, the prevalence of poor singing abounds because contemporary pop music requires unrefined vocal sounds—usually tight, straight, often harsh, and discordant.

Such vocal timbre can hardly be avoided. Its very prevalence in the marketplace—via television, radio (including Christian stations), CDs, phone, and general muzak—attunes people to the normality of such vocal production. Unless a singer has taken steps to avoid such pitfalls, the vocal modeling people listen to will become their vocal ideal. With a powerful microphone in hand, such a singer will influence the congregation to sing the same way. That is a problem because pop vocal style, being so individualistic, does not lend itself to establishing a common unified sound suitable for group singing. Pitch bending, vocal slides, glottal pops, glissandos, rhythmic delays, and anticipations are not conducive to community song. Clear, straightforward vocal sounds that are pure, in tune, and rhythmically accurate are necessary. Such vocal production has the best chance of influencing the congregation positively. A singer who bases his or her vocal style after a favorite pop or rock singer does the congregation a huge disservice. Congregations need leadership that uses proven artistic vocal technique so the people's singing will be all it can be as their praises are lifted to the Most High.

It must be remembered that contemporary popular music styles such as CCM and CWM are essentially performers' music. The improvisatory nature of the style and the labyrinth of complex melodic and rhythmic twists and turns do not easily lend themselves to communal singing. A congregation needs to pull together with one accord, with one voice. Realistically, programming complicated pop music reduces the chance of that happening.

19. Diction

I have noticed that most church bands playing popular religious music tend to perform the instrumental portion of their renditions far better than the vocals. Numerous factors work to put singers to a distinct disadvantage and cause the text of a song not to be understood by the congregation: an imbalance in the decibel level between instruments and singers (the instrumentation is too loud); a vowel quality that is misshapen or less than pure; a sound system not optimized for clarity; and improper mike handling technique.

But the central issue in not being able to understand sung texts is faulty diction. Poor or inaccurate consonant pronunciation and enunciation, often rendering words totally garbled, remains a constant and widespread weakness. Most bands seldom even think about it, let alone address the matter. Believing that projecting the words on a screen will take care of any deficiency, they tend to dismiss the matter as irrelevant. The result is a less-than-faithful rendition of the song.

Care in pronouncing and enunciating the English language is a study in itself. As part of every singer's training, good diction is essential to rendering sung texts intelligibly. It is so basic that professional music schools require students to enroll in semester-long courses that cover the subject in thoroughgoing detail. Knowledgeable voice teachers also include instruction in diction in their private lessons, depending on the need of the student. There are many available books on the subject that benefit choral directors and CCM or CWM bands. One of the best and most detailed is Madeleine Marshall's *The Singer's Manual of English Diction*.[53]

20. Lighting

All sixty-six books of the Bible recognize God as light; "God is light, and in him is no darkness at all."[54] The latest trend notwithstanding, it seems incongruous to meet with the body of Christ to worship He who "lives in unapproachable

---

[53] Madeleine Marshall, *The Singer's Manual of English Diction* (New York: G Schirmer, 1953). Marshall was an instructor in English diction at the Julliard School of Music and the School of Sacred Music, Union Theological Seminary. Her book is written in two parts, consonants and vowels respectively. The detail and clarity of her writing has made the book a classic in the field.
[54] 1 John 1:5 (KJV).

light"[55] in a dark and light-diminished room. I am not unaware of the rationale: the screens show an increased clarity, the "stage" becomes a center of attraction, the performers are more easily seen, and the darkness cloaks people in a cocoon of anonymity. But are these "benefits" truly benefits? A darkened room isolates individuals, wrapping up each person in his or her own little world, something not conducive to the collectivity of communal fellowship. The ambiance of a dimly lit sanctuary and brightly lit platform area produces an environment commensurate with show business. That is, such lighting results in a performer/audience orientation, exactly the opposite of the intent of corporate worship. Evangelical worship depends upon worshiping "with one accord,"[56] not with sitting back to "watch the show."

21. Printed Song Texts

There are advantages to utilizing printed song texts (such as those found in a hymnal or service bulletin). Screen imagery restricts the number of lines projected at any given time; no such restriction applies to the printed page. Singing from a screen means that the words of a song, sung as they are in isolated two-line units, are sung out of context. Any connection between one unit and another must be done via memory. Taking a look back to recall what the text just said, or ahead in anticipation of where the text will be taking us, is not possible.

Having the entirety of the text so that the various lines network together into a melded whole greatly assists the singer in more completely apprehending the full meaning of the song. Able to see the entire song at once, a person may review, meditate, and study it, something possible only when in printed form. It also helps the singer to commit the words to memory. Having a library of meaningful poetry resident in one's memory

---

[55] See 1 Timothy 6:16 in the New International Version (NIV), American Standard Version (ASV), English Standard Version (ESV), New English Translation (NET), New American Standard Bible (NASB).

[56] Acts 1:14; 2:1; 2:46; 4:24; 5.12; 8:6 (KJV).

is a blessing that benefits daily living and graces the long night hours.

Upon entering the auditorium, worshipers in many churches are offered a Sunday worship guide or worship bulletin. Including in it the words of the songs to be sung (especially if the music was included) would be of immense help in aiding the congregation to participate more fully. Worshipers would also learn new music more thoroughly and would be able to take the sung material home for devotional use during the week. Just as a reminder, the hymnal with actual music and all of the words may yet be one's best resource.

22. Music Reading

One of the fallouts of the CCM revolution has been a decline in the ability to read music. In the past, people could become musically literate by learning to read music from the hymnal. Following the ups and downs of the notes on the staff and beginning part singing have been helpful in developing basic music-reading skills and elementary musicianship for those who have had a special interest in music.

But everyone can follow to some degree the contour of melodies written on a music staff. This aids in learning unfamiliar music more expeditiously, as well as helping to recall previously introduced tunes. The assembly's worship benefits from the collective song of the people of God when everyone sings "from the same page."

It would be possible for people to participate more promptly and more completely if the music of the songs sung were available. This could be done in several ways, the most obvious of which would be to provide the congregation with hymnals. Projecting the melodies and words together on an extra-large video screen might be possible.[57] Experimentation would be necessary to outfit a particular setup, but I think the exploration

---

[57] For example, searching "digital songs and hymns" on the internet may prove helpful in this regard.

worthwhile. It would work best if the entire song (melody and words), or at least a goodly portion of it, could be projected at one time so that the singer could continually read ahead in the manner characteristic of reading any kind of printed matter.[58] Among the benefits would be the developing of basic music-reading skills for the uninitiated. For the musically proficient, the singing of new music as well as the expeditious recall of less familiar songs would be of help to everyone.

Another possibility to get music into the hands of the congregation would be to print the songs (words and melody) in the worship bulletin.[59] This would take substantial space. If that presents a problem, perhaps include just one song a week, or feature a song of the month. Repeating Sunday morning's music by carefully coordinating it with other church functions such as a preaching series, Sunday school lessons, home group study, prayer meeting, etc., would reap multiple benefits. Thematically tying together the different components of the church's corporate life via a common song sung in Sunday worship and then reiterated throughout the week would be of spiritual significance to the entire community. Carefully chosen by the leadership, such musical activity could give focus to the ministry of the Word as the song is sung either in a group setting or individually via audiation.[60] This is something done quite naturally and often without conscious thought, as in, "I can't get this tune out of my head." What better song to hear internally than one that extols God's work and magnifies the Lord?

Some churches may elect to make their own loose-leaf paperback song book (with music) comprised of material that the music ministry deems worthy of being part of the church's library of praise.[61] This has several advantages: it is relatively straightforward to do; it simplifies getting the church's song

---

[58] Be mindful of the need to comply with all copyright laws. Licensing is available.
[59] Ibid.
[60] Audiation is the hearing of music internally without any audible sound being present.
[61] Copyright licensing from such organizations as Christian Copyright Licensing International (CCLI) is available.

into the hands of the worshiper; there are no projection issues to contend with; songs may be added or deleted as desired; and the contents can be tailored to each particular congregation. By having a church-wide repertoire that is known to the people, it is conceivable that the congregation could take limited ownership of the musical worship by requesting that certain songs be sung from time to time. This would go far in keeping the show-biz performer/audience/spectator syndrome in abeyance. Having a good hymnal complete with music, loose-leaf or commercially published, goes far in helping to develop musical gifts in both young and old.

23. Standing

There is no question that standing is the best physical position for singing. Just ask any choral director. As the diaphragm and abdominal muscles do their work, the epigastric area expands to allow for the maximum of breath in the lungs, which in turn initializes the activity of singing.

The length of time that people can stand is largely age dependent. That being the case, it is not possible to put a limit on just how long a congregation can manage to stand. Young children get fidgety and old people tend to collapse. Having people stand continually for forty-five minutes might be fine for Generation Y but definitively not for the Silent Generation.[62] For this reason the worship leader needs to exercise discretion in how to handle the length of time people are to stand. Mentioning in the worship bulletin that those who are not able to stand are asked to participate seated would be a desirable inclusion.

24. More on Unaccompanied Singing

The voice, alone and unaccompanied, endures as the universal instrument of praise that God has given to everyone.

---

[62] The "Silent Generation" refers to people who were born between 1927 and 1945; "Generation Y" between 1981 and 2000.

Nothing more is needed—no other accoutrements, no other sound. With just our breath and voice we are able to praise God in song. Isaac Watts, in his hymnic paraphrase of Psalm 146, writes:

> I'll praise my Maker while I've breath;
> and when my voice is lost in death,
> praise shall employ my nobler powers.
> My days of praise shall ne'er be past
> while life and thought and being last,
> or immortality endures.

> I'll praise him while he lends me breath;
> and when my voice is lost in death,
> praise shall employ my nobler powers.
> My days of praise shall ne'er be past
> while life and thought and being last,
> or immortality endures.

To mention unaccompanied song in this context generally produces raised eyebrows (see no. 9 above). Some will declare, "I can't imagine that, in today's culture, instruments would give way to the voice. We live in an instrumental age after all." But there are great values in pursuing a cappella singing.

The sheer defenselessness and vulnerability of unaccompanied congregational singing promotes a unity among those involved that is not achievable any other way. Singing, voice only, is a manifestly personal expression and, when shared in this manner, a very personal act. In this context of a cappella singing, nothing is used but "ear and throat—along with mind and heart," Alice Parker (noted collaborator of the well-known choral conductor Robert Shaw) wrote. "When we sing together, we create a community, a communion in sound."[63] Singing together promotes a communal feeling of connecting with others

---

[63] Alice Parker, *Melodious Accord: Good Singing in Church* (Chicago: Liturgy Training Publications, 1991), 115.

in mind and heart, intellect and emotion, giving to all a unique sense of togetherness and fellowship. This type of commonality has to be experienced in order to be understood. Its deep-seated sense of brotherhood, particularly around the throne of God, binds brothers and sisters together as a people of God with ties that go beyond the temporal. Singing "is a paradigm of union with the creator."[64]

To develop unaccompanied singing in a church that has never done so takes courage. People no doubt will be timid and uncomfortable. Encourage them. Begin with more contemplative songs and move on to more overt praise songs as the weeks and months go by. In any case, stay the course. Singing without accompaniment is not weird. Quite the opposite; it is as normal as possessing breath and a voice.

25. Hymns

The singing of hymns is a time-honored activity of God's people. At the Last Supper Jesus and His disciples sang a hymn before they left to go to the Mount of Olives.[65] Paul and Silas sang hymns together while they were in prison.[66] Paul observes that when believers assemble together they sing hymns.[67] And in Ephesians and Colossians, Paul counsels the church to sing hymns.[68] Whatever we might personally think about hymn singing, it cannot be denied that it has been a universal practice of the church from the very beginning.

There are many reasons why the church found hymn singing to be a tried and true method of praising God and edifying the saints:

1.   Hymns are relatively simple, melodically speaking. One does not have to be a vocal acrobat to sing them.

---

[64] Ibid., 34.
[65] Matthew 26:30.
[66] Acts 16:25.
[67] 1 Corinthians 14:26.
[68] Ephesians 5:19; Colossians 3:16.

2. They are rhythmically straightforward. Not having complex patterns and funambulist syncopation, hymns allow everyone to do exactly the same thing at the same time, thereby being in one accord with one another—a state highly esteemed by Scripture.

3. Hymns are strophic, using the same music for each stanza. Such musical repetition makes the assimilation of a new tune practicable for the average congregation.

4. Hymnody is heir to a huge repertoire of texts and tunes. There is no problem in finding something to sing for every conceivable ceremonial, theological, or worship requirement.

5. A great variety of hymnals are readily available. Relatively inexpensive, they offer worshipers the advantage of having music and words together, unlike the projecting of words alone on a screen.

6. Hymns are the only form that are host to an encyclopedic compendium of texts that, together, thoroughly and systematically celebrate and recount every corner of evangelical theology and belief.

Hymns make an unsurpassed contribution to the church's worship. They flesh out in passionate form the biblical substance of our faith. As a "people's art" they are the common song of the people of God, past, present, and future. When hymns are sung fervently and ardently we are "carried aloft into another realm where truth becomes impassioned. It is as if words alone become inadequate and we are compelled to sing."[69] Biblical content inculcated in hymnic form is, in reality, the musical lifeblood of the church.

---

[69] Calvin Johansson, *Discipling Music Ministry: Twenty-first Century Directions* (Peabody, MA: Hendrickson Publishers, 1992), 127. Pages 128–131 give thirty practical suggestions to aid in familiarizing a congregation with the practice of hymn singing.

26. Psalms

Admittedly, Psalm singing, though normative in sacred writ, is not practiced in today's evangelical church, with the exception of the relatively few congregations that sing metrical (versified) psalms. For the most part the longest book of the Bible, the Psalter, has largely been ignored as far as singing them straight from Scripture is concerned.

However, the singing of psalms need not be circumvented. Psalm singing is possible. And it is not that esoteric.

Quite simply, psalm singing has one main ingredient—the singing of large amounts of text on a single note. Once that has been grasped the rest is relatively simple. Because the Psalms are not metrical but written as prose, they cannot be rendered metrically. So, for example, the Twenty-Third Psalm could be set:

Verse 1a, all sung on one note: "The Lord is my shepherd."
Verse 1b, all sung on a second note: "I shall not want."

Verse 2a, all sung on one note: "He maketh me to lie down in green pastures;"
Verse 2b, all sung on a second note: "He leadeth me beside the still waters."

Verse 1a has 6 syllables; verse 1b has 4 syllables. Now note: verse 2a has 11 syllables while verse 2b has 10 syllables. One can readily see that verse 1a and 1b do not match the syllabification of verse 2a and 2b. Hence a metrical tune such as a hymn tune is not feasible.

The solution to the requirement for singing the prosody of the Psalms is to use what is called a reciting note (which is unmetrical) for most of a given portion of text and then a cadence for the final notes of that portion. For each verse of the psalm, the reciting notes would have a variety of syllables (depending on the length of the verse), while the cadences would always have the same number of final notes. In actuality it works quite well.

In practice, the psalm verses could be sung by a soloist or small group with the congregation joining in on a refrain repeated every couple of verses. However, it must be said that once initiated into the practice of cantillation, congregations become adept at singing the reciting notes, especially if led by a choir.

There are numerous variants of this type of psalm singing. I go into detail and give examples in my *Discipling Music Ministry: Twenty-first Century Directions*. There are also excellent resources online such as *Psalms Made Singable* and other general helps.

For those who opt for singing the Psalms in metrical version, there are many publications available.[70] One example of a metrical psalm is:

1. The Lord's my shepherd, I'll not want,
    He makes me down to lie
In pastures green: he leadeth me
    the quiet waters by.

2. My soul he doth restore again;
    and me to walk doth make
Within the paths of righteousness,
    Ev'n for his own name's sake.

3. Yea, though I walk in death's dark vale,
    Yet will I fear none ill:
For thou art with me; and thy rod
    And staff me comfort still.

---

[70] Of the many psalters available, choose one that contains all 150 psalms. Be careful of publications that are titled "Psalter" but contain songs that are only vaguely connected to the Psalms.

4. My table thou hast furnished
       in presence of my foes;
    My head thou dost with oil anoint,
       And my cup overflows.

5. Goodness and mercy all my life
       shall surely follow me:
    And in God's house for evermore
       My dwelling-place shall be.[71]

This setting is in common meter (86 86) and can be sung to any common meter hymn tune such as *Azmon* "O For a Thousand Tongues to Sing" or *St. Anne* "O God, Our Help in Ages Past." The metrical versions of the Psalms were favored by John Calvin and many of his followers. As a matter of fact, his Genevan Psalter has been in continual use since 1539. Psalm versifications are, of course, one step removed from the translated Scriptures, being put in meter and generally in some sort of rhyme scheme. Nevertheless, for those who are not able to manage psalm singing straight from Scripture, the singing of metrical psalms is an excellent alternative.

27. Altar Calls and Prayer Time

Churches that practice a time of personal devotion at the conclusion of a service are traditionally surrounded by background music of one sort or another: loud, soft, sentimental, or wandering; vocal, instrumental, or keyboard; hymns, gospel songs, pop hits, and on and on. In an insightful remark one leader notes, "Our culture has duped us into thinking there must always be music in the background. I have started asking in many places where I minister that there be no music during the time at the altar."[72] Concentration is diminished when one's

---

[71] From the *Scottish Psalter and Church Hymnary*, Geoffrey Cumberlege, Oxford University Press., No. 23

[72] George O. Wood with Randy Hurst, *Core Values* (Springfield, MO: Gospel Publishing House, 2007), 74.

neural system is confronted with intrusive musical sounds. In actuality they hinder rather than help the task at hand. It would be useful to reduce—or, better yet, eliminate altogether—such background music, especially when significant spiritual activity takes place: a time of prayer, personal counseling, or leading unbelievers to Christ.

28. Applause

Many evangelical congregations expend considerable energy clapping for people who have rendered some beneficence during the worship service. Musicians, speakers, leaders, and sermonizers are applauded as a courtesy or way of saying thank you. As well-intended as that may be, it does tend to refocus attention from God to people. Yet the central point of worship is God, not people. Worship is not simply another public meeting. Worship has a specificity which is unique. Losing that definitive difference, worship morphs into something else.

The literal meaning of the word *applause* is "to give praise."[73] When we applaud someone we are praising them, an action which in worship belongs to God alone. While it might be contended that people clap not for the person but for what that person has rendered (which may indeed edify the saints), it remains that it is the person who receives the accolade. When the Psalmist pens, "O clap your hands, all ye people; shout unto God with the voice of triumph," the focus is on God, not on a human. Genuine clap offerings tendered to God alone may exist as a leader-led activity ("Let's all give a clap offering to the King of kings"). But it is unlikely that a congregation will do so spontaneously. No, in our society clapping remains associated with "the stuff of the theater, the concert stage, the comic routine, and the political speech."[74] It is best reserved for those situations.

---

[73] Paul Jones, "Applause: For Whom Are You Clapping?" in *Singing and Making Music: Issues in Church Music Today* (Phillipsburg, NJ: P&R Publishing, 2006), 9.
[74] Ibid., 9.

29. Silence

The world is a noisy place. Technology has the ability to cram consciousness with all manner of sound regardless of the desires of the individual. People are forced to shop, eat, exercise, work, worship, and recreate to music. Try finding a grocery store that does not ingurgitate the shopper with music, or being put on telephone hold without being forced to listen to endless loops of "elevator" music.

The church has bought into this noise-filled environment. Parking lots, foyers, halls, and worship spaces are often filled with canned music foisted on people. Video clips use background music throughout, often to the detriment of apprehending what is being said (hence its message). Above all, the pre-service piped-in music saturates the body to the degree that sometimes spiritual and physical unease result. In large measure all of this is just taken for granted, a customary convention. There stands no complex theory or intent behind such practice other than the belief that providing "atmosphere" and eliminating silence is expected.

On the contrary, Scripture enjoins the believer to meditate on the Lord, His precepts, law, works, statutes, Word. Such reminders are increasingly essential in our day. When daily life endures a blitzkrieg of competing obligations, a literal rat race to be run flat out, it would be wise to allow quiet time before a worship service for worshipers to reflect and meditate without the interruption of background music. The hush of contemplative stillness remains a desirable objective. "The Lord is in his holy temple: let all the earth keep silence before him."[75]

---

[75] Habakkuk 2:20 (KJV).

4 Furthering the Reach of the Church's Music Ministry

I. Specific Ministry Opportunities for Children, Youth, and Adults

A. The Family

The basic network in Scripture is not an army, nor a crowd, nor a crew, congregation, committee, or even friends. We find that the family takes precedence over all other groupings in Holy Writ. Fathers, mothers, sons, daughters, husbands, wives, and ancestry (which Scripture recounts in detail from time to time) form the prime associative unit. The family delineates the underlying building block of all of life and living.

Note the family references in Scripture. Christ is referred to as the Bridegroom of the church and the church as bride.[76] We become children of God through adoption[77] and, as adopted sons and daughters, are welcomed into the church with the requisite privileges and responsibilities of familial kinship.

God the Father, God the Son, and God the Holy Spirit form a family-like entity. They are three persons yet one, somewhat analogous to Scripture's view of marriage, in which a man and a woman become one through a spousal covenant; two persons forming a single family, Scripture's primary grouping. And, in

---

[76] See Ephesians 5:22–33; 2 Corinthians 11:2; Ephesians 5:24; Revelation 19:7–9, 21:1–2, and 21:9–10; also Matthew 9:15 and 25:1–13; Mark 2:19; Luke 5:34; and John 3:29.
[77] Some references are Romans 8:14–17, John 1:12–13, Galatians 4:4–7, and Ephesians 1:5.

the plan of God, families blessed with children are expected to bring up their progeny in the nurture and admonition of the Lord. Mothers and fathers are answerable for their children's well-being.

B. Children

Work with children constitutes one of the most important aspects of music ministry. Often thought of as the church of tomorrow, children are in fact the church of today.

The local church, the family of God, has a role to play in the overall welfare of its children. In today's culture a child's development, if left to the secular world, will begin to reflect the mores of that world. Public academia, not allowed to base its curriculum on a Judeo-Christian value system, will perpetuate the assumptions characteristic of the wider postmodern, post-Christian, relativistic thinking of today's society. Even if governmentally sponsored schools do not actively advance an anti-Christian agenda, the politically correct tolerance proffered produces a vacuum that is unpreventable and into which flow the standards of a lost world. Children from evangelical families who attend public schools need to be buttressed against the impact of six to seven hours a day of non-Christian influence. And for those who are fortunate enough to attend a Christian or parochial school, scarcity of resources often results in a less rich curricular experience for the student. Here God's people, the assembly, the adopted people of God, the bride of Christ, have the privilege of ministering to the children entrusted to them. The church, in its care for the young, must provision them for life in a world inhospitable to the gospel, hostile to Christian morality, and which has abandoned any connection between redeemed life and daily life. This must be of special concern. Above any other agenda, plan, or program, the nourishing of the assembly's children ought not to be forgotten.

C. Holistic Education for Children

Conventional thinking tends to compartmentalize children's education. For most Christians that boils down to perceiving education in terms of secular/sacred categories: secular, having to do with the three Rs of reading, 'riting, and 'rithmetic; sacred, with the three Rs of redemption, relationship, and responsibility. The first is thought of as school, the second as Sunday school; the first as academic, the second as religious; the first as a five-day, six-hour-long commitment, the second as a one-day, one-hour-long commitment.

A more holistic approach would be to integrate the sacred with the secular so that whatever program of education an individual church undertakes, it would all be conceived as spiritual ministry. With a priority commensurate with being given the greatest gift that individual and church families have, their children and young people, churches would do well to look into developing or sponsoring Christian schools. Cherishing and teaching, forming and guiding, are challenges not easily achieved. All kinds of impediments crop up. But with vision and determination, monetary and personnel support, the mission to educate the young to the best of a congregation's ability is possible. A home missionary calling to serve children and youth, part of the Great Commission given by our Lord, remains one that the church can ill afford to sidestep. If the church avoids this obligation, it does so to its own and the kingdom's detriment.

Of course the exact details of evangelical ministry to children depend on church vision, personnel, and resources. In general, the larger the church, the more potential exists for numerous well-developed educational offerings. But all sizes of congregations, even those with only a handful of families, have the ability to do something. The following is the usual disposition of Sunday educational opportunities found in evangelical circles:

D. Christian Education for All

1. Sunday school held for children during the morning worship service. Include in children's Sunday school music material taken (and adapted as necessary) from the church's congregational cadre of songs. Remember that songs such as "Tallis' Canon," "All Things Bright and Beautiful," "Let Us With a Gladsome Mind," "Sun of My Soul," "God of Our Fathers," and other like songs are completely suitable for the early elementary grades as well as middle school and high school.
2. Children's church (which may or may not contain a dedicated religious education curricula) held during the adult morning worship service.
3. Sunday school for everyone prior to the morning service. Children attend worship with their parents, staying for the entire service.
4. Sunday school for everyone. Children attend the worship service until the sermon whereupon they are dismissed to go to Children's church.
5. Sunday school for everyone. Children attend Children's church during the adult worship service.

   Other assorted types of educational venues are listed below. All have their place in the scholastic scheme of things as they tie their particular activity to specific and distinct biblical values. Doing so eliminates the sacred/secular worldview dichotomy and integrates redeemed life with temporal life. Both academic subjects and extracurricular activities become faith-related. This view of education opens up vast possibilities to the church, whose mission to advance and live out the good news is the prime directive.

E. Suggested Musical Topics for Adult Christian Education

(Note: The following topics are fairly broad.)

Utilizing six- to eight-week segments, adult education could include various types of musical studies. Held under the auspicious of the department of religious education, each topic might relate to Scripture, theology, the Christian life, or church history. The activity would consist of a forty- to fifty-minute weekly lesson, subdivided as necessary to further interest and the educational completeness of the topic at hand. Some of the possible topics include:

1. Large works such as oratorios or cantatas.
2. Hymns or other congregational songs. Include music and texts.
3. Music in the Bible.
4. History of some particular genre (anthem, chant, gospel song, metrical psalter).
5. The music of a particular composer(s).
6. A study of particular church music texts.
7. Liturgical music.
8. Types of and examples of musical textures used in sacred music.
9. A musical/textual study of the next month's upcoming assembly songs.
10. A historical study of the organ in worship.

Each topic would be configured so as to take full advantage of personnel, resources, and facilities. The depth of each study would somewhat dictate the amount of material covered in each session. For example, in a survey course, one oratorio could be covered each week. On the other hand, if depth is the object, a single oratorio would be more than enough to span a six- to eight-week period.

Another way to frame a study plan would be to organize it around the church year. The four weeks in Advent might serve to host the Advent section of

Handel's *Messiah*. And Christmas would be well-served by the Bach *Christmas Oratorio*. Lent would be a perfect time to reflect on one of the passions. There is no end to the variety of organizational possibilities.

In each session, time should be made for musical listening, lesson details, and group interaction. One characteristic of a musical study is the variety of activities available to the teacher and class, a veritable cornucopia of substantive potential.

F. Intergenerational Faith Formation

The psalmist tells us, "One generation shall praise thy works to another, and shall declare thy mighty acts."[78] Activities in which children and adults participate jointly enact the biblical concept of human connectedness. In addition to the present, Christians have a history that defines them as a people as well as a common future toward which they aspire. The family in the context of the family of God means we are all related. Belonging together, it is normal for children and adults to walk, work, help, and learn as kin.

One of the ways adults and children might function in concert is through specialized learning activities. Projects employing an extended time frame, such as the pre-Christmas and pre-Easter seasons, give ample opportunity to cultivate and build community between young and old. Single events to celebrate a particular biblical phenomenon (for example, the day of Pentecost or the Ascension of our Lord) are also useful. Even a collective activity to mark the opening of a church addition or the close of a special church-wide event is an occasion which benefits from the combined celebrative togetherness of the whole family of God. The particulars of each individual activity must, of course, be realized within the context of each

---

[78] Psalm 145:4 (KJV).

church assembly. Numerous helps published within the faith community are available.[79]

G. Outreach Ministries

There are a considerable number of programs that may benefit children and youth depending on family, church and community circumstances, and interest. It is possible for all of these to have specific/general faith connections. All are wholesome and are of value for the overall development of the young.

1. Missions projects
2. Short-term missions outreach trips
3. Puppet ministry[80]
4. Bible quizzes
5. Nursing home ministry (singing, visitation, short programs)
6. Church camp
7. Community service
8. Local food drives
9. Sports

H. The Academy, K–12

Churches may, singly or in conjunction with other churches, sponsor a K–12 school. This requires heavy capital outlay and a particularly dedicated staff. But it is a ministry of immense

---

[79] See Lois J. Johansson, *Hands and Hearts: Intergenerational Activities Throughout the Church Year* (Harrisburg, PA: Morehouse, 2006). This book contains activities with reproducible patterns and scripts for the main New Testament events. It also has a banner-making project appropriate for any time of the year. Each of these has its basis in a biblical passage or concept and is designed so all ages are able to participate together. Also: Mariette Martineau, Joan Weber, and Leif Kehrwald, *Intergenerational Faith Formation: All Ages Learning Together* (New London, CT: Twenty-Third Publications, 2008). Holly Catterton Allen and Christine Lawton Ross, *Intergenerational Christian Formation: Bringing the Whole Church Together in Ministry, Community and Worship* (Downers Grove, IL: IVP Academic, 2012).

[80] Many resources are available online ("puppet ministry for children") and from church publishing concerns such as Gospel Publishing House, (800) 641-4310.

importance in forming the life orientation of young people. Monetarily, a Christian educational institution has a better chance of long-term survival if the congregation understands it as a home missions project rather than as an entity that is required to be self-sustaining.

The impressions acquired during youth are particularly strong and enduring. It seems unlikely that a child indoctrinated along with his or her peers for twenty-five to thirty-five hours or so a week in the values of contemporary culture as found in the average public school can somehow summarily dismiss them in favor of what is taught during Sunday's religious education hour at church. The value of daily long-term spiritual formation cannot be overemphasized. The nurture provided by such a school is a gift to be treasured. This type of ministry takes vision and sacrifice. I would not recommend it to any congregation until there is pledged long-term commitment and monetary resources.

Churches that have K–12 youth in their congregation, but are unable to host a school of their own, ought consider sending their young people to a nearby Christian or parochial school, if one exists in the area. After careful scrutiny, should such an academy be found that meets muster, perhaps a church scholarship plan might be devised to help those students who need financial assistance. A school that stresses Christian formation throughout the entirety of the curriculum, and whose faculty and staff are resolute in the faith, would certainly qualify to receive church funds.

I. Choral Activities for Young Singers

There is value in having choirs for children and youth. Singing is an activity that, hopefully, will be included in Sunday school and children's church activities. However, if it is possible to incorporate into the offerings for young people a dedicated musical activity, leaders will find a long and rich heritage from which to draw inspiration, ideas, and musical resources. Often the young are believed to be incapable of anything truly musical. Designated or thought of as "kid's choir," such ensembles end up either providing cute entertainment for adults or free babysitting for parents.

As a young lad, Martin Luther entered the *Georgenschule* in Eisenach in 1498 and joined the *Kurrende*, one of the school choirs that sang for weddings and funerals along with forays into the neighborhoods of Eisenach. There they sang for alms that were applied to the cost of attending the school. Years later Luther referred to this discipline in his *Sermon on Keeping Children in School*, 1530:

> Therefore do not look down on the fellows who come to your door saying, "Bread for the love of God," and singing for a morsel of bread; you are listening—as this psalm says—to the singing of great princes and lords. I too was such a crumb collector once, begging from door to door, especially in my beloved city of Eisenach.[81]

Luther's contact with music in his childhood home, in school, and in his early years as a clergyman shaped his deep and abiding understanding of music in the church. He was fully cognizant of the importance of music in the lives of the young. In writing "To the Councilmen of All Cities in Germany That They Establish and Maintain Christian Schools" (1524), Luther stated: "If I had children and could manage it, I would have them study not only languages and history, but also singing and music."[82]

Later (1528), in his "Instructions for the Visitors of Parish Pastors in Electoral Saxony," Luther delved into curriculum management, suggesting that the children be divided into three groups. He recommended that the first, or youngest group, "shall also be taught music and shall sing with the others." Regarding children in the second, or middle division, Luther wrote: "All the children, large and small, should practice music

[81] Carl F. Schalk, *Luther on Music: Paradigms of Praise* (St. Louis: Concordia Publishing House, 1988), 14.
[82] Ibid., 28.

daily, the first hour in the afternoon." As far as the third, or oldest group, was concerned, he declared: "When now the children have been well drilled in grammar, the more excellent ones may be chosen for a third group. Along with the others these shall rehearse music the hour after noon."[83] When Luther acquired a family of his own, he followed his own advice:

> I am sending my son John to you so that you may add him to the boys who are to be drilled in grammar and music....And tell John Walther that I pray for his well-being, and that I commend my son to him for learning music.[84]

I would urge evangelicals to research the history of and capability of youth ensembles in the service of the church. From cathedrals to the local parish, children have been a consistent part of the main musical leadership of Sunday worship week after week after week. Children have ability. There is musical gold in the years of one's youth.

A remarkable quality of children is that they don't know they can't do something. With knowledgeable leadership, they respond to musical training with enthusiasm and developing facility. The young simply follow directions, leaving the result in the hands of the director. Children are quick to learn and have the ability to recall what has been taught. There is evidence that children who sing in choirs have, as a group, the best academic records, elevated personal and social development, and exemplary self-discipline.[85] The intricacies of singing well and reading a musical score are quite within the abilities of the youngest of choristers. Some of the finest ensembles in the world are mixed choirs for adults and children in addition to

---

[83] Ibid., 28.
[84] Ibid., 29.
[85] "The Chorus Impact Study" in Charlotte Kroeker, "The Church Choral Director: Leader of the Sacred, the Good, the Beautiful," *Choral Journal* 56, no. 11: 9.

the many dedicated boy choirs and girl choirs.[86] They integrate beautifully with adult singers. Hundreds of recordings are available that attest to this fact. The big secret is out: the young are an undeveloped musical resource of the evangelical church.

One zealous and knowledgeable leader, convinced that children have the capacity to lead the music of worship Sunday after Sunday, began at the outset of his tenure at a new church a concentrated choir program for young voices. He notes: "Seventeen years later, the program is thriving and we normally have between twenty-five and thirty young singers to whom singing good music well, in a loving ensemble, is one of the central identifying traits of their Christian life."[87] Young singers growing up in such a worship environment take for granted that they have a distinct contribution to make to the corporate worship life of the church. They become absorbed into the body of believers through the process of weekly participation and musical leadership.

The practical questions relate to structure. Is there a knowledgeable and gifted leader? Are there enough children to make up a viable singing group? When will rehearsals be scheduled? And lastly, do parents and church leaders support the project?

In general a choir program has one of three rehearsal options: weekdays, Saturdays, or Sundays. Weekday afternoons are often complicated because of transportation logistics and conflicts with other activities.

---

[86] Choirs of men and boys are a time-tested, church-related type of ensemble going strong in America and Europe. Men sing the bass, tenor, and alto parts; the boys the soprano line. Less prevalent are choirs of men and girls such as that found in the Washington National Cathedral. There are also stand-alone boys and girls choirs such as the All-American Boys Chorus, American Boychoir, St. John's Boys' Choir, Tucson Girls Chorus, San Francisco Girls Chorus, and the Portland Symphonic Girlchoir. However, mixed choirs (girls and boys together) form the bulk of the children's choirs in America both in churches and schools. Some churches have extensive choir training programs beginning with children ages four to five.

[87] Mark Howe, "From the Editor," *The Journal of the Association of Anglican Musicians* 27, no. 5 (May/June 2018): 9.

J. The Saturday Choir School

If, amid an already bursting schedule, Saturday morning could be reserved for a church related choral activity, the Saturday choir school has much to recommend it. Meeting for an hour and one-half in the morning, activities are broken into two periods of twenty minutes each (music reading and vocal training) with the remainder of the time spent in rehearsal. The choir (for example grades 3–6) is broken into two classes, grades 3 & 4 and grades 5 & 6. They rotate activities: during the first period 3 & 4 study sight singing while 5 & 6 have vocal training. During the second twenty-minute period 5 & 6 practice sight singing while 3 & 4 have vocal training. Then all join together for rehearsal during the third period, which lasts for about fifty minutes.

K. The Choristers Guild

The Choristers Guild continues to be an extraordinary resource for those involved in children's choirs. It was begun in the 1940s by legendary church music educator Ruth Krehbiel Jacobs who, after years of receiving "How do you do it?" queries, organized a Christian association that "enables leaders to nurture the spiritual and musical growth of children and youth." There are now about twenty-five local chapters disbursed throughout the United States, with approximately 4,000 members worldwide. It is headquartered in Dallas, Texas.[88]

The Guild offers numerous programs that benefit children's choir leaders, including a wide array of educational offerings, music for children, handbell music, periodicals, lesson plans, helps in starting a children's choir program, online teaching tutorials, and many other benefits. There are modest membership fees depending on the level of participation.

---

[88] Choristers Guild, 12404 Park Central Drive, Suite 100, Dallas, TX 75251. Tel. (469) 398-3606 or (800) 248-7478. www.choristersguild.org

The following time-honored prayer adopted by the Choristers Guild discloses the heart of the organization and is one I used with my choir school:

Bless, O Lord, us Thy servants who minister in Thy temple.

Grant that what we sing with our lips we may believe in our hearts,

and what we believe in our hearts we may show forth in our lives.

Through Jesus Christ our Lord. Amen

L. Other Choir Options for Children

Sundays are sometimes the only time a church can find to schedule children's choir. If the Sunday school time consists of an extended session that includes Christian education and children's church, time for rehearsal might be worked into the morning's activities. Characteristically there should be an abundance of singing activities even without choir (accompaniment not necessary). But unlike group singing, a choir focuses on performance and musical skill. Moreover, a choir has the potential for use in worship and outreach, which gives it a specific ministry focus. There is nothing like a children's choir to lighten the hearts of worshipers or those in assisted living and nursing home care.

Often church leaders have discipled children and youth with a predominance of informational activity: Bible reading, prayer lists, intellectual acquisition of Scripture knowledge. However, more may be needed in today's world. David Fitch wrote, "Although all of these approaches to discipleship are good, they do not address the forming of the soul, the shaping of imagination, the orientation of desire." He continues, "We need less *information* and more *formation*. We require practices that form our relationship with God in such a way that all things— minds, bodies and souls—are ordered under the lordship of

Christ."[89] I would contend that one of the prime ways formation will take place is through the practice of singing good music, music compositionally crafted with the highest artistic standards coupled with texts that are poetically and theologically sound. The surest way to deconstruct spiritual formation is to sing religious pop music, music which is inartistic and made with and for expendability and entertainment.

M. Adult Church Choir

The ministry of a choir is invaluable in worship. Choirs have a comprehensive role that encompasses spiritual support of the pastoral leadership of the church, the leading of congregational singing, and the rendering of special choir music.

Scripture documents a well-formulated and organized choir ministry. Singers had an ecclesiastical role, spiritual and musical, whose defined task was to minister to the Lord in music. These musicians were of the priestly tribe of Levi and were set aside and consecrated to work in the house of the Lord. The leadership role of the choir was unique, at once musical and also clerical. Even in our time it retains its ministerial and priestly function, being comprised of laity who by virtue of the priesthood of all believers are ordained to minister as priests unto God.

Among the considerations for developing choirs and choral ensembles in a church setting is the capacity of choral music to simultaneously reach people emotionally and intellectually. Music, having no material substance, is a prime vehicle for conveying intangibles. Being abstract and ethereal, music cannot be captured in time. Its very nonmateriality identifies it with the transcendent nature of the Divine. On the other hand, the texts of choral music being concrete and corporeal have a physical, immanental cast. Together, music and words are a formidable presence in a worship service. In listening to the choral offerings of a choir, congregations have every probability for receiving

---

[89] David E. Fitch, "Discipleship for Our Day," *Alliance Life* (November 2007): 10.

truth in full measure noncognitively and cognitively, affectively and cerebrally, emotionally and intellectually, provided that the piece being sung has the integrity and compositional quality (musically and textually) commensurate with the full gospel. Especially when texts are printed in the church bulletin so that people are able to follow the words clearly as they are being sung, is a special connection and identification with the content of the music possible. And, of course, developing the God-given musical talent of the individual singers in a church choir is not an insignificant aspect of music ministry. It would be appropriate for every church to set aside money in the budget for establishing and sustaining such a worthwhile ministry.[90]

If the church employs a small singing group or praise team and band, please note that the ministry of the choir in no way diminishes the smaller group's contribution or usefulness. The choir's input simply enriches the service. The following are some specifics useful in choral music ministry:

1. The ministerial mission of the choir

    Above and beyond its musical role, the choir functions as a spiritual force not only in embracing the work of the people (worship), but also in blessing the pastoral staff. This aspect of choir ministry is arguably one of its most important offices. In a sense, the choir stands between pastor and people, nurturing both through its prayers and steadfast support. Staff benefit greatly when undergirded by the impassioned intercessions of those in the ministry of music. When Christian *agape* love is the ambient medium through which the choir discharges its intercessory office, the unity of being in one accord strengthens the efficacy of their prayer. Choristers who practice their calling as "a

---

[90] In the 1930s an absence of adequate monetary resources caused well-known music director Healey Willan to tax his choristers ten cents per month! In Ruben Valenzuela, "Healey Willan (1880–1968): Establishing a Musical Legacy," *The Journal of the Association of Anglican Musicians* 26, no. 3 (March 2017): 6.

chosen generation, a royal priesthood, a holy nation, a peculiar people"[91] are a formidable spiritual presence to be reckoned with.

The spiritual energy of a dedicated group of singers focused on the pastoral leadership is a blessing beyond compare. It is not easy to be a pastor. Ministering in the midst of a culture that has largely rejected the tenets of biblical truth requires constant sustenance. The ever-present temptation of believers to give in to the world in little things commonly leads to an incremental collapse of larger issues. Christian standards become watered down, and the testimony of the Christ life less vibrant. Those in leadership are vulnerable; abandonment, discouragement, disillusionment are only an arms-length away.

The choir can be an enormous help here. What pastor would not welcome the heartfelt support and encouragement of a radiant group of choristers? As a matter of fact, all those on the front lines of ministry, whatever the specific area, benefit from the spiritual backing and sustenance that a choir is able to bring to the corporate life of the body of Christ. Prayer, of course, is the number one tactic for providing strength and refreshment to those in ministry. However, a personal word, a material token, or other expression of goodwill goes far in keeping a pastor and staff encouraged. Such gifts are beyond compare and are fully part of the ministry of the choir.

Choristers also assist in worship by their careful and enthusiastic attention to the worship leader of the moment. A choir's unreserved amenability sets an example for the people to follow. Requesting a show of hands, a call for extemporaneous prayer, extending the hand of fellowship to a neighbor, the giving of personal testimonies, or listening to announcements, a vocal

---

[91] 1 Peter 2:9 (KJV).

solo, report, or sermon, the choir has a responsibility to be a model of responsiveness and receptivity. It can do much to inspire congregational involvement in a worship service.

2. Choir and congregational song

The choir is an excellent leader of congregational singing. With every chorister thoroughly rehearsed on the songs to be sung, the unanimity and solidarity of praising the Lord together inspires wholehearted participation throughout the worshiping congregation. Such leadership is not only musical, it also communicates through facial expression, eyes, and general bodily demeanor. As a facilitator of worship, the choir shows the congregation the way to break out of the temporal and reach the heavenly. It exhibits a worship in spirit and in truth that encourages others to do the same. In taking the initiative, the choir inspires, helps, and leads. As recipients of the earnestness and enthusiasm of those in front of them, the community of believers experiences a deeper, more fervent worship than that which would be achieved without the priestly leadership of the choir.

On the other hand, a choir made up of disinterested, unenthusiastic, unresponsive individuals, or a group that executes its musical duties poorly for whatever reason, eliminates any advantage an ensemble might afford the worshiping community. It would be better not to have such a group.

To make the most of the choir's leadership potential, it is essential that the director rehearse the choir well ahead of time on any congregational music that is unfamiliar. Having a chorus of well-practiced, enthusiastic singers to lead the assembly will inspire worshipers to give of their best in rendering praise to the King of kings and Lord of lords. Every practice technique advantageous to learning should be used with the choir so that together, they and the congregation will form a musical commonwealth of believers whose hearts have been touched with the fire of God's love through the channel of singing in one accord.

The following are some suggestions for choir members and leaders involved in preparing for congregational song leadership:

a. Rehearse well ahead—as much as four or five weeks.

b. Rehearse thoroughly, working on melody and text until the choir is able to sing the song accurately, well, and with understanding.

c. Work diligently on enunciation and pronunciation, especially consonants.

d. After the group's initial introduction and rehearsals of an unfamiliar tune, be sure to practice with the specific accompaniment forces which will be used for the worship service, be they full worship band, keyboard alone, or with obbligato instruments, or just a single instrument such as acoustic guitar, piano, or organ, etc.

e. In the worship service have the ensemble sing in unison until such time as the congregation has learned the song well. This may take weeks or even months depending on how frequently a new song is repeated.

f. After the people are familiar with a song, a judicious balance between unison and part singing will lend variety to the choir's musical leadership.

3. Special choir music

In addition to having a pastoral role in worship
and in leading the church in congregational song, the
choir may, from time to time, provide special choral
music for the edification of the saints. Though not the
primary function of the choir, rendering an anthem
with refinement and grace is a ministry that has the
potential of reaching the deepest recesses of the heart.
Music, moving fleetingly in space/time, is an emotional
language that is caught rather than taught. It moves
us in ways that the spoken word is unable to do. For
some in the church, listening to the choir's singing
has the potential of ushering the listener into the very
Holy of Holies, the place where the heart of God and
the heart of man meet. Music here is not unlike the
ministry of the Holy Spirit: both are real, yet without
mass; felt, yet unseen; covert, yet effectual; amiable, yet
compellingly moving. In a sense, music operates much
like love: powerful, wordless, and intuitive. And when
coupled with worship texts that extol God Almighty,
music becomes more than just the sum of its parts. As
one author put it:

When in our music God is glorified,
and adoration leaves no room for pride,
it is as though the whole creation cried Alleluia!

How often, making music, we have found
A new dimension in the world of sound,
As worship moved us to a more profound
Alleluia![92]

---

[92] Words by F. Pratt Green; music, *Engelberg*, by Charles Villiers Stanford. In *The
Christian Life Hymnal* (Peabody, MA: Hendrickson Publishers), 56.

Leading up to his Aldersgate experience[93] when John Wesley felt his "heart strangely warmed," he attended choral evensong at St. Paul's Cathedral in London. The year was 1738, and his journal reveals that though there was characteristically no sermon from the pulpit at choral evensong services, there was nevertheless a sermon from the choir loft in the form of a verse-anthem. The one likely sung that day was William Croft's lengthy verse-anthem setting of Psalm 130, "Out of the Depths Have I Cried Unto Thee" for bass solo, four-part choir, and organ. In the anthem, Croft emphasized and reiterated the words "trust in the Lord," which is exactly what Wesley did later that day at Aldersgate. On the two subsequent afternoons he likewise was present at St. Paul's choral evensong services. They also contained psalm settings in the form of verse-anthems, Henry Purcell and Maurice Greene being the composers of choice those two days.[94] The sung Word is powerful when divine revelation is revealed through words set to music commensurate with that divine revelation. Good texts set to good music are a compelling and weighty combination.

Practical helps for the singing of special choir music:

a. Think of special choir music as congregational edification through the testimony of song.
b. Most, but not necessarily all, music should be within the capability of the congregation to grasp, musically and textually. Some music should be retained that will, over time, cause

---

[93] Attending an evening meeting in Aldersgate, there was a reading from Luther's *Preface to the Epistle to the Romans*. Wesley wrote: "While he [Luther] was describing the change which God works in the heart through Christ, I felt my heart strangely warmed. I felt I did trust in Christ, Christ alone for salvation, and an assurance was given me that He had taken away my sins, even mine, and saved me from the law of sin and death."

[94] Robin A. Leaver, "Celebrating With a Penitential Psalm: Psalm 130," a sermon preached at the 2016 Fair-Chester Conference, in *The Journal of the Association of Anglican Musicians* 25, no. 6: 11.

the congregation to expand their musical understanding.

c. The choir's music should be within their technical and vocal capability to render well.

d. Choose a variety of material. Don't neglect the historicity of the church. Include older music and styles of music from time to time.

e. Don't be afraid of simplicity. A Christmas carol, for example, sung well with some variety in voice-part divisions from time to time, can be moving and inspirational.

f. If there are choir people who sing particularly well, occasionally program anthems for them that include solo passages.

g. Be especially concerned with enunciation and pronunciation so that the congregation will be able to understand the words being sung. It is particularly disconcerting to people not to understand the text of a choral piece. If there is a worship bulletin, include in it the words of such special music. Doing so will not only render clarity to the choir's song, it will allow anthem texts to be used at home for meditation and for personal devotions.

II. General Music Education

Part of the contentious warring over music in worship resides in the public's adoption of pop music as its normative, everyday music of choice. The so-called worship wars of the 1970s through the first decade of the 2000s were essentially a style-based conflict. Popular music is what people were led to, drank deeply of, and were shaped by. The issue centered on what people liked, what was familiar to them, as opposed to what was appropriate and reflective of both historic practice and biblical norms.

It took over twenty years from the inception of rock and roll to Larry Norman's contention that rock music was congruous with worship (1969). Credited with opening evangelical doors to the genre, he is thought of as the father of Christian rock music. During those twenty years the fierce initial opposition to rock by Christians dissipated somewhat, and the battle for the musical soul of the church was on. Little by little leaders and people relented until finally pop styles were no longer just tolerated by the evangelical church but became the preferred worship music of most evangelicals.

A. Forging Musical Preference

The reason that the takeover of church music by various pop styles was accomplished relatively quickly and completely after 1970 was due to a number of factors:

1. The post–World War II cultural climate in America warmed to liberal progressivism on all fronts: education, law, politics, theology, psychology, sociology, and aesthetics. The general movement of the nation's worldview assumptions moved from an accepted, rather laissez-faire theism to an outright postmodern relativism. Having lived through this whole era, I experienced the changes in our culture firsthand and with singular clarity. In a nutshell, the last seventy-five years begat an almost total rejection of objectivity and, conversely, an unthinking acceptance of subjectivity. That is to say, individual preference, opinion, whim, taste, desire, caprice, likes, and dislikes became the new standard—entirely relativistic and subjective. This fracturing of the objectivism characteristic of Judeo-Christian theism resulted in a sweeping personal egocentrism which produced a nation on its way to

being out of control. As recounted in the book of Judges, "Everyman did that which was right in his own eyes."[95]

2. Such a widespread relativistic worldview affects all aspects of culture: moral standards depend upon individual preference; theological heresy is just a matter of accommodating the gospel to culture; American jurisprudence reads, interprets, and applies the law subjectively to the extent that the killing of unborn children is mandated to be a constitutional right; the spectacle of one court overturning the rulings of another (though both use the same law) occurs frequently; political parties move in lockstep with the philosophical fashion of the day; education incontestably mirrors the mores of the nation as a whole.

   It is no wonder that the country's discernment in the arts in general and music in particular has succumbed to the subjectivity of individual taste. For most people it is either baffling or ludicrous to speak of universal objective musical standards. The very idea that anything could trump one's own personal and individual musical preference with something more valuable seems incomprehensible. No longer is there an accepted good, better, and best in the arts. The fact that "I like it" is all that matters.

3. As subjectivism took hold of people's psyche, objective aesthetic value judgments were suspended, leaving people wide open to unconditionally absorbing all manner of music without the need for evaluation other than their liking it. And since people tend to like what they know, their preferences were leveraged by what was provided them. And what was supplied came through the juggernaut of popular media's business acumen and technology.

4. Technology coupled with business interests ushered in a new era. At the turn of the 20th century, ease of

---

[95] Judges 17:6; 21:25 (KJV).

publishing, electrical amplification, radio, recording, and television (beginning in the 1940s) provided wide-open, large-scale access to the public. Initially known as mass culture, this phenomenon gave rise to a new approach to music in which music became less of an activity and more of an inactivity; that is to say, more passive. The parlor organ gave way to hi fi and stereo, singing to listening. Homes, stores, automobiles, and any place where the public gathered was wired for "canned music." Recording studios, where technologically altering sound (an engineer's and studio musician's dream) became commonplace, turned out recordings by the millions. Background muzak comprised of popular musical styles was unavoidable. It was everywhere. The public was inundated with the music of a new era. Pop music, a disposable music, was a music that reflected the values commensurate with relativistic culture. There was no way to escape it.

As generations were born into this new world of sound, it became their world, the only world they knew. As a result, popular music in all of its various permutations and styles resonated with culture's nontheistic worldview assumptions and became the music of our time. Is it any wonder that the evangelical church adopted it?

B. A Broader Field of Vision—Continuing Education

The original Sunday school movement begun in England in the 18th century was not only concerned with the teaching of the Bible, but with secular subjects such as language arts and arithmetic. Classes were sometimes expanded beyond Sunday to weekdays as well. By 1800 there were 200,000 enrollees in England's Sunday schools, rising fifty years later to about 2 million. Those who pioneered the movement realized that illiteracy was no boon to the spread of God's word. Hence the curricular expansion into the "three Rs" served the purpose of religious education while simultaneously endowing children with basic educational skills.

The example of our spiritual forebears to combat the illiteracy of their time is abundant inspiration for us to do the same. Even as helping people to read and write gave people access to a richer faith life, so clarifying, ennobling, and opening up the language of music to evangelicals would give people access to deeper, more profound worship. As has been previously noted, a considerable portion of evangelical worship service time is music. Imbuing worship with musical elements of the pop world results in worship that is of the world.[96] The evangelical church would be well served and spiritually strengthened by moving away from the profane and carnally subjective-driven musical language of our post-Christian culture. Replacing it with a musical vocabulary commensurate with objective musical standards—those not based on the need to be popular—opens up treasure trove after treasure trove of good, solid, theologically affirming musical possibilities.[97]

Since the music of evangelicals is due to the largely unrecognized and unapprehended musical education its people have had imposed upon them by the wider culture, it is needful that the church do what it can to promote objective theistic musical values in its people. Making such music normative would be of immense benefit to the congregation and its worship. It would bring evangelicals into line with scriptural standards.

There are activities, outside of the usual Sunday school offerings, that would serve to cultivate increased musical discernment and appreciation. They are part of a broad approach

---

[96] See 1 John 2:15; Romans 12:2; James 1:27.

[97] Song books such as *The Worshiping Church* (Hope Publishing Company), *The Christian Life Hymnal* (Christian Book Distributors), and *The Hymnal for Worship and Celebration* (Word Music) contain a variety of serviceable materials. Among composers who write quality music useful to evangelicals are K. Lee Scott, Robert Leaf, Sue Ellen Page, Alice Parker, Martin Shaw, Helen Kemp, John Ferguson, and Mabel Boyter, as well as cherished standbys George Frideric Handel and Johann Sebastion Bach. This list is just a very small sample of possible composers.

to Christian life and living, therefore very much part of the educational work of the church. The following listing is but a sample of possible music education venues for children, youth, and/or adults:

1. Chime and bell choirs for children, youth, and adults. These ensembles would be able to play periodically for church services.
2. Weekday or Saturday choir school for children and youth (this has been discussed previously in the chapter).
3. If eliminating all background music throughout the church campus is too problematic to start with, a helpful beginning would be to turn down the volume and program pieces of substantive quality. The point in dispensing with muzak is to help foster active (attentive) listening rather than passive (inattentive) listening.
4. The use of church facilities for vocal and instrumental ensemble practice (especially for home-schooled youth) under the direction of a knowledgeable leader.
5. Allowing piano and instrumental lessons to be given by outside teachers.
6. A review in depth of a well-known, large-scale sacred music work such as Handel's *Messiah*, Mendelssohn's *Elijah*, Bach's *St. Matthew Passion*, or Matthew King's *Gethsemane*. Each work could be looked at from a textual and musical point of view. Listening would be an important component of the study. This may be accomplished by meeting once or twice a week in units of three or four weeks each.
7. Trips for children, youth, or adults to area symphony concerts, recitals, or choral programs.
8. The formation of an adult dinner/concert group.
9. Summer music camp such as New England Music Camp (West Sidney, Maine); Interlochen Summer Music Camp (Interlochen, Michigan); Baldwin Wallace Music Camps (Berea, Ohio).

10. Short-term groups of children, youth, and adults to practice Christmas carols for ministry to hospitals, nursing homes, and shut-ins.

11. Encouragement of the children and youth of the church to join the choir of the school they are attending. It would also be good if the church publicized the concert programs of these choirs to support the church's youth.

12. The church leadership should actively encourage their children to take piano or orchestral instrument lessons from qualified private teachers.

13. Church-sponsored recitals given by the children and youth of the congregation who are taking private music lessons.

14. Encourage intercultural musical activities for all age levels to further understanding and appreciation of the fine arts.

15. Teaching musical discrimination to the young gives early exposure to life skills in musical comprehension, disposition, judgment, and preferences. Since pop music, particularly rock, is injurious to the development of innate musical aptitude and talent, musical discernment from a Christian perspective (given in formal or informal settings) would be of great benefit.[98]

16. Music appreciation venues. Musical appreciation materials that emphasize the classics prime youngsters for a lifetime of comradeship with the great music of the ages. This music will become a benchmark by which all other music will be measured; musical judgment and musical values are enhanced when great music becomes the normal musical language of everyday life.[99]

17. Individual creativity. One of the ways to further the artistic enterprise throughout the congregation is by

---

[98] Kimberly Smith's books *Oh, Be Careful Little Ears* and *Let Those Who Have Ears to Hear* are particularly helpful in dealing with children and youth (Winepress Publishing). Also *Rock Music's Powerful Messages* by John Ankerberg, Dr. John Weldon, and Eric Holmberg is a useful beginning in addressing the question of the suitability of rock music for teenagers. There are numerous other resources available online.

[99] Numerous music appreciation courses and books are available online such as *Classics for Kids, Introducing Music Appreciation to Elementary and Primary Students, Learning the Grammar of Music Appreciation*, and *Squilt Music Appreciation—Music Appreciation Made Easy.*

encouraging the composition of personal works of art: music, drama, poetry, story, painting, etc. To further the goals of ministry, encourage such works to be made with a particular bent toward excellence as modeled in God's creation of the world and toward which church music aspires.[100]

18. Creativity festival. Adjusting for local circumstances, set aside a daylong, afternoon, or evening block of time for the celebration of works of art authored by members of the church family. Included may be anything original: painting, sculpture, writing, needlework, music, drama, drawing, poetry, photography, woodwork, etc. The purpose of the activity is to highlight and develop the God-given creativity afforded every person and to make the church a center for creativity and art. Holding a festival gives opportunity for displaying, performing, and sharing each participant's work.[101]

---

[100] *Some Suggestions on How to Pursue the Artistic Adventure* from "Notes on 'The Artistic Adventure,'" an address by Leland Ryken, Wheaton College, n.d.

(1) You already exercise your artistic ability, whether consciously or unconsciously. The challenge is to improve the quality of an artistic experience you already enjoy.

(2) Your quest for excellence in artistic experience must begin where you are. The point of departure is to understand the artistic principles in works of which you already have some grasp.

(3) In order to succeed in the artistic adventure, a person must be aware of what is happening in a work of art, music or literature. Response depends on an awareness of the artistic dynamics of a given work.

(4) The artistic adventure requires that a person learn what to look for in works of art, music and literature. To respond adequately, a person must come to a work with the expectations appropriate to the given form he is contemplating. College courses should be viewed as courses in methodology, designed to give the skills necessary to understand artistic works.

(5) The acquisition and exercise of any skill requires conscious discipline. The artistic adventure is no exception. More sophisticated kinds of art require more discipline than simpler forms require, but the rewards are usually greater where the expenditure of effort is greater.

(6) Artistic fulfillment is characterized by "serious non-seriousness;" that is, people enjoy contemplating artistic works because they want to, not because they have to. Yet, despite this lack of coercion, serious involvement is required for the artistic adventure.

(7) Given the large number of paintings, works of music, and works of literature that exist, a person must be selective in the painters, musicians, and writers he chooses to know well.

[101] When employed as a director of music at a Springfield, MO church, Grady Manley developed and used this concept with great success.

III. Technological Helps

The following are possible utilities which may be useful to the church musician.

A. Music Readers:

1. **ForScore** for an iPad (iOS8 or later) is a music reader. No more fumbling with awkward page turns (forscore .co, iOS).
2. **OnSong** for iPad is similar to ForScore (onsongapp .com, iOS).

B. Music Writing:

1. **MuseScore** works with the app for MuseScore.org (MuseScore, iOS and Android).
2. **Notion** is an iOS app for iPad, iPod touch, and iPhone. It may be used with a MIDI appliance (Notion, iOS).

C. Metronome:

1. **Metronome Plus** may be used in the customary manner but also has multitasking and customization features (Metronome+, iOS and Android)
2. **Pro Metronome** contains a whole range of rhythmic and screen features (Pro Metronome, iOS and Android).

D. Tuning:

1. **Cleartune** can tune any instrument that is able to sustain a tone (Cleartune, iOS and Android).
2. **Pano Tuner** covers the entire range of the piano and comes in a free version. It is available for iPhone, iPad, Android devices, and may be used on a computer by downloading the app from Google Play (Pano Tuner, iOS and Android).

3. **Pitch Pipe** is an uncomplicated, straightforward tuner for use in the keys of C and F (Pitch Pipe, iOS and Android).

E. Music Theory:

1. **Theory Lessons** is compatible with iPhone and iPad (Theory Lessons, iOS).
2. **Musictheory.net** contains online basic music theory lessons (www.musictheory.net).

F. Music Notation:

1. **Noteflight** is a particularly flexible online software music notation package. Free (www.noteflight.com).
2. **Finale** is a tried-and-true program for engraving music scores (www.finalemusic.com).
3. **Sibelius** is another sophisticated music engraving package (www.avid.com/Sibelius).

G. Vocal Music:

1. **Vocal Ease** contains exercises and helps for the singer's warm-up (Vocal Ease, iOS and Android).
2. **Choral Public Domain Library** contains a huge repository of downloadable choir music especially useful to those with minimal monetary resources (www.cpdl .org).
3. **IMSLP** (International Music Score Library Project) is also a public domain library that does have some MP3 recordings for some works (www.imslp.org).
4. **St. James Press** is a popular site for downloadable choral music available through subscription (www.sjmp.com).
5. **The Music Library.com** may be helpful in finding a wide variety of choral music for the church choir (www .themusiclibrary.com).

6. **The Royal School of Church Music in America** and **RSCMA Press** offers vocal training through its *Voice for Life* curriculum, choral materials, and links to a variety of choral music publishers (www.rscmamerica .org).

7. **Young's Music** specializes in used choral music (www .youngsmusic.com).

8. **CyberBass** provisions singers with rote aural methods for the learning of SATB choral voice parts (www .cyberbass.com).

H. Organizations:

1. **The Church Music Institute** provides church music resources for a wide variety of Christian persuasions. It has a 11,000-title eLibrary for members. Cost is a $75 fee for individuals; $200 for churches (www .churchmusicinstitute.org).

2. **The Hymn Society in the US and Canada** promotes congregational singing via annual conferences, a newsletter, and an online resource, *The Center for Congregational Song*. Annual membership for individuals and churches is $75 (www.thehymnsociety.org).

3. **The Choristers Guild** provides music for children, educational material, handbell music, lesson plans, and helps in starting a children's choir program. 12404 Park Central Drive, Suite 100, Dallas, TX 75251-1802. Tel. (469) 398-3606; (800) 248-7478 (www.choristersguild .org).

I. Other Online Resources:

1. **YouTube** may be of use to those who wish to hear recordings of particular choral or instrumental music.

2. **Evangelical Resources for Music Ministry** has a variety of helps which may be of use to church musicians.

3. **Oremus Bible Browser** is a multiuse site that allows Bible searches in various translations using a word or phrase common to the passage researched (bible .oremus.org).

4. **Bible Gateway** works well for looking up Bible passages in almost any translation. It is also extremely valuable in researching biblical topics, key words, reading plans, and devotional helps (www.biblegateway.com).

5. **Hymnary** is one of the most complete databases of North American hymnody available. Does not contain a concordance, however (hymnary.org).

PART II

5   Culture and Religious Popular Music

In the summer of 1959, as a student at Houghton College, I accepted the position of music director at one of the large churches in Olean, New York. It was a sleepy little town thirty miles from Houghton, and I found myself alone with not much to do.

During those months I made friends with Clarence Goudy, pastor of a small Pentecostal assembly. Rev. and Mrs. Goudy, formerly missionaries to Africa, lived in an apartment attached to the rear of the church, and they often invited me for Sunday dinner following our respective morning services. Their fellowship and counsel, let alone the sharing of a meal that I now realize was funded from very meager resources, were a great blessing. And so, whenever I was free, I attended Sunday evening services and, from time to time, during the week when special services were held.

That summer Pastor Goudy invited David Wilkerson, well-known evangelist and founder of Teen Challenge, to hold a series of meetings. By that time Wilkerson had already established Teen Challenge, a ministry to aid drug addicts and fringe people in New York City. On one particular night I recall his recounting the story of Teen Challenge's beginnings.

David pastored a church in Pennsylvania. A zealous and dedicated shepherd, he worked hard among the people to further the kingdom of God in that place. But one Sunday night following the evening service, he returned home prepared to collapse. "I was all in, tired, exhausted. I had preached my heart out. Drained, I initiated my usual Sunday night routine of flopping down in an easy chair with a large bottle of root beer to watch the late show on TV." He went on to explain that it was at this point that the Holy Spirit convicted him so powerfully and in such a way that he was compelled to intensify his pastoral work. Through a series of circumstances he went on to begin a ministry to the marginalized young people of New York, a work that eventually became known as Teen Challenge.

Wilkerson was a straightforward, no-holds-barred preacher pulling no punches. Highly opinionated and unbending, his preaching style was ardent, even bombastic at times. Above all, his impassioned pleas to follow Christ and live a life of holiness, separated from the world, the flesh, and the devil, were central to his message. No doubt he would be called a fanatic today. He would gladly have worn the label.

One of the families in Pastor Goudy's church had a wayward son for whom the church had been praying. The young man had joined a rock and roll band that played in the bars and night clubs of Olean. During one of the evening services I recall that Wilkerson, burdened for the soul of this teenager, left the meeting and went to the night club where the rock band was playing to reason and plead with the young man. During the time of Wilkerson's absence, the church remained in prayer, asking God for a favorable response to the evangelist's rescue mission. After some time he returned, alone and without the youth. "But," he told the congregation, "I have never seen a young man so under conviction." For whatever reason the rock 'n' roller just could not let go. At the time Wilkerson was well aware of the debilitating effect that rock music had on the spiritual lives of the young. That summer he published his "Rock and Roll, the Devil's Heartbeat" alerting thousands of families across the United States to the serious debilitating effects of rock and roll.[102]

---

[102] David Wilkerson, "Rock and Roll, the Devil's Heartbeat," *The Pentecostal Evangel*, July 12, 1959. David Wilkerson, *The Devil's Heartbeat: Rock and Roll!* (Philipsburg, PA: Teen-Age Evangelism, n.d.).

Basics of a New Music

Rock and roll music, with its mind-boggling number of permutations, is arguably the most influential music ever produced. It cannot be denied that more effort, time, money, and listener exposure has been given to it than to any other musical form in history. All music of this genre, derived from rock's explosive genesis in the 1950s, permeates the entirety of our society. Shopping, telephone holds, attending a professional sports event, watching a recent movie, background for educational videos, restaurant dining, commercials—even the time spent in a waiting room—often means some kind of forced musical exposure. And, as I discovered, it is normal fare in the evangelical church.

Wilkerson found rock music to be a collaborative partner in that triumvirate of "sex, drugs, and rock 'n' roll." While others initially railed against this music from a theoretical point of view producing hundreds of sermons, articles, and books, Wilkerson, to his credit, as one who worked directly with the young people who were affected by it, understood through observation the corrosive quality of this music. He sensed something in this form that caused him alarm. The wholesale rejection of Judeo-Christian values, evidenced by drug addiction, immorality, vacuous norms, and general lifestyles of rock enthusiasts, was not lost on him.

Rock was a revolutionary music. It was the result of, an expression of, and an influence upon many different aspects of national life. That is to say, one cannot divorce its creation from its creators, nor can it be divorced from the culture in which it was created, or from the influence it imposed on that same culture. For the music itself, derived from the value system of its makers, expresses the culture in which it was made, as well as having, in turn, a formative affect/effect on society.[103] Undeniably, rock was a musical expression of a deep-seated discord nested in the common psyche of Western civilization:

---

[103] There are many books and articles that chronicle the history of rock and roll in some detail. The internet also has summaries of its development.

musical nihilism, personal rebellion, spiritual anarchy, unrestrained sexual indulgence, and violence.[104]

Immorality and drugs fueled the fierce rebellion and mutinous unrest of rock's propagators and became the societal expression of rock's defiant and anarchistic sound. These essential characteristics are so deep-seated, so centered at the very core of this music, that none of the mutations and variations of this musical style can jettison them. The many spin-offs of rock music are all incapable—that is, are musically unable—to eradicate the nihilistic traits inherent in this music. While it is possible to become so hardened by listening to heavy metal or "gangsta rock," for example, that the Beatles actually seem bland, the existential unruliness of 1950s and 1960s rock is still present. All such notions are misguided and simply reveal the insensate perceptive condition of the listener. Contemporary rock music, regardless of species, cannot shed its parent's genes.

There is a spirit about rock music which is endemic to its style. It is crepuscular at best, dark at worst. The shadows that surround its fleshly appeal are rooted in a worldview out of sync with basic Christian theism. By this I do not mean that rock musicians did not believe in God. Rather, that rock musicians as a group developed music that, from a musical standpoint, was outside the orbit of Christian theism. Consequently rock music, at its heart, bears no theistic imprint.

Judeo-Christian Theism

Everyone has a worldview, an approach to life, an understanding of the world and one's place in it. Worldview presuppositions may or may not be consciously held. But not being aware of one's worldview—one's basic beliefs about life—does not mean that one does not have a worldview. Such unawareness simply becomes that person's worldview. Basic life assumptions (or lack thereof) drive actions, attitudes, beliefs,

---

[104] Don Feder, *A Jewish Conservative Looks at Pagan America* (Lafayette, LA: Huntington Home Publishers, 1993), 167–168.

feelings, character, and decisions large and small. Value systems stem from worldview presuppositions and are the foundation for all reflections on values of every kind, including aesthetic values. It follows, then, that an individual's worldview is the powerhouse that drives, regulates, causes, and controls the substance of every individual's values. Its dogma is of cardinal importance.

The difficulty is not that people are unaware of what they believe. Rather, the larger problem occurs when a worldview develops into an assortment of contradictory, even irreconcilable assumptions that yield life principles warped and mutilated. For a worldview remains sound only to the extent that it is coherent, comprehensive, and consistent, and connects all the dots in such a manner that one grand holistic design emerges. For Christians, that means that one's faith must be applied to all of life, not just in certain areas. "Christ, the Lord of all" the sweeping application of Christian theism to moral, aesthetic, sociological, political, and economic spheres emerges as the indispensable factor to living holistically and biblically. "Christianity is a way of seeing all of life and reality through God's eyes. That is what Christianity is: a worldview, a system, and a way of life."[105] In our day, such application takes great courage for it means living counterculturally, swimming as it were against the cultural mainstream.

Living in contradistinction to the prevailing norms of culture, many of which directly conflict with scriptural standards, remains difficult and requires constancy of purpose and spiritual resolve. Indeed, leading a countercultural lifestyle has emerged as the single greatest challenge that contemporary evangelicals face. How does the church testify in word and deed to a society which has little connection with, even hostility toward, gospel truth? Is compromise inevitable? Worldview,

---

[105] David Kinnaman and Fermi Project, *Unchristian: What a New Generation Really Thinks About Christianity* (Grand Rapids: Baker Books, 2007), 87. Of the 48 million people over the age of 42 who have made a profession of faith, 9 million practice a Christian worldview. Of the 29 million between ages 18–41 who have made a profession of faith, only 3 million practice a Christian worldview (pg. 76).

as we shall see, is of paramount importance, for it ultimately founds musical values.

Christian theism was the dominant Western worldview for 1,600 years.[106] But beginning in the early 18th century, cracks appeared as the Age of Reason and the Enlightenment elevated the importance of humanism in the overall scheme of things. Deism, as it was called, served as a bridge to a full-blown naturalism that questioned the very existence of God. Popularized in the mid-20th century, such thought eventually gave way to contemporary postmodernism, a worldview that denies any notion of objective truth. This post-Christian secularism has infected every aspect of contemporary life in some way, including Judeo-Christian values and beliefs.[107]

Among the queries that every worldview must address are the following fundamental questions:

1. What is above, beyond, and over self? Who is your God?
2. Who is man?
3. What is the basis of value?
4. What is the meaning of human history?
5. What happens at death?

From a faith perspective, a theistic worldview addresses these questions most satisfactorily. All other worldviews postulate suppositions quite at odds with basic Christianity.

Briefly, theism presupposes a creator God: infinite, personal, transcendent and immanent, omniscient, sovereign, and good.[108] Having brought the cosmos into being out of nothing (*ex nihilo*), God created mankind in His image. Man, alienated from God by man's own free will, needs redemption—a redemption

---

[106] The death knell of European Christianity as well as Europe's rejection of all moral absolutes is now an accomplished fact. Claire Berlinski, *Menace in Europe* (New York: Crown Publishing Group, 2006), 7, 122.

[107] Harry Blamires, *The Post-Christian Mind* (Ann Arbor, MI: Servant Publications, 1999), 77–79.

[108] This material is largely taken from James Sire, *The Universe Next Door: A Basic Worldview Catalog*, 3rd ed. (Downers Grove, IL: InterVarsity Press, 1997).

provided for in the death and resurrection of Jesus, God's son. God sustains the ongoing world by the power of His Word. His character establishes the basis for all value. History is the canvas upon which God (in the fullness of time) has revealed Himself to mankind. Death is the entrance to eternity.

Comprehensiveness is one of the built-in characteristics of theism. Such a worldview lays claim to all areas of life regardless of category. It cuts across the entire spectrum of human thought and experience. That is to say, Scripture does not influence certain areas of life to the exclusion of others. If there is one thing revealed in holy writ, it is that Christianity speaks to all of life. A grave distortion of the Christian faith results when applied to some spheres of common everyday existence and omitted in others.

This creator God has endowed humans with creativity and the ability to think and evaluate. At the end of the Genesis account of creation in chapter one, Scripture notes that "God saw every thing that he had made, and, behold, it was very good" (Genesis 1:31, KJV). That is a value judgment. Humans, made in the creative *imago Dei*, not only have the ability to create, but have been given the tools to evaluate what they make. In theism, objective good, better, and best do exist. In theism there are things that are right and others that are wrong. There is good and there is bad. And in theism God has provided the means to tell the difference. Music becomes Christian as each component part of its structure bears a theistic imprint.

Postmodernism

As a youngster, I attended a typical 1940s neighborhood grammar school not unlike the one pictured in the film *A Christmas Story* (complete with flagpole in the school yard).[109] The curriculum was the characteristic 1940s fare of "reading,

---

[109] *A Christmas Story,* a 1983 film directed by Bob Clark and taken from Jean Shepherd's book *In God We Trust: All Others Pay Cash,* 1966, and Wanda Hickey's *Night of Golden Memories,* 1971.

'riting, and 'rithmetic." But under the influence of John Dewey's educational philosophy, Massachusetts had begun a gradual shift to what was termed "progressive education" in which liberalizing subjectivistic trends were advanced.

As a fifth grader, I knew nothing of this. But I do recall certain things about Mrs. Grodin's class that, unbeknownst to me, embraced the new educational thinking.

As a ten-year-old, my only remembrance of Mrs. Grodin's teaching was her reluctance to give definitive answers. I found such methodology unsettling. I vividly recall sitting at my desk in the back of the room and thinking, "Why doesn't she just tell us? I'm not interested in the thinking of others who don't know." Somewhat impatient, perplexed, and even agitated, this was my first exposure to an adult who seemed to believe that there were no correct answers, or at least no best answers, to particular problems. She would ask questions and listen to replies, but then would leave things open. She did not guide us in critical thinking nor coach us in learning to think for ourselves. Facts, principles, or even an understanding of the problem were never part of the process. She provided no rationale for thinking through such questions as: "Were white settlers justified in taking land from the Indians?" or "Which of these drawings is the best?" And so the class ended up with twenty-one differing answers, each of which, according to her, were all equally valid. Authority, right and wrong, good and bad, beautiful and ugly became outmoded concepts. As a youngster, I was being exposed to postmodern value relativism.[110]

All these years later, postmodernism has finally become

---

[110] In a particularly insightful summary of value-free relativism, Edward J. Erler wrote, "According to this new morality, all value judgments are equal. Reason cannot prove that one value is superior to or more beneficial than another, because values are not capable of rational analysis; they are merely idiosyncratic preferences. In this value-free universe, the only value that is 'objectively' of higher rank is tolerance. Equal toleration of all values—what is called today a commitment to diversity—is the only 'reasonable' position. And note that it is always called a *commitment* to diversity. It is a commitment because it cannot be rational in any strict sense—it exists in a value-free world from which reason has been expelled. The only support it can garner under such circumstances is the simple fact that it is [subjectively] preferred." Edward J. Erler, "Who We Are As a People—The Syrian Refugee Question," *Imprimis* 45, no. 10 (October 2016): 1.

the broad underlying foundation of culture. Enumerating its more general characteristics, one can easily see why this is so; the properties of postmodernism conclusively stand outside the norms of Christianity. They are a veritable compendium of unbiblical precepts, a who's who of human selfism. Some of these are:

1. Extreme societal humanism—the self as self-serving god; acute egocentricity; meism as the dominant motif of contemporary society.
2. Hedonism—pleasure is the highest good.
3. Relativism—values are derived by subjective selection, not from objective revelation.
4. Absolute truth is only a myth.
5. Immediate gratification of individual desire.
6. Pluralistic acceptance of all paradigms.
7. Right and wrong do not exist.

These traits together give a broad overview (*Weltanschauung*) of contemporary society. With no universals, no standards, and no transcendent authority, perhaps it is not too strong to suggest that culture is out of control. For church musicians and other leaders particularly, understanding that these contemporary theorems largely govern the aesthetic realm of our society need to be acknowledged and understood. In fact, the arts are at the forefront of anarchistic societal development. They lead, suggest, infer, speculate, construe, and interpret value systems that people then adopt as their own.[111]

It is important for those whose church ministry is bound to and centered around the arts to be aware that: "In the last few decades our society has shifted from a Judeo-Christian foundation to a secular one. Some believe this philosophical shift has been accelerated by two cultural forces. The first (see

---

[111] John P. Newport, professor of philosophy of religion, provost, and vice-president for academic affairs at Southwestern Seminary, was a strong believer in the strength of the arts in formulating societal standards.

note 112 for the second) is the entertainment media (television, movies, rock music, MTV...)"[112] Empowered by the incessant drive of the popular arts to break with propriety and long-held theistic convention, people experience the results of this shift to postmodernism and its suppositions on a regular basis. Although it took decades to reach the person on the street, postmodernism pervades all of society, including the church. It is foundational to pluralistic aesthetics, the current prevailing approach of most people toward the arts in general and music in particular. Personal subjective taste becomes the operative standard. There are as many differing "aesthetic truths" as there are people. It is a philosophy of normlessness and vacuity. Thomas Oden has stated it so very well, "To proclaim generously that anyone's truth is as valid as anyone else's truth is to deny the existence of truth altogether."[113]

In a challenge to all authority, postmodernism sweeps away objective truth and enthrones subjective "truth." To have "truth" we fashion "my truth" erected according to individual desire. Rather than objective reference outside of the self, truth becomes a subjective, personal entity. It can be whatever I want it to be. Pluralistic to a fault, moral, ethical, political, musical, societal, cultural, scientific, historical, artistic, and theological relativism wins the day. Verbose discourse does not disguise the fact that intellectual anarchy is a fact of life. Having no conglomerate center, no objective reference outside of individual whim, fragmentation occurs. Subjectivity tolerates no norms. The fabric of society is rent.

Christian theism advances quite a different set of principles. Objective in its outlook, it calls Christians to consistently practice the tenets of Christianity in every aspect of life and living. Neglecting such comprehensive application leads to a

---

[112] J. Kerby Anderson, *Moral Dilemmas: Biblical Perspectives on Contemporary Ethical Issues* (Nashville: W Publishing Group, 1998), 59. According to Anderson, the second cultural force that expedited the shift from a societal Judeo-Christian worldview to a secular one is the radical content of present-day sex education whether in the classroom, by way of school-based clinics, the media, or in the home.

[113] Thomas C. Oden, "Why We Believe in Heresy," *Christianity Today*, March 4, 1996, 12.

splintered caricature of the faith. Regrettably, an analysis of the evangelical church shows it has not always been careful to apply its theistic belief system to its use of music in worship. Practicing a Judeo-Christian theism that has more in common with post-Christian ideals than Christian ones persists.

In addition, many prominent evangelical leaders have sidestepped the issue of popular music's negative influence on society (sacred or secular) or have taken positions that affirm its use. In a recent book, one well-known pastor/author takes great pains to document the changing values of contemporary popular culture. Pornography, depravity in the military and medicine, out-of-wedlock births, substance abuse, alcoholism, sports scandals, gambling, cheating, crime, divorce, and many more are seen as evidence of the country's decline. Warming to his theme, he calls for the believer to be willing "to be labeled a prude for avoiding movies, books, speech, TV shows, and activities that promote immorality, sacrilege, or ungodly values." Rejecting evolution, homosexuality, and abortion, while affirming the exclusivity of Christ, may cause Christians "to be scorned and thought of as the filth of the world"[114] (1 Corinthians 4:10, 13). Though popular music such as rock and its derivative forms are not mentioned, it would seem reasonable that they ought to be included in the list, as a case could be made for their being one of, if not the major influence upon, the development of postmodern relativism and its concomitant practices in our time. Other noted evangelicals have also affirmed a clear biblical worldview theologically but have been inconsistent in applying it musically.

The reality is that the evangelical worldview tends to be schizophrenic. That is to say, it is compartmentalized to such a degree that its comprehensive nature is frequently compromised. Evangelicals do speak out against relativism in the social, ethical, moral, and spiritual realm, but seldom concern themselves with the aesthetic realm. Here, taste-driven relativism takes over.

---

[114] David Jeremiah, *Is This the End?* (Nashville: W Publishing Group, 2016), 83.

And a relativistic idea accepted in one area affects others. It is the path of least resistance.

Many vehicles have contributed to setting up postmodern ideals as normative: philosophic literature, avant-garde art, television, movies, print matter, the attitude of the intelligentsia as it influences the thinking of society's leaders, the teaching of professors in the nation's institutions of higher learning, and the radical agendum of groups dedicated to implementing secular, nontheistic norms.

Postmodernism and Rock

Often overlooked is the part that rock and roll and its descendants have played in propagating postmodern values.[115]

From its outset rock has been an expression of defiance.[116] Reacting against societal norms, it shed any modicum of aesthetic excellence and goodness in its decibel overkill; in the driving, incessant pounding of beat; in the vulgar melodies and harmonies purposefully constructed to shun musical beauty; in its bending of pitch; in its mind-numbing repetition of rhythmic and melodic patterns; in its coagulation of syncopated figures to galvanize the pelvic movements connected to the name "rock and roll;" in the larger-than-life mechanical power of amplification; and in the grotesque vocal sounds that have little connection to singing. All of these musical traits combine to be the musical expression of nihilism, rebellion, hedonism, license, alcohol and drug abuse, illicit sex, and the overriding concept of having no restraint. Rock music is the perfect musical incarnation of postmodernism.[117]

Alfred G. Aronowitz, music critic for the *New York Post* and lifelong devotee of rock, confessed:

[115] A small review of influential rock musicians would be the Beatles, Grateful Dead, Jim Morrison, John Lennon, Whitney Houston, Alice Cooper, Led Zeppelin, Bad Religion, Van Halen, Black Sabbath, Against Me!, and Deafheaven. The list could go on and on.
[116] In conversing with a professional rock performer, I noted well his statement that rock is still, i.e. continues to be, a musical expression of rebellion.
[117] There are numerous books and articles that sum up rock's philosophical suppositions and their effect upon society.

If the establishment knew what today's popular music really is saying, not what the words are saying, but what the music itself is saying, then they wouldn't just turn thumbs down on it. They'd ban it, they'd smash all the records and they'd arrest anyone who tried to play it.[118]

Well-known rock and roll performer and composer Little Richard (Penniman) admitted:

I was using dope, marijuana, angel dust, cocaine and heroin with pills and drinking and all I wanted to do was have orgies... I was one of the pioneers of that music, one of the builders. I know what the blocks are made of because I built them.[119]

Punk rocker Jim Lindberg explains that punk rock "seethed with adolescent resentment and frustration. It was anti-fashion, anti-authority, anti-everything...We'd change the world with distortion, anarchy, and angst."

I don't wanna live, to be thirty-seven
I'm living in hades,[120] is there a heaven?
Live fast, die young
Live fast, die young
Live fast, die young [The Circle Jerks][121]

Rock's genesis cannot be chronicled without acknowledging the large part that nonmusical elements played in its creation. Still overlooked some seventy years later, they are important for understanding the medium. The internal workings of this music have not changed. They still do what they were originally designed to do.

To say that rock became postmodernism's musical advocate is putting it too mildly. I lived through the beginnings of rock and roll and witnessed its influence on society through the

---

[118] David A. Nobel, *Christian Rock: A Stratagem of Mephistopheles* (Manitou Springs, CO: Summit Youth Ministries, n.d), 6.
[119] Ibid.
[120] Original word changed as per WestBow Press requirements.
[121] Jim Lindberg, *Punk Rock Dad* (New York: Harper Collins Publishers, 2007), xvi–xvii.

years. My generation found this music foisted on us in one way or another: radio, TV, recordings, peer interaction, commercial establishments, restaurants, outdoor public venues, magazines, concerts, and music festivals. We absorbed it and made it our own. Successive generations experienced the same thing as the vast number of spin-offs continued to roll from the assembly line. The revolutionary agenda of rock, along with other postmodern societal influences, eventually effected sweeping, highly visible, and inescapable changes in the moral and cultural life of America. Rock in particular, but all pop music in general, "became the most influential of the arts in people's lives."[122]

David Wilkerson, though not always consistent, was right in his assessment of rock. Not always able to explain his belief in technical terms, he nonetheless was a prophet. He saw what others did not see. Working with and ministering to young people, coupled with intense dependence on the Lord and an extraordinary sensitivity to the Holy Spirit, gave him remarkable insight into this music. Against the tide of cultural acceptance he sums up his observations about this, the most popular music ever created. He wrote:

> Rock music was born in the womb of darkness and rebellion."[123] And again, "Rock music was born with more than a particular sound; it was conceived by a spirit, and it continues to be activated by that same spirit that gave birth to it. It is the spirit of Antichrist; and the more one becomes wholly devoted to Jesus Christ, the more readily he discerns that spirit.[124]

I realize that Wilkerson sounds old-fashioned and out of date. Yet his point that rock is essentially a music of rebellion continues to be confirmed by today's rock musicians. In a recent interview with a knowledgeable rock bass guitarist, I was surprised by his understanding and affirmation that

---

[122] Dan Peters and Steve Peters with Cher Merrill, *Why Knock Rock?* (Minneapolis: Bethany House Publishers, 1984), 33.
[123] David Wilkerson, *Set the Trumpet to Thy Mouth* (Lindale, TX: World Challenge, 1985), 96.
[124] Ibid., 100.

contemporary rock's underlying foundation continues to be rebelliousness. Recounting the outlandish accoutrements, mannerisms, and gestures of the rock style, his was not an apologetic admission; rather, it was something he took for granted: rebellion is a working credo. His encyclopedic grasp of rock history and his vast experience as a performer, along with what I knew of his lifestyle, caused me to realize that his rock music and belief system were intrinsically linked.[125]

From the very inception of this musical form then, rebellion has been a driving force in rock's makeup. Evident in one of the first rock and roll songs, "Rock Around the Clock," a tumult of clamorous sounds, this sentiment may be found even in much Christian contemporary music whose rock-like cast has sometimes been described from within their own ranks as "smashmouth," "music to melt your face off," bands that are "cheesy, in-your-face," "tone deaf," that speak of praising God "till your ears bleed;" and which elect to title record labels "Morphine, Worthless, Screaming Giant, and Grr."[126] Whether or not someone likes the rock style is not the issue; it remains, regardless, a music of dissent and defiance. Antagonistic toward established values, this "passionate, amplified music was the message much more than the words sung."[127] Rock music has been the heart of an insurrection; its goal: to establish the normalcy of post-Christian dis-value.

A thorough analysis of this music and its many musical spin-offs[128] expose the darkness that makes up its prevailing essence—its signature. People can deny this fact of course. After all, listening to rock constantly would harden anybody to it. And studies have shown that just between grades seven and eight alone, adolescents expose themselves to this music for thousands

---

[125] Conducted in April 2017.

[126] John Makujina, *Measuring the Music: Another Look at the Contemporary Christian Music Debate* (Willow Street, PA: Old Paths Publications, 2002), 182.

[127] Arnold Perris, *Music as Propaganda* (Westport, CT: Greenwood Press, 1985), 182–183.

[128] Some of the spin-offs are progressive rock, hardcore punk, crossover thrash, hip-hop, gangsta rap, horrorcore, electroswing, hard bop, pop, doo-wop, post-punk, adult contemporary, grind core, etc.

upon thousands of hours.[129] Moreover, the postmodernism endemic to our culture supports a pluralism that admits the caprice of individual desire as a "truth for me," regardless of evidence to the contrary. In this environment, believing rock to be an unsullied musical form is entirely acceptable.[130] But that does not negate the point that the spirit of rock music and the popular music derived from it has, at its center, a heart and spirit of discord at the least and, at most, as Wilkerson put it, a spirit of Antichrist.

The Heart of Christian Contemporary Music

Larry Norman, acknowledged father of CCM, put religious lyrics to rock music because he was unsatisfied with the traditional music of the church. Believing that the music of rock and the lyrics of rock were two separate entities, he saw no problem in establishing what became known as "Christian rock."[131] Though unintended, his 1972 song "Why Should the Devil Have All the Good Music?" actually acknowledges the locus of this music. The song title clearly bears out the fact that this "Good Music," this rock music, is the Devil's; exactly what Wilkerson contended. Norman's question, "Why should this devil music, this music of darkness, not be used in Christian worship?" occurs to fewer and fewer people today. Yet I would have thought the answer to the question would be obvious. Offering to the Lord that which is pernicious is an abomination.

This musical form, coupled with religious lyrics, was given various labels: Christian contemporary music, contemporary Christian music, commercial Christian music,[132] contemporary

---

[129] Elizabeth F. Brown and William R. Hendee, "Adolescents and Their Music: Insights Into the Health of Adolescents," *Journal of the American Medical Association* 262 (September 22/29, 1989): 1659. Found in John Ankerberg, *Rock Music's Powerful Messages* (Ankerberg Theological Research Institute, 1991), 13.

[130] More on the aesthetics of value judgments in 6, "Music."

[131] Larry Norman explained his views in an appearance recorded in Hattern, The Netherlands, in the 1970s.

[132] It was Stan Moser, former head of Word Records and CEO of Star Song Records, who suggested the designation of "commercial Christian music" for Christian popular music (Christian pop). "We Have Created a Monster," *Christianity Today*, May 20, 1996.

worship music, or simply praise and worship music. As popular music, they are all derivatives of rock,[133]and cannot shed rock's spirit of disorder and dissent—traits endemic to the style. When there are rock characteristics in the musical texture itself, there is no objective way of getting around the fact that the music in question belongs to the rock family.

Medium and Message

Kimberly Smith tells the story of an elderly lady whose life experience had led her to equate rock music with crime. While waiting at a crosswalk for the traffic light to change, she was accosted by blaring rap music emanating from a stopped auto packed with young people. Her concern mounted until the car moved on. Then, reassured, the woman gratefully breathed a sigh of relief.[134]

For whatever reason, this woman became afraid because of the music; she associated it with lawlessness. In this scenario her anxiety was not caused by an actual crime but by the musical stimulus.

Significantly, the music emanating from the car was "Christian" rap. But she was not able to discern that fact. The text was unintelligible. To her it sounded like the rock music that she associated with evil.

The message received came through the music and the music alone. There was no difference in the content of the music, be it "sacred" or "secular." The fact that it had Christian words did not change anything. The message was in the musical medium.

There exists much misunderstanding on the part of the clergy and laity alike concerning this matter of message and

---

[133] Some of these forms are Christian metal, contemporary gospel, CCM, praise and worship, Southern gospel, Christian pop, and Christian rap. Performers include Newsboys, Hillsong United, Phil Keaggy, Petra, Matt Redman, Gaither Vocal Band, Skillet, Amy Grant, Newsong, and many more.

[134] Kimberley Smith, *Let Those Who Have Ears to Hear* (Enumclaw, WA: WinePress Publishing, 2001), 15.

medium. The widely held belief that communication methods such as music (the medium) have no intrinsic message continues unchallenged. Taste-driven musical subjectivity commensurate with no objective right or wrong is an accepted norm of evangelicals. On the other hand, when it comes to texts, religious lyrics (the message) must subscribe to objective truth as revealed in scripture.[135] Relativity concerning musical methods is admissible; relativity concerning gospel texts is inadmissible. Such a disconnect between medium and message has been the reason for much controversy concerning the use of popular music in the church. When post-Christian relativistic values are thought acceptable when applied to music yet unacceptable when applied to divine precepts, there arises a relativistic dichotomy between the two of gargantuan proportions. The wholeness of the full gospel, the gospel for all of life including the arts, is fractured into countless pieces.

The music of the developing secular rock scene shows less disunity. Enmeshed in one holistic structure of music/text, both parts of the form (music and text) generally communicate the same thing via their respective idioms (music-words). Perusing the lyrics of rock we find themes of "violence, vandalism, rape, murder, drug abuse, suicide, human sacrifice, degradation of women, children and human life, bestiality, sadism, masochism and other perversions."[136] The music is constructed in a manner that gives voice to such themes. Its stylistic components blend together in such a way so as to create the spirit Wilkerson calls darkness. This ethos of unrestrained license, nihilism, amoralism, paganism, hedonism, and the shock-and-awe mutilization of the neural system does not reflect the spirit of the gospel. And should the text include such gospel words as peace, joy, love, tenderness, humility, worship, or any other biblical term, the message the music delivers is still that of another gospel.

---

[135] Eddie V. Rentz, "How to Kill a Youth Ministry," *Enrichment* (Winter 2001): 18.
[136] John Ankerberg, *Rock Music's Powerful Messages* (Ankerberg Theological Research Institute, 1991), 12.

Musical Characteristics

First and foremost, rock music is a musical language. Its imprint, a musical/neural one, reflects the nature and character of the music. That includes CCM. Put all the religious words in the world to a rock-generated song and you still get music with a rock-generated disposition. In the world of musical aesthetics, music always trumps text. It is a significant fact, one that evangelicals need to grasp. "Music is never just words. Its expression is total, even more in the melody, rhythm and harmony than in the words."[137]

Drums are the most obvious instrumental characteristic of CCM. The frenzied, throbbing, pounding beat that is the gene pool of rock carries over unmistakably into CCM. This is not rhythm in the musical sense, for rhythm means flow. Rather, the loud, incessantly driving beat of CCM communicates a sense of being stuck in endlessly repeated throbbing. It lacks any forward movement. This is the only genre of music that requires such an outright across-the-board exacerbation and intemperate accentuation of a basic musical element; namely, the beat. All other genres have a rhythmic mellifluousness and judicious correspondence between compositional ingredients. At best, the overpowering turbulence of the drum set causes the listener to become insensate. At worst, it annihilates the God-given capacity for appreciating beauty.

I recall that one of our children, at about the tender age of three, was suddenly and unexpectedly thrust into a situation of excruciatingly loud rancorous sound. She froze, unable to move, face contorted and paralyzed. It was only after she was extracted from the cacophony that she returned to normal. Any auditory paroxysm, including that of the drum set, is enough to overcome the nervous system as well as damage hearing.

Repeated exposure to sound levels as low as eighty-five decibels can cause permanent hearing loss. CCM may subject congregations to levels of 120–150 decibels (a chain saw

---

[137] H. R. Rookmaacher, *Art Needs No Justification* (Downers Grove, IL: InterVarsity Press, 1978), 49.

operates at 100 decibels!). From the standpoint of hearing loss, the evangelical church has much to answer for.[138] Overpowering the senses with musical sound needs rethinking.

The melody of CCM, subsumed into the composite texture, may be hard to find and identify. With drums, guitars, bass, electric keyboard, and obbligato instruments, it can easily be lost in the amplified ensemble. Nevertheless, the melody, obscure though it may be, is often repeated incessantly along with a nontraditional harmonic structure. Not the simple repetition germane to good art, rock melodic restatements are mind-numbing in their seemingly endless barrage of repetitive patterns.

The vocal style of CCM and CWM is derived from that of secular rock. CCM melodies are sung with a straight sound, harsh and strident. Constant syncopated melodic twists, turns, and anticipations give to the vocal line a kind of careless and indolent quality. Moreover, the general phonic style of all popular music, sacred or secular, calls for amplification. It is now considered the "'norm' and the unamplified voice, 'unnatural.'"[139]

Along with drums, stylized vocals, and melodic line, the mandatory amplified guitar(s) have an important position in the ensemble. Of particular note is the bass guitar, which gives a definitive pitch foundation to the ensemble in the midst of the concussions emanating from the trap set and the vocals resounding above it all.

In addition to the necessity for drums, CCM depends heavily upon mechanical sound augmentation. Without amplification this genre of music loses its characteristic essence and clout. What is more, the necessary amplification unique to the style must be at an ear-splitting level. In all of my visits to churches

---

[138] Dan and Steve Peters note that teenagers tend not to be concerned about their hearing (though continual exposure to anything over 90 decibels is harmful. Rock is known to generate about 120–125 decibels). They listen constantly. Silence seems to be anathema. Dan Peters and Steve Peters with Cher Merrill, *Why Knock Rock?* (Minneapolis: Bethany House Publishers, 1984), 199.

[139] Robert P. Commanday, "This Here Millennium Thing," *The Journal of the Association of Anglican Musicians* 7, no. 6 (July/August 1998): 5.

that used Christian contemporary music, I have seldom been subjected to less.

All in all, the internal workings and sounds of Christian contemporary music based on the rock style appear musically malnourished, some would say vulgar—perhaps even pagan. Since music affects humans via the subconscious, the subconscious absorbing musical stimuli that cultivate in the listener feelings, emotions, attitudes, and actions according to the spirit and temperament of the music listened to, people are manipulated over time much more than they suspect or care to admit. Without a doubt, the rise of rock and CCM contributed to the far-reaching adoption of postmodern values. In spite of its immense popularity, CCM might just be a wolf in sheep's clothing. Christian texts cannot elevate this music out of darkness into the light. The musical heart of CCM shows it to be light starved—some of it, a black empty abyss.

CCM Foundational Issues

From the beginning rock was intended to be entertaining. But more than that, it was a musical way to make philosophic, moral, and aesthetic statements. As such it had a far greater impact than simple entertainment. People, however, were not generally concerned with rock's revolutionary agenda; for the most part their attention was focused on the immoderate and outlandish sounds of rock's larger-than-life entertainers.

As such, rock became very much a cultish, star-studded entity. Devotees became fans, fans became aficionados, aficionados became fanatics, and fanatics became groupies. Performers were idolized, their road to fame paved with egregious sounds. Teenagers identified with this music, made it "their sound" on into perpetuity.[140] Christians as much as

---

[140] Moving in the direction of hip-hop and contemporary R&B, current rock musician Kirk Franklin has sold millions of records and won scores of awards. He is considered "the most successful contemporary gospel artist of his generation." Vinson Cunningham, "How Kirk Franklin Is Pushing the Boundaries of Gospel," *The New Yorker*, January 16, 2017, 27.

non-Christians bought into the idolization and adulation of rock stars. Their magnetism caused the cult of personality to flourish among all those who appreciated the music and the lifestyles of these popular music celebrities.

By the late 1960s rock was firmly and intractably entrenched in the popular culture of the day. So widespread had it become that Christian conferences, such as those hosted by the InterVarsity Christian Fellowship, adopted the rock idiom. Secular events such as Woodstock, a 1969 rock festival held in rural Bethel, New York, drawing a crowd of over 400,000 fans over a period of four days,[141] became a model for a host of Christian gatherings where CCM was featured as the main draw. The Passion Conference in Atlanta, 2007, was typical. With 21,000 young people in attendance, the conferees were subjected to "worldly, sensation-stirring, high-decibel, rhythmic music...Christian hip-hop and rap lyrics...uniting the doctrines of grace with the immoral drug-induced musical forms of worldly culture."[142] Presently, the Rock and Worship Road Show advertises itself as "Christian music's most uplifting and entertaining concert series for the whole family." It is not inexpensive to attend.

The roots and evolution of CCM confirm that, at heart, CCM persists as a pop music entertainment form, a product of the boomer generation[143] and the mindset of the 1960s–1970s Jesus hippies. Its musical construction, performance practice, and association with the entertainment industry all corroborate this fact. Note the following:

First, CCM, by definition, lacks musical depth, an aesthetic characteristic of all popular music. As discussed previously, its approach can be noted in its melodic configuration, simplistic harmony, and heavy reliance on constant percussive drumming

---

[141] Such gatherings continue. Two weekends in October 2016 saw the classic-rock showcase Desert Trip, near Indio, California, gross $165 million, the largest take of any music festival anywhere. A V.I.P. ticket sold for $1,599. John Sealbrook, "The Immaculate Lineup," *The New Yorker*, April 17, 2017, 30.

[142] Peter Masters, "New Calvinism – The Merger of Calvinism with Worldliness," *The Sword & Trowel* (2009, issue 1), 1.

[143] People born from about the 1940s to 1960s.

to elicit bodily response. These traits are idiosyncratic to every variety of pop music. Without them music takes on some other style. In addition, non-musical features such as bizarre outfits and antics are used to "distract from achingly bad music."[144] Pop avoids the musical characteristics of art music (sometimes described as classical or serious music) because in utilizing the features of serious composition, pop music loses its triviality and becomes something else. One cannot get around the fact that the *raison d'etre* of the music of CCM is levity. Though some would argue that its locus is worship, yet being devoid of profound musical depth it cannot help but become an entertainment, a veritable repository of musical satisfaction.

Second, CCM is a disposable music. Not wearing well, titles are steadily dropped and replaced by new ones in a constant assembly line of musical product. The Top 40 are a case in point as are the Top Christian Airplay Songs, Billboard's Praise and Worship Songs Chart, and the year-end charts of Hot Christian Songs.[145] The novelty of Christian pop music, like its secular counterpart, requires regular revamping. Banal and trite musical components do not wear well and are endemic to the style. In contradistinction to the creativity and longevity of great art, pop requires constant replacement and refashioning—a throwaway music with built in expendability. Pop's jettison-like character appears the opposite of what we know of God's creating.

Third, CCM/CWM along with all of its substyles is a performer's music. It does not lend itself easily to group singing. For the most part, people just listen to it. When visiting evangelical churches that use CCM, I observed that,

---

[144] Kate Ryan, "This is How I Learned Pop Music Can Be Garbage and Still So Catchy," *Elite Daily*, March 28, 2016, www.elitedaily.com/music/pop-music-can-be-garbage-and-catchy/1437817.

[145] The widely disseminated newspaper *USA Today* publishes in its Life section lists of the most popular pop music for a given week. Categories include Top 40, Hot Adult Contemporary, Active Rock, Alternative, Urban Adult Contemporary, Adult Rock, Adult Contemporary, and Christian (CCM). It is worth noting and utterly revealing that Christian contemporary music (CCM) is included along with all the other pop types. Whatever else one might say about CCM, its musical home is with secular pop. Its generic roots and particular style characteristics show it to be but another pop genre, compatible with its secular counterparts.

in general, they showed quite limited musical participation. Many people just stood and stared at the musicians on the stage. Some congregants just watched the lyrics on the front screens; others moved their lips while still others, familiar with the songs, tentatively sang along. The fact remains that Christian contemporary music does not enable and advance group participation. It is very much a solo-performer entity.

Fourth, Christian pop is built on the principle of immediate gratification, the reverse of the aesthetic principle of delayed gratification, a gospel precept. The speed of musical gratification is an indicator of its value. Leonard Meyer, noted theorist and aesthetician, shows that when musical goals [cadences] are "reached in the most immediate and direct way,"[146] aesthetic value is slight. He notes that the difference between:

> ...art music and primitive music lies in speed of tendency gratification. The primitive seeks almost immediate gratification for his tendencies whether these be biological or musical. Nor can he tolerate uncertainty. And it is because distant departures from the certainty and repose of the tonic note and lengthy delays in gratification are insufferable to him that the tonal repertory of the primitive is limited, not because he can't think of other tones. It is not his mentality that is limited, it is his maturity." Pop "operates with such conventional clichés that gratification is almost immediate and uncertainty is minimized.[147]

A difficulty with the use of CCM in worship is that its aesthetic foundational principles are incompatible with the gospel's foundational principles. Whereas pop music strives for immediate self-gratification, the New Testament reveals a penchant for delayed gratification. Someday Christians will sit down at the Messianic banquet. Someday there will be no pain or sorrow; someday we will receive an incorruptible body; someday the lion and the lamb will lie down together. Someday

---

[146] Leonard Meyer, "Some Remarks on Value and Greatness in Music," in *Aesthetic Inquiry: Essays on Art Criticism and the Philosophy of Art*, ed. Monroe C. Beardsley and Herbert M. Schueller (Belmont, CA: Dickenson Publishing, 1967), 263.
[147] Ibid., 178.

Christ will come again. We have the resurrected life now, but not in its entirety. We live in hope.

Not receiving now everything that will eventually come to us, we wait until the fullness of time. That is delayed gratification, a divine time line. Though someday we will be completely vindicated, for now we must wait. The life process of maturing prevails as a gradual process, a progressive advance of becoming conformed into the image of the Son. The time frame and travail of making us into what God intends us to be is a mark of how God has ordained life.

God instituted delayed gratification as a basic life principle. Observe the natural world: life comes from seed that then grows toward maturity. Difficulties and detours impede the process; we reach the goal only over time. These incursions make life a circuitous route, comings and goings that have purpose. They make us into the people God wants us to be. They give meaning and shape to existence.

One can see that CCM presents a different aesthetic locus than the life formation found in the gospel. Pop principles recompense the listener immediately, whereas gospel principles favor delayed fulfillment. It would seem that when portraying biblical truth in an art form, a better medium would be one which exemplifies and inculcates in its internal workings that which it hopes to communicate—namely, gospel process.[148]

Why CCM?

What is there about religious popular music such as CCM or CWM that causes church leaders to mandate its use?

First, contemporary popular music finds wide use in worship because popular music has become the music of the people. Sensitive musicians dislike this fact, but it can hardly be denied. This type of music is normative. Whatever style

---

[148] This material comes from my chapter on "Pop Music and the Gospel" in *The Christian and Rock Music: A Study on Biblical Principles of Music*, Biblical Perspectives 15, edited by Samuele Bacchiocchi (Berrien Springs, MI: Biblical Perspectives, 2000), 275–299.

or substyle the mainstream populace prefers, it will almost certainly be connected to pop traits in some way. Pop's reach grips the unguarded through marketing; it moves adolescents on to adulthood with the accompanying baggage of teen musical preference. Society's constant, continual, chronic, and consistent exposure to this type of music emanates from every corner of the everyday world—radio, TV, personal listening devices, background "muzak," church, DVDs, videos, film, public transportation—the list could go on and on. Popular music, pervasive and invasive, cannot be avoided. People become accustomed to it, a matter of self-preservation. Ears become dull of hearing and aesthetic senses are impaired; "join 'em rather than fight 'em" becomes the prevailing convention.

Moreover, living in an egalitarian, pluralistic society gives reign to the despising of any hint of aesthetic elitism, an anathema in the world of music. Thinking all music uniformly valid, the practicing of musical discrimination that would omit some of it is believed to be harshly judgmental and intrinsically misguided. Postmodern philosophy compels listeners to accept anything. And as they do so, what they are fed becomes, in turn, their own.

In an insightful look at the evangelical movement's interrelation with popular culture and its adoption of religious rock complete with a wide assortment of business interests, author Alan Wolfe concluded "that perhaps those fundamentalists who warned against the temptations of popular culture may have known a thing or two. At least Faust was aware of the consequences of the pact he signed."[149] Might it be well to rethink our wholesale adoption of pop culture's CCM and move to redress that which we have lost? David Wilkerson's assessment of rock early in his ministry may yet have something to say to us.

Second, CCM has become the music of evangelicals because of their particular understanding of accommodation. Are there

---

[149] Alan Wolfe, *The Transformation of American Religion: How We Actually Live Our Faith* (New York: Free Press, 2003), 213.

limits to what the church will allow in its quest to make the gospel relevant to a culture in need of saving grace?

Since the most prevalent music of our culture is popular music of some kind, the conclusion generally reached is that the evangelistic church ought to adopt popular musical style as its church music. It is an accommodation made on the basis of popularity and taste, an accommodation that expresses the gospel in terms of the dominant musical motif of the 20th- and 21st-century culture—trendy, fashionable, rebellious and aesthetically dissident. How do we musically accommodate the gospel to a sybaritic culture? We give in to culture's demand for a musical mirror image of itself: profane, defiant, turbulent, disorderly, and anarchistic.

How to enculturate the gospel to fit culture remains one of the most arduous and problematic difficulties that believers face. While it is true that Christianity stands above culture yet, if unable to communicate to culture, it becomes irrelevant and of no use. Evangelicals believe that music is a communication method. They hold that text alone has the responsibility for bearing the gospel message; the music has none. Believing then that faith is not at risk, the kind of music used depends upon the likes and dislikes of the people. This was precisely the attitude of Rick Warren in that oft-quoted passage cited in chapter one that disclosed his belief that people's preferences should determine the specific kind of music used in church.[150] Such a consumer-driven model of shaping the church and its musical values emerge because evangelicals take the position that form and content can be separated. They posit that form (in this case pop music) has little bearing on content (the message conveyed). The message is a separate entity and the purview of words; music is exempted from communicating the message and is just a matter of pleasing sounds. Both are free to go their own way—a dualistic concept severing spiritual and

---

[150] See chap. 1, n. 9.

temporal realms.[151] Such dichotomy may be seen, for example, in the worldview of those who believe in absolute truth in some areas of life yet maintain a dogmatic relativism in others. For evangelicals, such a worldview dualism may often be observed between the spiritual and musical realms.

The takeover of the church's music by CCM did not happen overnight. The years of contentious "worship wars" through the 1970s and 1980s were decidedly direct and plainspoken, often belligerent, graceless, and insensitive. But we would do well not to dismiss these often heated conversations as much ado about nothing. Jack Wheaton said, "One of the greatest victories of Satan in the past fifty years has been his ability to convince musicians, pastors, elders, deacons, priests, and congregations that rock music belongs in a worship service."[152] David Noebel has noted thirty reasons why Christian rock music is inconsistent with Christianity.[153] Nevertheless, the church at large moved with the times. Attempting to conform to contemporary musical fashion for the sake of accommodating the gospel to culture, the evangelical church gave up its musical heritage for being in and also of the world.

God used the incarnation as the principal event in His self-disclosure to the human race. As such it was a form of communication. Transcendent, dwelling in light unapproachable, God became flesh and dwelt amongst us. The immanence of God, fleshed out in Jesus His Son, came to us in a form we could relate to. God the transcendent one revealed Himself immanently in human flesh.

Evangelicals would profit from practicing the scriptural methodology concerning accommodation. Jesus, in taking on the form of a man (as in a fleshed-out musical form) never acted in contradistinction to the message (as in the text of a musical

---

[151] The Geek dualism of "visible" and "invisible" worlds has its counterpart in the heresies of Gnosticism and Arianism.

[152] Jack Wheaton, *The Paganization of Worship* (Bethany, OK: Bible Belt Publishers, 2004), 64.

[153] David Noebel, *Christian Rock: A Strategem of Mephistopheles* (Manitou Springs, CO: Summit Youth Ministries, n.d.), 23–30.

form) he taught. In other words, Jesus as messenger and Jesus as message were united. There was no dichotomy between what Jesus said and what Jesus did; the one bore out the other. Form and content were one.

Third, the reason why CCM has taken hold of evangelical worship, in addition to its being relevant to culture and in its being thought of as an incarnational musical accommodation, is the belief that music is but pure neutral agent. Simply consisting of melody, harmony, and rhythm, it harbors no worldview. Believing that right and wrong do not exist when it comes to music, evangelicals conclude that music remains aesthetically value-neutral, its worth totally dependent on a thoroughgoing individualistic subjectivity, its objective value but a myth. Such an understanding exactly mirrors the culture in which we live: pluralistic, relativistic, individualistic, and hedonistic.

This belief in the neutrality and vacuity of music is the underlying foundation upon which contemporary evangelistic music-making rests. It stands as the "granddaddy" of all philosophies related to the use of popular music in the evangelical church, and the most important. It will be dealt with in the next chapter.

6   Music

P ostulating that music is aesthetically value-neutral, the majority of evangelicals hold that any music of any style of any quality may be rightly used anywhere for anything. This democratization of music, which allows music to be whatever one wishes it to be, emanates from the nonjudgmental attitude and pluralism of the wider culture. David Tame addresses this very point when he wrote:

> But, if we look deeper, we realize that a society's very conception of the nature of music is itself conditioned by the entire general philosophical viewpoint upon which that society is based.[154]

The hollowness of postmodernism is an indication of the depth of its repudiation of the concept of value. A musically inert meaningless void suits evangelicals perfectly; it allows churches, in good conscience, to embrace the normality of having no musical restraint. A veritable Pandora's box of possibilities is opened up.

Evangelical Underpinnings

When Christian lyrics began to be set to rock and roll, a gradual erosion of prevailing musical norms was initiated: melodies suitable for congregational singing, common practice-period harmony, rhythm devoid of syncopation, clear formal structure, and supportive accompaniments most often for piano or organ. It is true that many evangelicals railed against the

---

[154] David Tame, *The Secret Power of Music* (Rochester, VT: Destiny Books, 1984), 28.

devolution of these musical components as the incursion of popular music into church worship gained momentum. But despite a rash of books, articles, lectures, conferences, and sermons, the church as a whole gradually changed its position.

An increasing number of influential leaders saw the handwriting on the wall. That, combined with the tremendous societal pressure of a post-Christian culture to affirm the secularization of the church, caused musical thinking to be drained of its power of discernment. One highly influential evangelical leader wrote:

> Worship has nothing to do with the style or volume or speed of a song. God loves all kinds of music because he invented it all—fast and slow, loud and soft, old and new. You probably don't like it all, but God does. If it is offered to God in spirit and truth, it is an act of worship.[155]

When all music is thought equal it becomes a candidate for anything. Even if music rings out with merry-go-round sounds or orgiastic din or bombast of drug-induced cacophony, all would be considered fitting vehicles for the worship of almighty God, provided they were "offered to God in Spirit and in Truth."

Implicit in Warren's quote is the philosophy that all music is created equal, unable to be constructed in a fashion that would do worship a disservice. But every language has the ability to express and differentiate, rightly or wrongly. In casting music upon the ash heap of meaninglessness, all music literally becomes equal to all other music—a nihilistic understanding. Viewing music as pure neutral agent strips it of its ability to express anything, to communicate anything, and to support anything. Music is neutered. Enter the world of the absurd.

The truth is that no matter what a person believes about music, music by its nature remains a language. As such,

---

[155] Rick Warren, *The Purpose Driven Life* (Grand Rapids, MI: Zondervan, 2002), 65. His thinking on the matter of musical style goes back to the 1980s when he founded Saddleback Church in Lake Forest, California.

it communicates as dictated by the internal workings of its component parts regardless of what someone may think about it. According to Frank Burch Brown, using "Rudolph the Red-nosed Reindeer" as accompaniment to Psalm twenty-three:

> ...discerns that the music expresses a register of feeling that goes much better with holiday escapades and shopping sprees than with private devotion or public prayer. Even after one gives all due credit to the social construction of musical meaning, it must be said that this music is not, after all, infinitely malleable or suited to all purposes.[156]

The music of "Rudolph," constructed in such a fashion that it communicates a flippancy inconsistent with the text of the twenty-third Psalm, expresses a point of view to the listener. Denying this expressive dimension flies in the face of musical reality. While it is possible that someone might use "Rudolph" in worship, doing so does not legitimatize its use; it simply reduces worship to comedy.

Music is a Language[157]

While not exactly analogous to written and spoken languages, music has similarities to them. Both use an alphabet: music, the twelve tones of the scale; English, twenty-six letters. By itself the alphabet remains devoid of meaning. Only after the alphabet is arranged in certain ways does meaning begin to appear, as music does with its phrases and English its sentences. Eventually these groupings form paragraphs, sections, and ultimately an entire work. Deryck Cooke in his treatise *The Language of Music* quotes Felix Mendelssohn:

---

[156] Frank Burch Brown, *Inclusive Yet Discerning: Navigating Worship Artfully* (Grand Rapids, MI: William B. Eerdmans, 2009), 96.

[157] Thanks to Kurt Woetzel, who researched much of the material in this chapter.

The thoughts which are expressed to me by a piece of music which I love are not too indefinite to be put into words, but on the contrary too definite.[158]

In Cooke's analysis, "music does function as a language."[159] It has a grammar and syntax with specific principles for making a composition intelligible. Mendelssohn understood this, although its precise message may be too deep to be translatable into spoken language. Music is not a blank slate, barren and hollow. As a language it reveals thought, emotion, beauty, or ugliness; and it has a spirit about it that is discernable. Music is not value neutral.

Arranging the letters of the English alphabet into a particular sequence, it is possible to make the statement, "Water is wet." On the other hand, it is possible to configure the letters to say, "Water is dry." The first is correct, the second false. The letters by themselves are meaningless. They are inert, neutral. But as soon as they are put together intelligibly it is possible that their assertions may be right or they may be wrong.

A person could claim, "The Lord is my shepherd," or on the other hand assert, "Satan is my shepherd." Both may be true, but only the first would be affirmed by Christians; the second would not. Its use in worship is inconceivable. The same alphabet, arranged in different ways, has the capacity to say vastly different things, the first appropriate for worship, the second quite inappropriate.

Characteristic of all language is the ability to differentiate, be it literature, poetry, painting, sculpture, or music. A particular vocabulary has the capability of expressing vastly different things. All painting is not equally fitting for display in the Louvre; nor are all architectural designs uniformly beautiful. The same goes for all the other arts. Without the possibility of dissimilitude in artistic worth, artistic language becomes nonsensical. To say that all music is appropriate for worship

---

[158] Mendelssohn to Marc André Souchay, 5 October 1842, in Deryck Cooke, *The Language of Music* (New York: Oxford University Press, 1959), 12.
[159] Ibid., 72.

presupposes an absurdist worldview. It does not square up with reality or the nature of language.

It was Arnold Schoenberg, 19th-century composer, who said that music is "the language in which a musician unconsciously gives himself away."[160] I am not suggesting that music is a literal image of words. It is a musical language, a nonverbal communication to be sure and one that has an ambiguous relationship to the specificity of the spoken word,[161] with:

> ...qualities that make it, in some respects, analogous to language. The music teacher can correct musical writing in much the same way that the English teacher can correct essay writing. Musicians know the difference between what works and what doesn't and have highly developed, self-critical awareness of how well something is played or made. For a musician, listening to badly written music is like taking part in an inane or even nonsensical conversation. Teachers know the disorientation and the frustration that sets in when reading an essay with badly constructed sentences and poorly presented ideas; exactly the same can apply to musical essays—bland, overly repetitive, and unoriginal.[162]

Being nonverbal does not inhibit its communicative ability. Music exists as "a wordless language and yet gives powerful *impressions* that are reacted to in a common way by listeners."[163] "Sit, march, run, walk" are word commands that cannot be literally rendered musically. But music is able to portray quietness, or martial step, or a fast spurt, or a moderate pace by the composer's shaping the musical vocabulary in specific ways. Music addresses a person through a labyrinth of means: emotionally, rationally, physically, mystically. Combined, they have the capability of moving the listener to heights and depths unreachable by words alone. The content of music, the *what* of

---

[160] Ibid., 273.

[161] Stephen McAdams and Emmanuel Bigand, *Thinking In Sound: The Cognitive Psychology of Human Audtion*, (Oxford: Claredon Press, 1993), 232.

[162] Julian Johnson, *Who Needs Classical Music? Cultural Choice and Musical Value* (New York and Oxford: Oxford University Press, 2002), 97.

[163] Joseph Eger, *A Conductor's Notes on Music, Physics, and Social Change* (New York: Penguin Group, 2005), 130.

the musical dialogue, has everything to do with how it is said. Content cannot be separated from form.[164] The form of the music, its grammar and syntax, will determine the nature of music's content.[165] Music embodies meaning according to the way the music is put together. Style shapes content.[166]

In his insightful book *Art Needs No Justification*, H. R. Rookmaacher writes penetratingly concerning this matter of form, value, and communicating meaning:

> Communication and form are the two facets, the two qualities of art. The communication is always through form, and the form always communicates values and meanings. It can depict reality outside of ourselves, as understood and seen by ourselves. That reality can be the things we can see as well as the things we experience—realities like love, faith, care, righteousness and their negative, evil counterparts.[167]

Sir Roger Scruton, former professor at Boston University, writes in his essay "Teaching Judgement" that "songs can have a moral character, not by virtue of their words only, but by virtue of their musical setting."[168] This has been the experience of many cultures over the centuries. Music has the ability to form the self. Philip Ball agrees with Professor Scruton that music influences character. It is a "character-forming force."[169]

Music's Power

History shows that many nations understood that music was powerful, something not to be taken lightly. Three thousand years before the coming of Jesus, China held to a remarkably

---

[164] Julian Johnson, op. cit., 104.

[165] Neil Postman, *Amusing Ourselves to Death* (New York: Penguin Group, 1985), 42.

[166] Michael Horton, "Is Style Neutral?" *Modern Reformation* 5, no. 1 (January/February 1996): 5.

[167] H. R. Rookmaacher, *Art Needs No Justification* (Downers Grove, IL: InterVarsity Press, 1978), 40.

[168] Roger Scruton, "Teaching Judgement," Future Symphony Institute, www .futuresymphony.org/teaching-judgement.

[169] Philip Ball, *The Music Instinct: How Music Works and Why We Can't Do Without It* (London: The Bodley Head, 2010), 15.

constructed philosophy that music had the capacity to affect emotional states and physical well-being. "Yet one effect of music was considered above all others to be the most important, and this was its moral influence."[170] India too forged a society in which music and religion were inseparably linked.[171] And of course the music of ancient Greece, with its doctrine of ethos[172] codified by Pythagoras and his disciples, is well known.[173] The moral force of music is also confirmed in the writings of the prophets Amos and Isaiah according to theologian and musician Erik Routley.[174] Music is not the benign reality many believe it to be. "The dilemma of what is right and what is wrong in music is basically a moral question."[175] The hard and fast vapid neutrality of the language of music, though largely accepted by society, is more wishful thinking and myth than proven certitude and fact.[176]

From the very beginning of Christianity, the early church exercised restraint in its use of music. It was not because Christians disliked music; if anything, it was acknowledged that music could be liked too much and believers could be tempted away from their commitment to separation from the world.[177] Practicing the implications of musical ethos that codified the power of music for good or ill, Christian leaders were circumspect in its use. Music's capability to influence was not taken lightly.

About the time that rock and roll was gathering momentum,

---

[170] David Tame, op. cit., 34.

[171] Bonnie C. Wade, "Some Principles of Indian Classical Music," in *Musics of Many Cultures*, ed. Elizabeth May (Berkeley: University of California Press, 1980), 83.

[172] The doctrine of *ethos* codified the understanding that music was an ethical and moral force that affected human behavior.

[173] George Farmer, "The Music of Ancient Mesopotamia," in *New Oxford History of Music*, Vol. 1, *Ancient and Oriental Music*, ed. Egon Wellesz (London: Oxford University Press, 1957), 252–253.

[174] Erik Routley, *Church Music and Theology* (Philadelphia: Muhlenberg Press, 1959), 17. See Amos 6:4–6 and Isaiah 5:11–12.

[175] David Tame, op. cit., 72.

[176] See Kurt Woetzel, *Is Music Amoral* (Greenville, SC: Majesty Music, n.d.)

[177] Lucian, *De Dea Syria 50* (III 361 Jakobitz) in Johannes Quasten, *Music and Worship in Pagan and Christian Antiquity* (Washington, D.C.: National Association of Pastoral Musicians, 1983), 37.

noted historian and scholar Alec Robertson invoked the musical wisdom of the church fathers:

> Every musician today is aware of the morally debilitating elements in popular music and of how mistaken are those who wish, with a sincere intention, to introduce the idioms of such music into the Church to draw the people in. They will be able, therefore, to sympathize with the views of the early Fathers on the kind of music Christians heard, unavoidable, in the pagan schools in which they went to study and, avoidably if with difficulty, at parties or in the theatres, and they did not mince their words. "It must be banned," cries St. Clement of Alexandria (c.215), "this artificial music which injures souls and draws them into various states of feelings, sniveling, impure, and sensual, even a bacchic frenzy and madness. One must not expose oneself to the powerful character of exciting and languorous modes, which by the curves of their melodies lead to effeminacy and infirmity of purpose."[178]

Ephrem, 4th-century hymnist, warns against the songs of pagans:

> Let us come before his presence with praise and rejoice before him with psalms! With psalms and not with ribaldry; with psalms and not with diabolical songs. Do not sing psalms today with the angels so as to dance tomorrow with the demons. Far be it from you to be today one who loves Christ and listens to the Scriptures as they are read and tomorrow is a traitor who despises Christ and listens to cithara music.[179]

Basil of Caesarea confirms the importance of discerning the ethos of church music:

> For passions, unfree and base, are wont to arise from this kind of music. But we must seek out the other kind of music, which is better

---

[178] Alec Robertson, *Christian Music* (NY: Hawthorn Books, 1961), 25.
[179] Ephraem, *Uber die Enthaltung von weltlichen Lustbarkeiten* 5 (BKV, Kempten 1870, Singerle I, 414) in Johannes Quasten, *Music and Worship in Pagan and Christian Antiquity* (Washington, DC: National Association of Pastoral Musicians, 1983), 134–135.

and which leads to the good, which David, the composer of holy songs, made use of to free the king from his melancholy.[180]

That better music, Basil suggests, has power under the Holy Spirit to blend:

> ...the delight of melody with doctrines in order that through the pleasantness and softness of the sound we might unawares receive what was useful in the words.[181]

Basil, certain in his knowledge of musical ethos, noted that some music is dangerous and warns Christians to "not be drawn down by the pleasantness of the melody to the passions of the flesh."[182] Augustine too understood that music had an effect on the actions and ethics of humans. In his *De Musica* (in thirteen books) he concludes that there is good and bad music.[183] His autobiographical *Confessions* offer that good music, devoid of frivolity and baseness, is useful in building up the spiritual man, enabling him to avoid sensual revelry and embrace music that leads to holiness. Andrew Fletcher's "Give me the making of the songs of a nation and I care not who makes its laws"[184] sums up well music's strength to produce particular ends.

In the centuries following the early church, the concept flourished that music had power to affect human virtue, thinking, and activity. Music, though a gift from God, could be altered to serve the fallen creature rather than the heavenly Father. Living in a world inhospitable to the gospel, wisdom in its use was called for. Music's power to mold those who ingest it required careful monitoring. It would be prudent, even today,

---

[180] Basil, *De legend, libr. Gentil. 7* in Johannes Quasten, *Music and Worship in Pagan and Christian Antiquity* (Washington, DC: National Association of Pastoral Musicians, 1983), 138.

[181] Oliver Strunk, *Source Readings in Music History* (NY: W. W. Norton, 1950), 65.

[182] Ibid., 66.

[183] Goulburn W. Crossley, review of *St. Augustine's De Musica: A Synopsis*, by W. F. Jackson Knight, *The Musical Times* 92, no. 1297 (March 1951): 127–129.

[184] Andrew Fletcher, 18th-century Scottish philosopher [stated in 1703].

not to dismiss out of hand the wisdom of the ages in the matter of musical choice in general, and church music in particular.[185]

Luther

The 16th-century reformers Martin Luther, Huldreich Zwingli, and John Calvin all had a marked respect for the power of music to shape people. Therefore, it is not surprising that they were circumspect in its use.

Luther, composer of that great chorale "A Mighty Fortress" (based on Psalm 46), believed music a beneficent provision of the Creator. He saw music as "part and parcel of the way the world is made, and which contributes to its preservation. It is not primarily an art or a science; it is a creature of God."[186] Time and again he reiterates this assumption:

> I would certainly like to praise music with all my heart as the excellent gift of God which it is and to commend it to everyone.... And you, my young friend, let this noble, wholesome, and cheerful creation of God be commended to you...A person who gives this some thought and yet does not regard it [music] as a marvelous creation of God, must be a clodhopper...Music is an endowment and a gift of God...Music is an outstanding gift of God and next to theology, I would not want to give up my slight knowledge of music for a great consideration....I place music next to theology and give it the highest praise.[187]

Music was a force to be reckoned with. More than just a pleasurable pastime, music actively moved people. In his preface to Georg Rhau's *Symphoniae Iucundae*, Luther wrote:

---

[185] Christopher B. Warner, "Church Fathers and Church Music," *The Catholic World Report*, September 12, 2013, 3. The author contends that the fathers of the Church can help us today in refining church music after fifty years of pop usage.

[186] Eugene Brand, "Luther: The Theologian of Music," *Pastoral Music* 8, no. 5 (June–July 1984): 21.

[187] Carl F. Schalk, *Luther on Music: Paradigms Of Praise* (St. Louis: Concordia Publishing House, 1988), 33, 34.

> For whether you wish to comfort the sad, to terrify the happy, to encourage the despairing, to humble the proud, to calm the passionate, or to appease those full of hate...what more effective means than music could you find?[188]

Music's power even extends to the physical. Friedrich Blume cites a report by the physician Matthias Ratzeberger that listening to music cured Luther of a fainting spell. As the musicians played, Luther gradually began to recover. "Then he found that as soon as he heard music, his weakness and depression were ended."[189]

His cheerful and positive attitude toward music contributed much to the spread of the Reformation. Luther encouraged all people to engage in the singing of the gospel, believing that the power of music would in its own right propel the Protestant message into the hearts and minds of the people. Singing:

> ...leads the man who practices it to God, teaches him to understand better God's Word (it is primarily sacred vocal music that Luther had in mind), and prepares him for the reception of divine grace, while making him a better man and a happy Christian and driving out the devil and all vices.[190]

Nevertheless, Luther also recognized the depravity of mankind and the ability of people to defile the gift.[191] The operative insight into Luther's use of music is to note how carefully he screened the material he used. Of the thirty-seven chorales of Luther, fifteen of the tunes were composed by Luther himself, thirteen he derived from Latin hymns or chants, four he adapted from religious folk song, two from pilgrims' songs, two are of unknown origin, and one is from a secular folk song.[192] Notwithstanding the common practice

---

[188] *Luther's Works*, vol. 53 (Fortress Press, 1958–1967), 323.

[189] Friedrich Blume, *Protestant Church Music* (New York: W. W. Norton, 1974), 10.

[190] Ibid., 10.

[191] Ibid. (See chap. 1, n. 5).

[192] Robert Harrell, *Martin Luther, His Music, His Message* (Greenville, SC: Majesty Music, 1980), 18.

of *contrafacta*[193] in Luther's day, Luther composed the music of almost half of his thirty-seven chorale texts himself. In the preface to Johann Walter's *Eyn geystlich Gesangk Buchleyn*, or so-called "Wittenberg Hymnal," Luther writes a cautionary note concerning the carnality of certain songs and pieces and the necessity for musical wholesomeness.[194] Clearly, he did not accept the blanket whitewashing of the language of music into bland neutrality. It can be sullied at the hands of humans and made less than it might be. Theologian and musician, Luther opted for the best in music, not the least. Music's power for good or ill depended upon compositional quality, character, and integrity. This understanding was very much part of his thinking and *modus operandi*.

Moreover, the culture of the day, dominated as it was by a prevailing theistic worldview, exhibited a musical unity that minimized sacred and secular stylistic differences. Hence it was entirely possible to find music in the folksong repertoire of the day, for example, which had the requisite musical integrity and weight necessary for carrying biblical truth. The concept of "pop" music (a development of the 20th century) did not exist. Today's huge disparity between the musical vocabulary, grammar, and style of contemporary rock and pop music and the musical vocabulary, grammar, and style of art music was nonexistent in the 16th century. Musical unity in the broader culture, stemming from a common worldview, minimized differences between sacred and secular music. Even so, Luther's fifteen-stanza chorale, *Vom Himmel Hoch* ("From Heaven Above to Earth I Come"), was set in 1535 to the familiar secular song *Ich Kumm aus frembden Landen her* ("I Am from Foreign Lands") but reset in 1539 and published in *Geistliche lieder auffs new gebessert und gemehrt, zu Wittenberg*. D. Marti. Luther (Leipzig 1539). It is likely that Luther did this because of the former tune's strong association with a well-known popular ring dance. Though he did not attach his name to the new tune, scholars

---

[193] The substituting of one text for another using the same music for both.
[194] Carl Schalk, op. cit., 23. Friedrich Blume, op. cit., 78. *LW* vol. 53, 316.

believe Luther composed it.[195] It has been given the tune name *Vom Himmel Hoch*.

Much has been made (erroneously) in evangelical circles concerning Luther's perceived use of "bar" tunes for his chorales. "If Luther did it, why are we not justified in doing the same thing in our day?" it is asked. "Why should we not put our religious texts to 21st-century popular music?"

The answer is straightforward. Luther's "bar tunes" had nothing to do with drinking establishments. "Bar" is a musical form with a structure of AAB. The A section of the music is repeated (AA) before the single statement of the B section. Sometimes a rounded bar form is used in which there is an abbreviated reference to the A section (a′ prime) in the B section, AABa′. "A Mighty Fortress" is an example of rounded bar form.

Luther, then, believing music to be a God-given gift, showed remarkable discrimination in his musical choices. This is all the more noteworthy given the fact that there prevailed a basic stylistic unity between the various musical genres of the day. The singular influence of Christian theism affecting all of life, including the arts, produced a foundational stability and shared vocabulary in keeping with a principled musical aesthetic. In other words, the music of the day enjoyed a propensity toward musical virtue. Even so, Luther—well aware of music's power—was particularly judicious and skillful in finding the finest music available for equipping the Reformation with song.

The power of music was not lost on Luther. He hypothesized that people could sing their way to faith. To that end he sought out the foremost composers of his day—Josquin des Prez, Ludwig Senfl, Johann Walter, Georg Rhau, and Heinrich Finck—to fund the new movement with high quality music.[196] For Luther, music (apart from text) had the potential to be the gospel in musical action insofar as gospel traits of "honesty, integrity, truthfulness, and winsomeness"[197] were inculcated

---

[195] Raymond F. Glover, ed., *The Hymnal 1982 Companion* (New York: The Church Hymnal Corporation), 80.

[196] Carl F. Schalk, op. cit., 21–25.

[197] Ibid., 51.

into the music by the composer. Music proclaims the gospel as it possesses the requisite qualities of musical goodness and value, attributes that flow from a Judeo-Christian worldview.

Calvin

John Calvin, the great Genevan reformer, was fully aware of music's power. While Luther emphasized music as a gift from God useful in His service, Calvin saw music more as a force in need of control. In the preface to the Genevan Psalter of 1543, Calvin wrote:

> But still there is more: there is scarcely in the world anything which is more able to turn or bend this way and that the morals of men, as Plato prudently considered it. And in fact, we find by experience that it has a sacred and almost incredible power to move hearts in one way or another. Therefore we ought to be even more diligent in regulating it in such a way that it shall be useful to us and in no way pernicious. For this reason the ancient doctors of the Church complain frequently of this, that the people of their times were addicted to dishonest and shameless songs, which not without cause they referred to and called mortal and Satanic poison for corrupting the world. Moreover, in speaking now of music, I understand two parts: namely the letter, or subject and matter; secondly, the song, or the melody. It is true that every bad word (as St. Paul has said) perverts good manner, but when the melody is with it, it pierces the heart much more strongly, and enters into it; in a like manner as through a funnel, the wine is poured into the vessel; so also the venom and the corruption is distilled to the depths of the heart by the melody.[198]

Harking back to the ancient doctrine of ethos, Calvin minces no words about the aptitude or, in his terminology, "the incredible power" of music to shape outcomes. A right music, stylistically chaste, modest, and dignified, functions as

---

[198] John Calvin, *Preface to the Psalter* (Geneva, 1543).

a "safeguard against the natural, lascivious powers of music."[199] For this reason he exercised extraordinary fastidiousness in determining an appropriate musical praxis for the reform movement sweeping Europe.

Specifically, Calvin, consumed as he was with *sola scriptura* (the belief in Scripture as the only and infallible rule of faith and practice), mandated the exclusive use of psalmody in Reform services of worship, although the 1543 version of the Genevan Psalter contained the *Song of Simeon*, the *Lord's Prayer*, the *Ten Commandments*, and the *Apostles' Creed*. If the Holy Bible is everything to Reformed Christianity, then it follows that merely basing song loosely on Scripture is somewhat anorexic. What is needed is to sing the Word itself, straight from Scripture. Consequently, the 150 Psalms of David became the primary songbook of Calvinism.

However, this would have required the use of Gregorian Psalm tones or some other formulary for singing prose. Instead, Calvin adopted the practice of metrical psalmody and included a number of poet Clement Marot's Psalm versifications in his 1539 Psalm book. Eventually the Genevan Psalter contained all 150 rhymed versions of the Psalms, fifty by Marot, with the rest completed by a variety of authors. One hundred twenty-six tunes were used, twenty-four being used more than once. An example of a metrical psalm would be the familiar *All People That on Earth Do Dwell*, a versification of Psalm 100. Its companion tune, *Old 100th*, is best known as the melody to which the doxology, *Praise God from Whom All Blessings Flow*, is sung. *Old 100th* made its first appearance in the Genevan Psalter of 1551.

In spite of Calvin's desire to sing texts straight from Scripture, it must be recognized that reworking a Psalm so that it has meter and a rhyme scheme renders it a paraphrase, no longer a literal rendering of Scripture. A metrical psalm, then,

---

[199] Oskar Soehngen, "Fundamental Considerations for a Theology of Music," in *The Musical Heritage of the Church*, vol. VI, ed. Theodore Hoelty-Nickel (St. Louis: Concordia, 1963), 14.

bears the distinct imprint of human intervention, and singing that psalm is a step removed from singing Scripture verbatim. Nevertheless, metrical psalms do retain a generic essence of the original. They are useful because their straightforward hymnic (strophic) form make them a viable, well-known song type. But they are not the infallible Word of God. However, psalmody of this order is indeed closer to the Bible than what might be termed "hymns of human composure" such as John Newton's well-known "Amazing Grace! How Sweet the Sound."

The English reformers also adopted metrical psalmody as their congregational song. As early as 1548 the first collection of nineteen Psalms by Thomas Sternhold was issued. By 1562 all 150 were published, the first complete Psalter in English. Known as *Sternhold and Hopkins*, it remained standard fare in England for 200 years until Isaac Watts, the father of English hymnody, finding some of the versifications less than inspiring and in need of "Christianizing," reworked the genre. But metrical psalmody continued in use until the hymn form finally gained ascendancy over the singing of metrical Psalms. In America, the early settlers brought this type of psalmody with them, the Massachusetts Bay Colony issuing the famous *Bay Psalm Book* in 1640.

In one of his ordinances, Calvin abolished the use of instruments in worship, believing that the early church sang their praises a cappella. He held that as New Testament Christians, Reform congregations would do well to do likewise. There emerged from such practice a refreshing simplicity that significantly enhanced reform worship.

The Strength of Music

All this shows there is an ethos regarding music that should not be dismissed. Throughout history beginning with ancient civilizations, philosophers, scholars, and others recognized the power of music. Over the centuries numerous religious notables, including Protestant Reformers such as Luther and Calvin, understood that music was dynamic, a language that, in some ways, possessed more might than words. Music has the ability to work unobtrusively, clandestinely, secretly. For good or ill the subliminal workings of music remain a mystery. Music is wordless and intuitive; simultaneously visceral and cognitive, emotional and intellectual. When all is said and done, music's power remains unexplainable, inexplicable.

In a speech given in October 1944, Winston Churchill referred to the destruction of the House of Commons during the bombing of London on the night of May 10, 1941. A recognized wordsmith and inspiring orator, Churchill's plea was that the House be restored to its former glory. Understanding the power of the art of architecture, he delivered that now-famous line, "We shape our buildings and afterwards our buildings shape us." It was a remarkable insight, for the power of the arts to effect outcomes is recognized only by a few, unrecognized by most, and affects absolutely everyone. Considering Churchill's statement in reference to the music of Herbert Howells, author Jonathan Clinch paraphrases Winston's remark by declaring, "We shape our MUSIC, and afterwards our MUSIC shapes us."[200]

Considering the widespread acceptance of popular musical forms (especially rock and roll and its derivative styles), William Kilpatrick wrote: "Music has powers that go far beyond entertainment. It can play a positive role in moral development by creating sensual attractions to goodness, or it can play a destructive role by setting children on a temperamental path that leads away from virtue."[201] Music is never neutral, bereft of power. On the contrary, it is an efficacious dynamic. A steady diet of driving drum set volleys, strident vocalizations, ear-damaging decibel levels, musical incoherence, and endless repetition of melodic and harmonic irrationality are bound to create in the listener a like spirit: coarse and defiant.

---

[200] Jonathan Clinch, "Shaping the Living and the Dead," *The Journal of the Association of Anglican Musicians* 25, no. 10 (December 2016): 1.
[201] William Kilpatrick, *Why Johnny Can't Tell Right From Wrong* (New York: Simon & Schuster, 1992), 188.

Andrew Fletcher was right: the nation's songs are more effectual than its laws.[202] Musically, we tend to become what we sing. Mark Noll said simply, "We are what we sing."[203]

Nuts and Bolts

Music does not have the brute power of a locomotive. It cannot coerce the listener to submit to its control. Rather, it shepherds, compels, and therapeutically heals.[204] Music has influence, subtle and unobtrusive, to affect its listeners in one way or another. It works by inference. As a matter of fact, its very subtlety is its might. Its ability to invade unsuspectingly, a characteristic of all the arts, means that musical styles and genres bear careful scrutiny.

Music, then, is not a uniformly causal agent; it cannot make you *do* anything. But it is a powerful invitatory. However one views music, there is no doubt that it will never leave the listener untouched. Whether concert hall, rock festival, informal sing-along, grocery store, or CCM church service, listeners will be affected. If they are not all affected in the same specific way, they are, nevertheless, affected in the same general way. This ability to effect broad ends can be seen in the appreciation one has for the beauty of a symphony; the edification received from J. S. Bach's Cantata 140, *Wake, Awake, for Night Is Flying*; the activity of "Dancing Queen" (Abba, 1976); the turmoil of "To Kill" (Bounty Killer, 2009); the aimlessness of "wallpaper music;" the resounding inspiration of Luther's "A Mighty Fortress;" and on and on. Naturally, different listeners bring different aptitudes and backgrounds to the music: intellectual, emotional, psychological, experiential, associational, all of which colors music's impact. Yet beneath the differences something beckons in a particular direction: wordless, intuitive, innate, instinctual. Such musical bidding result from many elements, the most basic

---

[202] Andrew Fletcher, *An Account of a Conversation Concerning a Right Regulation of Governments for the Common Good of Mankind* (London, 1703).
[203] Mark Noll, "We Are What We Sing," *Christianity Today*, July 12,1999, 37.
[204] Julius Portnoy, *Music in the Life of Man* (Holt, Rinehardt and Winston, 1963), 103.

being the configuration of the music itself. The aesthetic of a piece of music is the result of compositional craft, the internal artistry of music's nuts and bolts.

Value and Music's Message

One would think that in a postmodern world the concept of value would be an outmoded one. Regardless of society's insistence on a broad expansive relativism, there still is retained in our culture pockets of looking for good, better, and best. Competitions abound. Judging happens. Humans habitually evaluate, and for good reason: God has made the world such that we must make choices.

Ah, but on what basis does one choose? That is the question.

I believe that musical value is based on universal artistic principles placed by God in creation.[205] They are cross-cultural and timeless and may be summarized as unity, variety, dominance, economy, tendency gratification, and creativity.[206] A musical composition is good to the extent that these principles are carried out throughout the piece.

The component parts of music, rhythm, melody, and harmony all come under the jurisdiction of these aesthetic fundamentals. Lest the reader feel that such constraint limits a composer's freedom, just the converse is true. Igor Stravinsky explains:

> My freedom will be so much the greater and more meaningful the more narrowly I limit my field of action and the more I surround myself with obstacles. Whatever diminishes constraint diminishes strength. The more constraints one imposes, the more one frees one's self of the chains that shackle the spirit.[207]

---

[205] More on this in the next two chapters, "Church Music and Aesthetics: Theological Insights" and "Scriptural Discernment Extended."

[206] Ibid., 102. The author lists several traits a musical score should possess: logic, consistency, unity, coherence, variety, contrast, repetition, and appropriate length.

[207] Igor Stravinsky, *Poetics of Music in the Form of Six Lessons*, trans. Arthur Knodell and Ingolf Dahl (Cambridge: Harvard University Press, 1977).

Rhythm is the fundamental ingredient of music. Without it music ceases to be. A pithy definition of music might be: "Thought or emotion expressed in terms of rhythmically moving tone." This essential of rhythm needs to be differentiated from beat. Beat is merely the pulse of the rhythm. Rhythm is organized around the beat. When beat dominates, rhythm (which means flow) suffers. Value is diminished.

Melody is another indispensable constituent part of music. Commonly believed to be music's primary component, melody has enormous potential for establishing the intended effect of musical composition. By building a balance between conjunct and disjunct motion, a variety of high and low pitches, creative unity between phrase members, and a sense of cadential arrival,[208] melody reaches its greatest expressive potential. Melody is patently the most identifiable of music's elements— the one that people most often use to identify particular pieces. Melody may also have harmonic implications, strengthening the underlying chordal structure of the music. This vertical aspect of music is governed by principles of dominance between primary and secondary chords,[209] providing harmonic color to the overall musical texture.

There are numerous other constituent factors which go into the making of music: mode, polyphony, orchestration, dynamics, form, timbre, and texture, to name a few. Each element plays a distinct role in the general aesthetic of each composition. These elements can be structured to sound beautiful or ugly, virtuous or rebellious, uplifting or depressed, pessimistic or optimistic, funny or serious, noble or vile, and so forth. Music's components are the vocabulary of the language of music. They give voice to the composer's intentions and convey the composition's musical message, the real message of music being in the music itself.

There exists a certain ambiguity in trying to explain in words the exact meaning(s) of musical language. The question is: "Can

---

[208] *Conjunct* means progression by step, *disjunct* by skip; phrase members are analogous to sentences in linguistics; cadences are musical closes.
[209] Primary chords are those built on the first, fourth, and fifth degree of the scale. Secondary chords are those built on the second, third, sixth, and seventh scale degrees.

you state in so many words what the meaning is?"[210] Probably not. Nevertheless, "the music in its total impact in the melody, the rhythm, the harmony, is expressive of a mentality, a way of life, a way of thinking and feeling, an approach to reality."[211] Its power works at the intuitive level more than at the cognitive level. This makes musical communication obscure. In working behind the scene, its communicative power is formidable.

Because of the inferential power that music possesses, music shapes worship after its own image to a far greater extent than is commonly discerned. The emotional and intellectual character of the music sets the overall temperament of worship. Since the whole complexion of worship is subject to the disposition of the music chosen, prayerful, informed, and Holy Spirit–guided choice is a responsibility that every music director and song leader needs to take seriously.

[210] Aaron Copeland, *What to Listen For In Music* (New York: McGraw-Hill, 1957), 12. Found in Chris Dobrian, *Music and Language*, 1992, music.arts.uci.edu/dobrian/CD.music.lang.htm.

[211] H. R. Rookmaacher, *Art Needs No Justification* (Downers Grove, IL: InterVarsity Press, 1978), 48.

7 Church Music and Aesthetics: Theological Insights

Remarkably, the world that we inhabit is one world, one creation, a unified whole. In considering aesthetics in the light of Scripture, we find in God's Word great and glorious principles, principles that are cross-cultural and timeless, principles upon which great art rests. However, there are no explicit God-given prescriptive formulas for the making of art, music included. "Whereas the scriptures provide a wealth of commandments to guide our behavior and character development in the moral sphere, they provide few explicit commandments about what is expected in the aesthetic sphere."[212]

What we do find in Scripture are broad-based principles applicable to the constructing of all forms of art. Although exact unequivocal aesthetic guidelines are given for the building of the temple, this is the exception and not the rule. However, God's provident instructions for the erecting of such structures do highlight the Almighty's concern for matters artistic. In reading the passages relating to the building of the tabernacle and temple, we cannot help but be struck by the requirements that the Lord gave the builders and artisans.[213] These structures and

---

[212] Michael Palmer, "The Role of the Bible in Shaping a Christian Worldview," in *Elements of a Christian Worldview*, ed. Michael Palmer (Springfield, MO: Gospel Publishing House, 2012).

[213] See 1 Kings, chapters 6–9 and 2 Chronicles 3 concerning the building of the Temple. The making of the Tabernacle may be found in Exodus 25–31. In Exodus 31:3–5, the Lord tells Moses about Bezalel, the artisan: "And I have filled him with the Spirit of God, in wisdom, and in understanding, and in knowledge, and in all manner of workmanship to design artistic works, to work in gold, in silver, in bronze, in cutting jewels for setting, in carving wood, and to work in all manner of workmanship" (NKJV).

their furnishings show a well-defined symmetry, proportion, grace, and elegance,[214] the artistry of which is undeniable.[215] Even the priestly garments were specifically designed "for glory and beauty."[216] God's prescript is precise and well-defined, the taste of the builders subject to the ordinance of the Almighty. But as far as music goes, other than an obvious requirement for artistic excellence, these passages do not render specific guidelines for music. No definitive citations concerning the exact music or musical style to be used by the church in its worship exist. Nevertheless, Scripture is replete with theological guidelines that are foundational to making right choices in all areas of life including the choice of music in worship.

The underlying presupposition is that evangelicals need a Judeo-Christian worldview that is broadly comprehensive. The Christian faith must not be compartmentalized thereby affecting only certain select areas of life. On the contrary, a theistic worldview is the foundation upon which all of life, i.e. every aspect of life, is built. This includes the arts and, specifically, music.

Yet I have heard dozens of times, "The Bible says nothing about the kind of music to use in worship," inferring that there are no scriptural guidelines for music. The assumption is that anything is all right, regardless. But if this is so, the all-embracing scope of the parameters of the Christian faith gets lost, for how can one's faith be comprehensive when artistic areas of life remain untouched by Scripture?

The answer is clear: it can't. Cutting the arts free from theistic reach gives it an autonomy incompatible with Christianity. Axiological schizophrenia[217] results.

One cannot find the word abortion in Scripture; nor does it mention the words illegal drug use, physical or mental abuse, or pornography. Evangelicals label these as sins, and

---

[214] Exodus 25–28; 30:1–5; 39–39; 1 Kings 6–7; 2 Chronicles 2–3.

[215] Exodus 26:1, 31, 36; 35:31–35; 1 Kings 6:29, 32, 35; 7:29, 36.

[216] Exodus 28:2–28, 33–34, 40. John Makujina, *Measuring the Music*, 2nd ed. (Willow Street, PA: Old Paths Publications, 2002), 155.

[217] An expression coined by Dale Jorgenson.

their justification for doing so rests upon biblically extrapolated principles ordained by God for holy living. Not including particular words such as these in Scripture does not indicate approval of them. Biblical presuppositions beyond the mention of a particular word governs the Christian faith.

To reiterate, the Bible does not contain proof-texts concerning illegal drug use, physical or mental abuse, or pornography. But you will find broad biblical principles that relate to the same: care of the body, kindness, and sexual morality.

The same is true of music. Scripture is laden with aesthetic principles that undergird all music-making, including the music of the church. Music has the responsibility to proclaim in its own right (apart from text) the sterling qualities of the uncompromised gospel: truth, grace/law, and goodness. The Lord who is truth and goodness, but not beauty, is not the God of Scripture.[218] God, in making us in His image, gave us the ability to produce that which is beautiful. On the other hand, the sin nature provides humankind with ample capacity for generating ugliness. Depravity prevents us from achieving perfection, yet we can continue to strive for excellence. To that end we need to practice theological/aesthetic discrimination in the music that the church provides for the worship of the Almighty. Church music, in its contextual surroundings, should blend rhythm, melody, and harmony in wholesome combination whose total impact, being more than the sum of its parts, is a musical witness to gospel integrity. The precise measure of musical rightness for doing so comes from following the lead of scriptural norms as expressed through the grammar of music.

The Preeminence of Special Revelation

An effective musical worship aesthetic in our postmodern world must have the capacity to speak to culture with authority.

---

[218] John Mason Hodges, "Aesthetics and the Place of Beauty in Worship," *Reformation and Revival* 9, no. 3 (Summer 2000): 64.

Giving the church a musical version of the very society the church hopes to save hinders the church's mission. What is needed is an authoritative aesthetic that has its basis outside of culture, something supra-cultural. That something is Scripture. Christians from all sides agree: "Scripture will govern not just what we say but will also govern how we say it."[219] What is necessary is judicious understanding and comprehensive application of Biblical principles.

Divine revelation is the only viable instrument with the capacity to guide the course of church music in today's world. In general, people hold assumptions (consciously or unconsciously) that work against the forming of discipled musical parameters. In evangelical worship, unrestrained license is by far the general ground from which particular musical compositions or musical genres are chosen. Such practice is entrenched in the modern psyche of normlessness. Traits such as immediate gratification (the quickest way to satisfaction is the best), hedonism (pleasure as the highest good), unenlightened democracy (decisions based on self-interest), individualism (selfishness), and solipsistic relativism (values are a matter of personal choice, each no better or worse than any other) mitigate against any kind of uniform commonality. Such a value-neutral worldview leaves reason helpless, aesthetic principles non-existent, history irrelevant, and standards meaningless. No basis remains for establishing musical norms for worship. Therefore, to construct an appropriate aesthetic for the evangelical church, nothing short of divine revelation will be effective.

Society's cast for pleasure drives its self-indulgence. Even the worship services of many evangelicals are designed to be entertaining and fun. Though not stated, providing the "audience" with a good time remains high on the list of priorities. Most church leaders tend to view musical enjoyment in worship as entirely normative.

---

[219] Joe Carter, "Debatable: Is Christian Hip Hop Ungodly?" *The Gospel Coalition Blog,* December 2, 2013, www.thegospelcoalition.org/article/debatable-is-christian-hip-hop-ungodly/.

Special revelation paints quite a different picture. It does not contain a sybaritic gospel. On the contrary; our Lord clearly taught that Christians are to deny themselves, take up their cross, and follow Him. Pleasuring the self is hardly the aim of saving grace, nor fun the goal of living. In an age consumed by frivolity and levity, God calls us to crucify the self. The test of good church music is not that it pleases the listener but that it speaks truth via its melody, harmony, rhythm, and form. Musical value, not frippery, is at the heart of the matter.

In a society that denies universals and downplays reason, we cannot expect normal rational argument and conversation to be the basis for church music convention. In a culture as relativistic and hedonistic as ours, resistant to thoughtful consideration of the issue, this loss of reason appreciably weakens the church: "One of secularism's most useful devices for weakening the Christian Church has been the policy of relativizing and individualizing values and beliefs."[220] Choosing one's truth on the subjective basis of taste is anathema to Christian theism. Considering the comparably few explicit commands concerning aesthetics in Scripture, Michael Palmer comes right to the point. We cannot conclude that:

> ...art is simply a matter of personal taste and that no standards (norms) can be brought to bear in judging what is presented as art. The biblical narratives assist the patient reader in thinking about appropriate standards. They do this, for example, by providing models of significant contexts (such as worship or celebration) within which artifacts and works of art were exhibited.[221]

Nevertheless, culture exerts so strong an allure and the tastes of popular religious leaders are so influential that dichotomizing *what* is said (the text or "message" of a song, for example) and *how* it is said (the music or "medium" of a song, for example) seems right as rain. As we have seen, it was this understanding that led

---

[220] Harry Blamires, *The Post-Christian Mind: Exposing Its Destructive Agenda* (Ann Arbor, MI: Servant Publications, 1999), 79.
[221] Michael Palmer, op. cit., 32.

Pastor Rick Warren to choose the worship music genre (middle-of-the-road rock) for his church in Lake Forest, California. Since 97 percent of attendees preferred that sound, middle-of-the-road rock was the music chosen.[222] In other words, Warren selected the music for Saddleback on the subjective basis of people's individual preferences. Objective musical valuation was ignored. One of the downfalls of postmodernism is that it has no compass.

For evangelicals, this leaves special revelation as the one and only truth that has the power to break through modern consciousness. If it is possible to show that Scripture has an authoritative word on the subject of church music, chances for evangelicals to reorient it from its subjective foundation to a biblical truth foundation increase. Evangelicals, as people of the Book, have a divine bedrock on which to build up and strengthen the music of the church. In turning to God's Word, we have a foundation that will weather all cultural incursions.

Music/Gospel Analogue

Throughout the Old and New Testaments, witnessing characterizes the people of God. For evangelicals, witnessing defines the very heart of what it means to be evangelical. Evangelicals evangelize. They witness. The great commission found in Acts 1:8 is a rallying cry for the evangelization of the world. Jesus charges: "and ye shall be witnesses unto me both in Jerusalem, and in all Judaea, and in Samaria, and unto the uttermost part of the earth" (KJV). Today's English version, New International translation, and James Moffatt all use the word *witnesses*. The Living Bible uses the word *testify*. And of course a witness does just that: a witness testifies.

Music is a testimony.[223] Its general style discloses a position on purity and holiness.[224] That is to say, the rhythm, melody,

---

[222] See chap. 1, n. 9 for Warren's full explanation.
[223] We are considering music apart from text.
[224] Donald P. Hustad, *True Worship* (Wheaton, IL: Hope Publishing Co., 1998), 187.

harmony, texture, and vocal quality are the show-and-tell of the music's witness. Not only is there an internal spirit about the music as a whole, it is also possible to evaluate its component parts in the light of Scripture.

Just as giving or withholding the proverbial cup of water speaks volumes about one's faith, so the music we program indicates to those who encounter it our concept of God. Church music serves as a musical re-presentation of the gospel. It is the gospel translated into musical action. Or, put another way, church music is an analogue of God's revelation to the human race. The characteristics of the church's musical language should show, or witness to, or be a musical analogy of the very gospel itself. That's a big order because it requires evangelical musicians and congregants alike to view church music in an entirely new light—counter-culturally and theistically holistic. The scandal of Scripture is its claim to exclusivity. The cultural relativism and unchecked openness of postmodernism is in direct contradistinction to Scripture's absolutism.[225] New Testament Christianity requires that Christians take a different road from that of our relativistic post-Christian culture.

In order for church music to witness well, it must be disciplined and shaped by that which it represents. That is to say, God's principles must inform musical principles. The musical language of the people of God is God-speech, similar to that found in nature. The Psalmist's observation that the "heavens declare the glory of God" has its counterpart in the realm of music. Both are a form of general revelation. Moreover, when any music is composed well (meaning written within the parameters of the principles placed by God in creation) by Christians or non-Christians, that music gives testimony to the God of the universe.[226]

The following, then, are gospel-related principles that form

---

[225] Steve Badger, *Evangelizing Our Postmodern World: Training Christians to Bear Witness on the Postmodern Battlefield* (Springfield, MO: self-pub., 2000), 9, 18, 21, 39, 45.
[226] Virginia Ramey Mollenkott, "Christianity and Aesthetics: Conflict or Correlation?" in *Man and His Culture: A Compilation of Readings* (Springfield, MO: Evangel College, 1973), 27.

the framework upon which a church music aesthetic may be erected. These principles will guide us in the choice of musical genres and in the selecting of particular repertoire.[227] What we are after is the discovery of broad theological principles that apply to the making of church music. Taking the macro view, we look to Scripture as the authority on which to establish a faithful church music gospel analogue.

Creation

"In the beginning God created..."[228] This pronouncement not only introduces the entirety of Scripture, it opens both the Nicene Creed and the Apostles' Creed. The Christian church cannot dismiss the fact that the God it worships is a Creator God—"the maker of heaven and earth." Whatever else God is, Scripture reveals God as conceiver and framer of that which only He can imagine.[229] God is the cosmic artist, one who brings into being that which is not. That is what artists do: they make things; they originate the unknown.

God creates *ex nihilo* (out of nothing), something humans are unable to do. Artists depend on preexistent "stuff" to fashion their works. Pitch, timbre, and harmony all come from the natural world. That makes the musician dependent. On

---

[227] It must also be added that there are numerous practical considerations of an important and often thorny nature that need to be dealt with in determining the music to be utilized. What do you do with an uncooperative singer or an influential leader who wants to sing the same songs every Sunday or a pastor who wishes to emulate the musical style of a particular megachurch? How important is the congregation's musical understanding and experience? What is the budget for expenditures on music, etc.? The answers to these and other such questions are important and can also be dealt with from a scriptural point of view.

[228] See Hebrews 1:2; John 1:3; John 1:10; 1 Corinthians 8:6; Colossians 1:16.

[229] The cosmology uncovered by researchers and the inner world of quantum mechanics probed by scientists continue to baffle and amaze the human mind. With instruments such as the Keck telescope in Hawaii and the gains afforded by Hubble, investigators are continually at the brink of one new discovery after another, with no end in sight. Can anyone really imagine the infinitesimal dark-energy unit density strength of space at .(decimal point and 122 zeros) 138? *Newsweek*, May 28, 2012, 24. God and God's making is truly beyond our ability to comprehend.

the other hand, artists are simultaneously independent. The decisions made in the shaping of a work of art are entirely up to the artist. Their autonomy gives them a certain exaltedness, their dependence a sense of humility.

Creativity breaks new ground with imagination and integrity. Contemplating His creation on the sixth day, Scripture records, "And God saw every thing that he had made, and, behold, it was very good."[230] That pronouncement is a statement on quality. Our creations too, within human limitations, must also be good. When someone produces art along the lines of God's creative handiwork, that art, as an *a priori* assumption, witnesses to and reflects something of God Himself.

It follows then that church music requires the spark of genuine creativity if it is to reflect the creative nature of God. It is injurious to attempt to image the master Creator through a musical creativity that is gaunt, feeble, and shallow. Music with little creative depth cannot reveal God's creative nature. There are, of course, levels to creativity. It is not a matter of all or nothing. But our calling to utilize musical materials with as high a degree of creativity as possible in any given situation ought not be disregarded.

Pop music of whatever stripe lacks genuine creativity in its conception, execution, and consumption. It entertains and pursues fun. It is constantly in flux, displaying ever new permutations of musical fashion commensurate with changing societal standards and taste. But newness does not guarantee creative integrity. In truth, popular music of all types avoids substantive creative depth. This trait distinguishes it from art music. Pop is a light music. Its creativity is shallow; it is geared to producing a superficiality that wears out relatively quickly. The ever-changing pop music charts bear out the trendy, transient nature of popular music. To attempt to use pop to musically communicate unchanging theological truth is to completely miscast it. Let pop be itself. Just because people like it—find it entertaining and amusing—is no reason to bring it into the

---

[230] Genesis 1:31 (KJV).

house of the Lord. The thin, emaciated creativity that defines popular music falls far short of the human capability to emulate the creativity found in creation. The creator God has given us the ingredients of true creativity: imagination and integrity.

The music of the church must be patterned after the creativity shown by God in creation. Theism is value-laden. It does not shrink from evaluation. It acknowledges differences between good and bad. Theism makes aesthetic judgment possible and necessary. In theism there is a creative imperative. Church music must model in its very bones the fact that we serve a Creator who does all things well.

The Creation Mandate

In making the world, God ordained that humanity would have a part to play in the ongoing process of *creation continua*, the continuing of creation. This mandate, given initially in embryonic form, has God instructing Adam and Eve to "be fruitful, and multiply, and replenish the earth, and subdue it; and have dominion over the fish of the sea, and over the fowl of the air, and over every living thing that moveth upon the earth" (Genesis 1:28, KJV). And again in Genesis 2:15, "The Lord God took the man, and put him into the garden of Eden to dress it and keep it," including the task of naming the animals (Genesis 2:19–20). Mankind does have a responsibility for the care and sustenance of the world. This mandate not only extends to the physical world, but to the spiritual world as well. All that God has made He has designated as our responsibility. And for Christians, the Great Commission is just as much a part of the creation mandate as are, for example, environmental concerns. Our charge is a wide one.

The Creative *Imago Dei*

It is worth noting that when God gave Adam the job of naming the animals, He did not tell Adam what to name the animals. Rather, Adam used his God-given creativity to do so. This is possible because Scripture tells us that God made man in His own image.

But what constitutes that image?

Up to the point in the scriptural record where the text notes, "And God said, Let us make man in our image, after our likeness" (Genesis 1:26, KJV), there are but two things that God has revealed about Himself, namely, that He exists and that He is a creator. Therefore, reading the Bible as one would read any other book, that is, from the beginning, the reader is compelled to conclude by verse 26 of Genesis 1 that (1) there is a God and (2) the image that man has been made into is the image of a creator. That is to say, we are compelled to conclude that humankind is gifted with creativity, an endowment from the creator God that reflects, in part, divine creativity. No other deduction fits the narrative.

Of course human creativity, wonderful as it is, does not match God's supernatural creativity. We are created creatures. Our creativity is a derived one. Moreover, our creativity is affected by the fall, and in our creating we are obliged to overcome the heaviness of the world through creative struggle and travail. True creativity, endowed with characteristics of godly creativity, is very much like childbirth: it takes effort.

To be truly creative, a work must have certain characteristics likened unto the pristine creativity of the Almighty. Some of these translate into the language of music as:

1. The Subjective Phase of Creativity.
    Here the composer relies on intuition, talent, and inspiration to birth new musical ideas.

2. The Objective Phase of Creativity.

This relates to the skill of the composer in fleshing out musical ideas. True musical creativity is dependent on knowing and understanding the grammar of music (similar to that of a fiction writer needing to know the grammar of the English language) and the ability to express thought and emotion in terms of tone.

3. Compositional Integrity.

This means embracing musical craft that eschews the frivolous and embraces the profound. The type of music determines the level of compositional technique. Popular music, fashioned for easy satisfaction, requires a less intense and sophisticated musical language than does musical art that requires more weight. Notably, God's making is not facetious. It is purposive, profound, virtuous, and principled.

4. Goal Inhibiting Writing.

The best music uses goal-inhibiting technique as found in God's economy, a pattern for achieving that which is worthwhile. God has set up life so that as Christians we "run the race," "attain unto perfection," "press toward the mark." We do not reach the final goal until our life course is over. Someday we will be vindicated. Someday heaven will be our home. But not yet. Now we are but strangers and pilgrims on a journey.

Woven into the warp and woof of the gospel is the concept of delayed gratification. The eschatological thrust of Scripture begins in Genesis 3 (when God explained that one day Eve's descendent, Jesus, would crush the head of the serpent, Satan) and continues throughout the book until the end of Revelation. While regeneration is complete at salvation, full vindication of the human condition is postponed until the Last Day. There will come a time when the lion and the lamb shall lie down together. Someday there will be no pain or suffering. Crying and sorrow will flee away. The Eucharistic acclamation, "Christ has died, Christ is risen," goes on to affirm, "Christ will come again." Delay is a theistic norm. Waiting is part of God's plan. There is a destination and it takes a journey to get there. As Paul notes, now we see through a glass darkly, but then face to face.

Composition that achieves its musical goal quickly, easily, and without travail is bound to be less valuable, artistically speaking, than a piece that wrestles with substantive musical issues, delaying final consummation of its musical goal until the concluding cadence. Certainly the banal "Rudolph the Red-Nosed Reindeer" has not the musical value of Cesar Franck's *Panis Angelicus*. Franck's music, with its deliberate pace, exquisite melody, and canonic imitation[231] on the second strophe[232] leads us to a final conclusion not a moment too soon. The musical journey culminates in reaching its musical goal only after taking a circuitous route. Goal-inhibiting compositional technique is necessary to achieve musical value. Aestheticians such as Leonard Meyer and Herman Berlinski find that:

> ...while "pop" music whether of the tin-pan-alley or the Ethelbert Nevin variety makes use of a fairly large repertory of tones, it operates with such conventional clichés that gratification is almost immediate and uncertainty is minimized."[233] "If the most probable goal is reached in the most immediate and direct way,

---

[231] The technique of overlapping a melody throughout the musical texture at a variety of intervals and beats.

[232] A strophe is a poetic stanza-like section.

[233] Leonard B. Meyer, "Some Remarks on Value and Greatness in Music," in *Aesthetic Inquiry: Essays on Art Criticism and the Philosophy of Art*, ed. Monroe C. Beardsley and Herbert M. Schueller (Belmont, CA: Dickenson Pub. Co. Inc., 1967), 178. Herman Berlinski, "Pop, Rock and Sacred," II, *Music 5* (1971), 48.

given the stylistic context, the musical event taken in itself will be of little value.[234]

Contemporary society puts a premium on immediacy. This penchant for immediate gratification has its musical expression in popular music. In fact, immediate gratification is the pop music principle. The ability of pop to please in the easiest, quickest, and most direct manner is what, at bottom, distinguishes it from artistic music. Popular music avoids the journey. Achieving its musical goals directly and quickly, abstaining from the excursions and developmental characteristics of more mature musical expressions, pop pleases the listener without the need for wrestling with substantive musical material. It has no travail. The listener "gets it" right away. Musical gratification, elementary to be sure, is rapid and complete.

Delayed gratification, then, as a mark of musical value, is founded in the very nature of how the Creator has ordered life. The church music which best models God's creative work is music of value, music that eschews immediate gratification and embraces the postponing of musical goals until the musical argument is fully worked out. Genres of music focused on popularity achieve their end by circumventing weighty writing. Constructed of light musical idioms, popular music of any type is unable to show the essence of God's creativity because it is constructed of weak musical components. What is needed is music that wears well, that goes for the long haul, that has objective value, that goes beyond popular cliché. In other words, the music of God's people is best achieved when it exemplifies (as much as is humanly possible) the creativity of our creator God.

---

[234] Meyer, op. cit., 263.

5. Musical Form.

Genesis, chapter 1, begins by asserting that in making and ordering the world God imposed form upon formlessness. It is a telling statement. Form is antithetical to chaos and a necessary ingredient for intelligible creativity. I have occasionally listened to salon piano players who wander over the keys with no shape, rhyme, or reason to their renditions. Sometimes referred to as elevator or wallpaper music, this type of background music has no frame, no architectural plan. Improvised melodies and harmonies go nowhere wandering from chord to chord and note to note, formless and shapeless. Music, if it is to have value, must have a format.

God's creative acts instruct us in this regard. Imposing form upon the unformed is a basic characteristic of creativity.

It is worth recognizing that God's forming of the universe does not imply that the created order can be fully and formally known to us. Science continually discovers new wonders of nature. While His ordering of matter may become intelligible to us, the depth of His making is such that everything is not immediately apparent. There are levels to God's forming. We have discovered much about the planets in our solar system, for example. But we don't know everything. There is more to uncover.[235] Artistic making follows this pattern, though from afar. The best music has an overall form readily apprehendable on the macro level. But the micro level contains artful and subtle diversity; knowing the form of a piece becomes a process of unfolding its form-giving twists and turns over the course of the entire composition and, depending upon its intricacy, over

---

[235] Astronomers at the California Institute of Technology have postulated from indirect evidence the existence of a ninth planet (sometimes referred to as Planet X) in our solar system. Thought to have ten times the mass of the earth, it is believed that one orbit around the sun would take from 10,000 to 20,000 years.

the course of repeated hearings. God's making provides a blueprint for shaping the form-giving of the best of human art.

6. The Historical Imperative

Scripture shows an orderly process in God's revealing Himself to mankind. From Genesis to Revelation we note the historical progress that builds on the past as the future is addressed. The old covenant is not dismissed as irrelevant but is utilized in a process whereby the new covenant fulfills the old. God reveals Himself in a time frame. Historicity is revered. In Acts 3, 10, and 13 Peter and Paul do not deliver metaphysical discourses. They tell the story of God's acts in history. And Stephen before the Sanhedrin recounted the long history of God's intervention in the lives of His chosen people:

> Men, brethren, and fathers, hearken; The God of glory appeared unto our father Abraham, when he was in Mesopotamia, before he dwelt in Charran, And said unto him, Get thee out of thy country, and from thy kindred, and come into the land which I shall shew thee (Acts 7:2–3, KJV).

Stephen continued with the story of God's acts in history, bringing Israel ever closer to the revelation of Himself in Jesus Christ. The Christian faith is grounded in past events and the continuing of that faith a matter of remembering and interpreting those events. "In short, He is the *Lord of history*, working through men and nations whom He has raised up to fulfill His purpose."[236]

How does history relate to our music-making as recipients of the creative *imago Dei*? It shows that the

---

[236] George F. Thomas, "Central Christian Affirmations," *The Christian Answer*, ed. Henry P. Van Dusen (New York: Charles Scribner's Sons, 1945), pg. 104.

ongoing process of revelation and the remembering of history is very much how God has set up the world. The arts are part of a people's story for they contribute to clarifying a community's unique identity and composite character. For the church to reject the past is to reject the conglomerate center of who we are as a people. "As memory is necessary to the sanity of personality, so tradition sustains the collective personality of a people."[237]

Every church musician must see to it that the traditional music of the faith is not eliminated from the repertoire of the congregation. Rejecting the musical history of our faith disembowels us from our roots. Forgetting our heritage leaves us wandering minstrels subject to the whims of a secularly commercialized popular culture. More than architecture, preaching style, dress, stained glass, or liturgy, music defines the selfhood and identity of a people. My assessment simply is, "Tell me what you sing and I will tell you who you are." To reject the birthright of 500 years of Christian hymnody, for example, cripples faith and compromises witness. Heritage matters. It is time to treat the musical past in the manner of God's revelatory process: namely, retain and build on history.

The Incarnation

The doctrine of the incarnation yields penetrating insights into understanding biblical relevancy, message and medium, aspects of musical communication, and the pastoral ministry of the church musician. Scripture shows the "infleshment" of God (commonly referred to as the incarnation) to be the pivotal event in God's self-disclosure to the human race. Having been foretold by Jewish prophets for centuries, the coming of Jesus (the second member of the Trinity) separated the Old and New

---

[237] Paul Waitman Hoon, *The Integrity of Worship* (New York: Abingdon Press, 1971), 97.

Testaments, the era of the law and that of grace, and the age of animal sacrifice for the forgiveness of sin and the crucifixion and resurrection of God's Son as the propitiation for sin.

Relevancy

We could not by our own initiative connect with God. Before Christ, sinful humanity had no direct path to Him. God, living in light unapproachable, whom no one has seen or can see,[238] was estranged from the creature He had made. The Holy Uncreated and the unholy created were cut off from one another. Mankind was forever lost, undone, and alone.

Scripture reveals that since we could not go to Him, God, in the fullness of time, came to us. He became unmistakably relevant to our situation. Coming in a form to which we could relate, He became one of us. Jesus, the Son, fully human and simultaneously fully God, came as the redeemer of mankind, to bridge the chasm between the Holy and the unholy, between God and man. And He came with a message spoken in terms that we could understand. This message, "God loves us," so easy to say yet so impossible to truly understand, needed relevant demonstration.

How could humans personally experience the love of God? It was only when God revealed Himself in the God/man Jesus that the love of God was revealed in all its fullness. Jesus not only taught us to love, He showed it throughout His life, and ultimately in the crucifixion.

The Gospel of John, chapter 13, gives the account of the Last Supper. Here Jesus taught the disciples about love and the selflessness characteristic of true love. The Lord of the universe, the King of Creation, poured water into a basin and began to wash the disciples' feet. Peter forbade him, but Jesus persevered: "If I wash thee not, thou hast no part with me" (John 13:8, KJV). So Jesus continued, and when He had finished He said: "Know ye what I have done to you? If I then, your Lord and Master,

---

[238] See 1 Timothy 6:16 (NIV).

have washed your feet; ye also ought to wash one another's feet" (John 13:12, 14, KJV).

It is a telling object lesson. God's people minister from a position of humility. Eschewing arrogance, pride, and one-upmanship, church musicians serve in the way shown by our Lord.

God's self-disclosure in the incarnation was, then, among other things, a communication method. In humility, Jesus came to us on our level. He spoke in a language we could understand, yet his message and communication method was never compromised in word or deed. He did not indulge in or utilize anything that jeopardized His message and mission. In short, Jesus was relevant without compromise.

Relevancy and the Evangelical Church

Historically, the *prima facie* issue in the *modus operandi* of evangelical methodology has been the preponderance of being relevant to the unbeliever. That is, the evangelical church has made sure that its preaching, teaching, and singing was in the common language of the people. Evangelization has not been primarily esoteric and abstruse thought-provoking discourse. Nor has it "evangelized" by saying nothing and in silence assume the sweeping pluralism of universalism will fulfill the Great Commission. No, evangelicals have pretty much used the common language of the wider culture so that the relatively circumscribed message of New Testament Christianity, couched in culture's existent language, will be disseminated without misunderstanding.

Note the incarnational idea in the use of contemporary language for the various translations of the Bible. Each one translates from the Greek, Aramaic, or Hebrew into the vernacular of a particular culture. For example, the *Eight Translation New Testament*[239] includes in one volume the entire New Testament as rendered in the *King James Version, The*

---

[239] *Eight Translation New Testament* (Tyndale House, 1974).

Living Bible, Phillips' Modern English, Revised Standard Version, Today's English Version, New International Version, The Jerusalem Bible, and *The New English Bible.* The concept is to faithfully transcribe the original language into modern usage so that the inceptive meaning of thousands of years ago will become crystal clear in today's nomenclature. Incarnating the ancient text's message into contemporary literary forms makes the subtleties of the original communicable to today's readers.

Those who lean toward the preservation and perpetuation of a particular ecclesiastical heritage in the configuration of public worship devalue any attempt to alter its makeup. Inherited tradition, pristine and unchanged, is highly revered. With unquestioned belief in the historic assumptions of one's inheritance, traditionalists tend to be closed, static, and immovable. They plant deep roots, abhor change, and believe in "holding the line." Existing in a contemporary culture that abhors traditional values, the conservation of the church's birthright is thought to be something for which to contend.

On the other hand, progressive theory values change. Believing that change is synonymous with progress, the elimination of the old in favor of the new is highly favored. The cornerstone of liberalism embraces a wide pluralism on a level playing field of acceptance. It is not concerned with preservation as much as with generation, with the past as much as the future, with antecedent as much as consequent. Nontraditionalists believe they are enlightened and as a rule move in lockstep with the overall progressive agenda of the wider culture. They generally repudiate transcendent authority, objective value, and any type of absolutes, but they do affirm the self as ultimate authority, embrace subjective value, and espouse broad-based relativism. Liberalism does not impose preconceptions and restrictions. Freedom means license without constraint.

Neither liberalism nor conservatism can exist as a working basis for the musical communication of the gospel. The internal contradictions of liberalism as practiced in the workaday world are clearly apparent: liberals who supposedly maintain an openness to anything are the first to be closed to some things—among them conservatism! There are things that liberals rail against, things with which they disagree. And liberalism taken to its limit will, in the end, lead to anarchy and chaos. There must be boundaries to life. To be open to the possibility that a red traffic signal light means "go" and a green one means "stop" because someone believes it so "for me" is to invite an automobile accident. Tolerance for openness must be screened. Without some objective parameters, life cannot exist. The result would be a broad-based nihilism, the negation of life.

Conservatism, too, has its limitations. No matter how much conservatives are closed to change, it must be admitted that conservatism is fundamentally at odds with how the natural world works. The changing seasons, the reshaping of the seashore from year to year, the second law of thermodynamics, even the self-disclosure of the Almighty in the fullness of time, are testimonies to the reality that process and progression are part of life and living. One might have the most restrictive standards possible only to find that no one is capable of keeping such law; to err is human. Conservatives can live only if allowances are made, if one's regulative box has sides that have the capability of coming down, if the rigidity and dogma of position is undergirded by the humility of human frailty. Idealistic conservatism is simply not attainable. The fluidity of life cannot be circumvented. Immovability must give way to mobility. As in liberalism, conservatism can achieve perfection only in the absence of life.

Scripture gives guidance in reference to such positions. The relevancy needed to communicate the gospel musically is not a matter of embracing one or the other of these contrasting and fundamentally differing philosophical points of view. While some evangelicals are intractable conservatives and others unbending liberals in the matter of embracing contemporary culture's communicative methodology, the fact is neither position is adequate. Conservatism opts for an inert changelessness; liberalism for continual change. Conservatives believe cultural relevancy a sell-out; liberals believe it to be the holy grail. Neither one is dynamic enough to cope with the reality of musically communicating gospel truth to the modern world. In the last analysis, the categories of conservative and liberal, traditional and contemporary, are not truly germane to music ministry. Neither position embraces enough of a thoroughgoing and comprehensive Scriptural teaching to found the music of the church. Only the full contrapuntal truth of God's Word will do.

In general, most evangelicals believe they are fulfilling the Great Commission by intractably practicing one or the other of these fundamental positions in reference to the musical accommodation of the gospel to culture. Historically, in fact, the vast majority of the evangelical movement disavowed conservative ideology when it came to music. Making a clear distinction between the theological rhetoric of words and their oft unknowing belief in a nontheological musical rhetoric, evangelicals have approached musical/gospel accommodation fairly liberally. In the 18th century, hymnody of a more "popular" type appeared in the revivals and camp meetings of the First Great Awakening.[240] And the next century's Second Great Awakening featured a continuing trend toward popularism in the form of Negro spirituals,[241] camp meeting songs,[242] and gospel hymnody.[243] The music was unsophisticated and appealed to the masses. They liked this music. It was enjoyable, even fun. In present-day parlance, it communicated.

This trend toward popular hymnody continued as an avalanche of gospel songs descended upon evangelicalism. Finally in the 1950s we had the beginnings of a more radical shift as rock music eventually became standard popular fare.[244] At this point the evangelical church struggled. But the concept

---

[240] "Amazing Grace" of John Newton (1725–1807) would be an example.

[241] "Swing Low Sweet Chariot," "There Is a Balm in Gilead," "Down By the Riverside."

[242] "All Praise To Him Who Reigns Above" ("Blessed Be the Name"), "Camp-Meetings With Thy Presence Crown."

[243] "Blessed Assurance, Jesus Is Mine!," "What a Friend We Have In Jesus," "Hold the Fort."

[244] See 3, *CCM*, for a more complete picture of the switch from the gospel song to rock.

of being relevant to contemporary society, using popular culture's musical dialect for what evangelicals believed to be the propagation of the gospel, largely won the day.

Extreme Relevancy

In a day and age where liberalism, individual rights, and personal freedom have been extended to an ever-widening circle of applications, including designer faith, it is not surprising that church music has, as a whole, become increasingly susceptible to fragmentation. Subjective taste has to be acknowledged. The answer to providing church attendees' consumer demands for a satisfying musical experience has been the commodification of the church's music. Satisfying individual taste has required that church music become acutely attuned to popular musical trends. In doing so the church musician has had to assume the role of product provider.

The question is, "How far ought the church go in accommodating the gospel to culture?" Or, to put it another way, "Just how much of the world can the church adopt in order to be relevant before its message is diluted or even obliterated?" These are not easy questions to answer. Evangelicals are so in tune with taking the gospel to the unsaved that methods are often adopted that seem to be appropriate, but which, in the last analysis, hinder the overall long-term mission of the church. Good intentions aside, following the unprincipled trends of popular culture makes such trends into a kind of golden calf. Blamires noted, "The idolatry of changing fashion is an aspect of post-Christian thinking that ought not to be allowed to infiltrate Christian communities and infect the Christian Church...The strength of the Christian Church lies in the essential changelessness of what it stands for...It is the world at its worldliest that makes fashion a god and forever seeks after novelty.[245]

---

[245]   Harry Blamires, *The Post-Christian Mind: Exposing its Destructive Agenda* (Ann Arbor, MI: Servant Publications, 1999), 87.

184 /   STRENGTHENING MUSIC MINISTRY
                 IN THE EVANGELICAL CHURCH

The church communicates the changelessness of the gospel by its own internal stability and changelessness. The Great Commission to bring the lost to Christ is paramount to evangelicals; yet fulfilling it is not a simple task. Blamires asks, "Does the Church exist to convert and refine the world? Or does it exist to water down its faith and practice until the post-Christian world can embrace it as its own?"[246] Wayne Brouwer believes that "Church 'culture' and non-church 'culture' are entirely different."[247] Our quest is to be in the world but not of the world.

One example of relevancy taken to extreme is CCM: when the church uses any popular music that has taken on musical characteristics having more in common with the world that needs saving than with the gospel that does the saving, mixed messages result. At the least, these diverse messages cause confusion; at most, there is a radical corruption of truth. Gospel attributes are joy, peace, longsuffering, gentleness, goodness, faith, meekness, and temperance.[248] Rock and roll, CCM, or any other derivatives of these styles are generally not peaceful, not longsuffering, not gentle, not meek, and not temperate. On the contrary, we find that this type of pop music is made to be "in your face:" disconcerting, agitating, raucous, unruly, discordant, and disordered. It is not surprising that one can find in this music more in common with current societal worldview attributes than with Christian ones.

Yes, Jesus was relevant to His time. But He never adopted societal values that were inconsistent with His message. He taught that a radical transformation of life was necessary: "ye must be born again." He used the language of the people but made sure the language He used was appropriate to the message. One does not find in His discourses any hint of subsuming the gospel to principles that would dilute the potency of that gospel.

Pragmatism is often the dominant methodological

---

[246] Ibid., 88.
[247] Wayne Brouwer, "Look Before You Leap!" *Reformed Worship* no. 39 (March 1996): 6.
[248] Galatians 5:22–23.

philosophy of evangelical music ministry. If something works, it must be right. A church that uses a band and contemporary song fare, is growing, and has the goodwill of the congregation might seem like its music ministry is all that it should be. But more needs to be said.

Judas's betrayal of Jesus bore good fruit. The fact that a good end resulted from a despicable act does not justify that act nor make it right. Note that Moses' disobedience in striking the rock to get water rather than following God's plan does not justify his disobedience even though water was acquired. In each case there was a cost: Judas committed suicide and Moses was prohibited from entering the Promised Land.

Church Music Relevancy and Scripture

Musical relevancy from a biblical perspective has more to do with large-scale musical systems than with taste and likeability. To be relevant, as modeled in the incarnation, was a matter of basic communication and general correspondence, not a matter of providing merriment and enjoyment. Likewise, musical relevancy is not dependent upon the provisioning of individuals with their favorite music or musical styles any more than it was for Jesus to tickle the ears of His listeners by saying what they wished to hear. On the contrary, Jesus' discourses were often onerous and astringent. True, He spoke in Aramaic, the language of the people. But He did not put the letters and words of that language together in a manner that was crafted to please the crowd. Their pleasure had little to do with His ability to communicate. Whether anyone approved or didn't approve, liked or disliked His speech, was not the issue. He communicated with the people because they understood basic Aramaic.

There are numerous musical language systems: some divide the scale into five steps, for example, some into seven, some sixteen, some twenty-two, some twenty-four. Western music divides the octave into twelve semitones and utilizes a diatonic scale of seven notes. The musical languages of ancient China, for example, or India, Egypt, or Mesopotamia, are not relevant to us. Such scales, intervals, and tonal combinations are unfamiliar and far removed from our experience and therefore essentially meaningless. They would sound like gibberish to the average person in the West. In other words, such music is not relevant to our situation, hence not useable as church music in our culture.

The Key Point

Musical relevancy in worship is not dependent upon preference but upon the basic underlying musical vocabulary. Since any music that can be envisioned as a possibility in evangelical worship is bound to be contextualized in the common musical language of Western culture, the issue of relevancy is then settled. At that point choice moves on to concerns of musical/gospel value and issues concerning appropriateness and practicability.

The Bible indicates that when one accepts the Savior, a new way of life is in order. As an immigrant to America, my father learned English; for him it was a brand-new language. Christians also have a new life language to learn—a whole new way of speaking, thinking, loving, parenting, learning, socializing, hearing, valuing, and so on. It is not unreasonable to expect that believers accept music that is fully consonant with and disciplined by the faith. Such expectation should be overtly taught and explained, perhaps in a church membership class, Sunday school forum, Bible study, or other venue. The point is that the exaggerated, overdrawn belief that church music must replicate the world's musical style if we are to attract and communicate with unbelievers is but another ploy that waters down musical/gospel witness.

The Problem of Incarnational Relevancy

The challenge in finding a church music for a particular congregation is to find music that is within the limits of their basic comprehension but that does not limit or alter biblical truth. Musical language, having its own vocabulary, grammar, sentence structure, form, and construct, has every ability to communicate idiosyncratic meaning that may or may not bear witness to the truth of the gospel. One musical characteristic not widely perceived is its ability to color and change gospel truth when the music itself is far removed from gospel norms.[249]

Music cannot convey direct gospel witness. That is the domain of verbal language. Music is unable to quote Jesus' statement, "Ye must be born again." That is clearly and unequivocally beyond its capability, a particular that fuels the belief that music is, after all, pure neutral agent, unable to convey meaning beyond itself. This view of music allows any music to be matched with any text without concern that the selected music may alter the meaning of the words.

However, music does have an indirect witness capability. Its rational and emotional content may affect text, effecting changes in word sense via subtle levels and shades of meanings. The nursery rhyme tune "Ring Around the Rosie," for example, minimizes a text extolling the awesomeness and magnificence of God Almighty. Compositional quality indirectly, yet forcefully, has the ability to enhance, support, or detract from song texts be they congregational, solo, or ensemble lyrics.

And, to further make the point, music has an indirect witness capability through implementing in its internal workings the creative traits placed by God in creation. Special revelation[250] indicates that God Himself found His own making "good," a term indicating quality.[251] Music may also be "good" in exhibiting compositional principles placed by God in the created

---

[249] Such as those listed in Galatians 5:22–23: love, joy, peace, longsuffering, gentleness, goodness, faith, meekness, temperance.
[250] The term theologians use for Scripture.
[251] Genesis 1:10, 12, 18, 21, 25, 31.

order: form, unity and variety, delayed gratification, creativity, and rational development. Good composition witnesses, albeit indirectly, to the character of God. His making is a model for the music-making of the church.

Form and Content

Evangelicals generally assume that "the message doesn't change, but the method may" or that "the content hasn't been altered, just the form." This understanding eases evangelicals onto the slippery slope of a colossal disconnect between what (content) is communicated and how (form) it is communicated. Musical forms then follow the twists and turns of culture's changing preferences. Gospel texts remain unchanged, faithful to scripture. The result of this fracture is a garbled message.

We find in the incarnation, however, an inseparable unity between content and form. In Christ we discover a message borne out by His actions: content expressed through form, an insoluble concord between what He said and what He did. Christ taught, "Thou shalt love the Lord thy God with all thy heart, and with all thy soul and with all thy mind. This is the first and great commandment. And the second is like unto it: Thou shalt love thy neighbor as thyself."[252] Such content as this was in turn acted out in material form. Jesus demonstrated love by healing, casting out demons, and ultimately by going to the cross—content and form incarnated.

Unity may be negated between message content and musical form when the music contains sounds of rebellion, lewdness, discord, and rapacious decibel overkill. Assuming the integrity of a given text, church musicians need to carefully and contemplatively evaluate the sounds of a song in the light of gospel distinctives.[253] While there are other things to consider in making choices, music that displays gospel attributes should

---

[252] Matthew 22:37–39 (KJV).

[253] This may be accomplished by hearing the music physically, or by audiation, the process of hearing music internally, its sound not physically present.

have a certain priority. The adage "We are what we eat" applies here: "We become what we sing."

Servanthood

In the incarnation we find the God of the universe taking on human form and becoming a servant. Paul spells this out most clearly in Philippians 2:6–8. "Who, [Jesus] being in the form of God, thought it not robbery to be equal with God: But made himself of no reputation, and took upon him the form of a servant, and was made in the likeness of men: And being found in fashion as a man, he humbled himself, and became obedient unto death, even the death of the cross."

Jesus' example is a model of how church musicians should actualize their ministry. We are to become washers of feet, leaders who eschew self-interest, and embrace *agape* love. In so doing, we emulate the pastoral stance of our Lord. Such a basis for ministry stems from a servants heart, a stream from which all true ministry flows.

Pastoral musicians exist to serve their congregations. This may seem to mean providing for people their every desire. But while paying attention to and attending to their requests and inclinations is important, it must be remembered that Jesus, the incarnate Son of God, was the servant of God, not the servant of humankind. Jesus did God's bidding, not the bidding of people.

In serving their congregations, what are musicians to serve up? Fare that comes from the caprice of people's temporality, though pleasing, may very well not be good for them. As with any other ministry, judicious choice is required. Jesus' servanthood often countered people's wishes. But whether Pharisee or commoner, He never gave in to their Adamic cravings. Before any other consideration, pastoral servanthood takes into account the holistic and final well-being of people. Musical fun and entertainment, having little to do with authentic worship, does not spiritually mature the saints of God. In providing more biblically discipled music, music of artistic grace and worth, music leaders serve their congregations well.

In finding music for the assembly, it is right from an incarnational point of view to take into account the various permutations of a people's profile: geographic location, general educational level, musical education, musical preferences, race, social strata, religious background, wealth, average age, and so forth. We want to ascertain just where their musical center of gravity is. In doing so, we have a general musical context from which to choose music that best fulfills the purposes of God for their spiritual formation and growth.

Music as Gospel Analogue (continued)

In these foregoing pages we have been considering theological topics that flesh out principles from God's Word to help the church musician identify music that embodies gospel traits.[254] Because of the widespread convention of worldview fracturing into objective and subjective, absolute and relative compartments, biblical norms in evangelical music have generally not been identified or sought after. Theological truth is believed objective and absolute; musical truth thought subjective and relative. Such a rift shatters the unity of theism, a worldview which calls for all of life to come under the Lordship of Christ. Relativistic, taste-driven church music rather than objective biblically-driven church music is, in fact, the norm for much of the evangelical world. Though such praxis is believed inconsequential and of little account, making no difference one way or the other, the truth is that music always makes a statement. It witnesses whether we want it to or not. The question is not, "Will music witness?" but rather, "What will be its witness?" Will it, through its musical style characteristics

---

[254] The following were mentioned: Creation, the Creation Mandate, the *Imago Dei*, Delayed Gratification, Form and Content, the Historical Imperative, Incarnation, Relevancy, and Servanthood.

and quality of composition, advance post-Christian values or those of Judeo-Christian theism?

Church music, then, is a musical metaphor of the gospel. It serves as a musical manifestation and embodiment of the faith when it embraces qualities of objective musical worth, characteristics commensurate with Christianity and quite opposite those of post-modern culture. We must understand that the features inherent in good, wholesome church music are in fact the antithesis of contemporary popular music both secular and religious. First-rate musical/gospel metaphor embraces edification, not amusement; excellence, not mediocrity; permanence, not transience; emotion, not sentimentality; creativity, not novelty; beauty, not glamour; depth, not shallowness; integrity, not flimsiness; substance, not insignificance; profundity, not fatuousness; weightiness, not lightness.

For the music of evangelicals, the best answer to the question of what music to adopt is to find a music that scrupulously exemplifies the gospel message in the music's structure as well as in its texts. In today's culture such music will not be particularly popular, being in a vein that circumvents pop music characteristics. But it can be a music understandable to the congregation and one in which they are fully able to participate.

8

Scriptural Discernment Extended

The primacy of Scripture—not tradition, reason, or magisterium—continues to be the readily acknowledged heart of evangelicalism. That Word, the lifeblood of every congregation claiming to be evangelical, must be clearly understood and applied comprehensively to every aspect of the church's life and mission. It is true that the array of differing theological positions, all purporting to be based upon that same Word, indicate a certain variety of hermeneutical processes. Yet there are central themes on which all branches of the evangelical church agree; themes which could profit church music in general and church music witness in particular.

Some of these broad themes need a new emphasis in our time. The present cultural milieu, casting a dark shadow of worldview relativism over society, tends to dismiss many biblical leitmotifs germane to church music as simply much ado about nothing. Yet God's work does contain a holistic mandate to bring all of life under its jurisdiction. Doing so gives believers boundaries and direction, a paradoxical freeing up of the human spirit to witness in word and in deed. Some of these biblical motifs have been addressed in chapter seven; more follow in this present chapter.

Stewardship

An important scriptural theme germane to music ministry is the whole sweep of Christian stewardship. The motivation for tending what God has given us comes from the fact that God is literally the creator and owner of everything. Our charge is a managerial one. Genesis 2:15 (NIV) explains, "The Lord God took the man and put him in the Garden of Eden to work it and take care of it." Charged with being caretakers of a garden, humans are responsible for what has been entrusted to them.

Evangelicals have a broad array of responsibilities. Scripture not only indicates stewardship of the material world but also of the personal endowments given each person. Consider Matthew 25:14–30 (KJV):

> For the kingdom of heaven is as a man traveling into a far country, who called his own servants, and delivered unto them his goods. And unto one he gave five talents, to another two, and to another one; to every man according to his several ability; and straightway took his journey.

> Then he that had received the five talents went and traded with the same, and made them other five talents. And likewise he that had received two, he also gained other two. But he that had received one went and digged in the earth, and hid his lord's money.

> After a long time the lord of those servants cometh, and reckoneth with them. And so he that had received five talents came and brought other five talents, saying, Lord, thou deliveredst unto me five talents: behold, I have gained beside them five talents more. His lord said unto him, Well done, thou good and faithful servant: thou hast been faithful over a few things, I will make thee ruler over many things: enter thou into the joy of thy lord.

> He also that had received two talents came and said, Lord, thou deliveredst unto me two talents: behold, I have gained two other talents beside them. His lord said unto him, Well done, good and faithful servant; thou hast been faithful over a few things, I will make thee ruler over many things: enter thou into the joy of thy lord.

> Then he which had received the one talent came and said, Lord, I knew thee that thou art an hard man, reaping where thou hast not sown, and gathering where thou hast not strawed: And I was afraid,

and went and hid thy talent in the earth: lo, there thou hast that is thine. His lord answered and said unto him, Thou wicked and slothful servant, thou knewest that I reap where I sowed not, and gather where I have not strawed: Thou oughtest therefore to have put my money to the exchangers, and then at my coming I should have received mine own with usury. Take therefore the talent from him, and give it unto him which hath ten talents. For unto every one that hath shall be given, and he shall have abundance: but from him that hath not shall be taken away even that which he hath. And cast ye the unprofitable servant into outer darkness: there shall be weeping and gnashing of teeth.

Parables, one of the methods Jesus often used in teaching, are genuine art forms. Universal in scope and theme and adaptable to all manner of situations, this particular one has a special poignancy for church music ministry. Connected to the creation mandate to care for what the Lord God has given us, the parable of the talents clearly shows God's expectation for the use and development of gifts given each individual. Its message, couched in artistic language and form, is readily and directly applicable to those gifted with artistic ability, including musical talent.

God, the owner of the talents, distributes to everyone as He deems best. There is no equality of gifts. Not having a choice in the matter, individuals need to accept what they have been given and use it to the best of their ability.

At the heart of the parable we find the master returning and calling for an accounting of his investment. It is instructive to note that the reward given the two profitable servants was not based on the aggregate sum that each servant acquired, he with the larger amount receiving a greater reward. On the contrary; the measure of God's accounting was faithfulness. Both servants received a reward commensurate with their utilization of what was given them by the master, not by the accumulation acquired. Both were made ruler over many things. Both entered into the joy of their lord.

This parable yields two important principles for the music ministry of the evangelical church.

First, God never requires more than we are capable of. Objective artistic standards must be seen in the light of the parable. Artistic merit is not the sole criteria for choosing the music to be used in church. Music that maximizes the talent and resources of a congregation, whatever its objective standards might be, fulfills in God's eyes His intention for His people better than those congregations that have the talent and resources to do the best music but are content to settle for less.

Second, it must be remembered that preference and taste are not sufficient criteria for choosing music for a congregation. The parable stresses the necessity for growth: stretching, learning, and achieving new horizons.

The subjective standard of doing one's best must be balanced with the objective standard of maturation. If one relies only on the first principle (doing one's best), a passive ministry is likely to develop resulting in limited musical maturation. If, on the other hand, only the second principle (growth) is applied, the striving and merit-based pursuit of music may very well make a congregation discouraged and dispirited. Music ministry does not flourish with such onesidedness.

However, both stewardship principles together yield a beneficent balance. Subjective standards are necessary and serve as a basis from which objective standards may be enacted. Musical maturation flourishes in such an environment.

Believers are on a life pilgrimage, a journey of becoming, a process that should be holistic and comprehensively integrated. But frequently people view spiritual growth as separate and removed from material existence. The parable of the talents shows that view of life to be a dichotomy, false and unfounded. For the Christian, life is one grand design. Signs of spiritual maturation are readily noted in the barometer of temporal existence: anger, malice, hate or long-suffering, patience, and love are emotions that clearly reveal spiritual condition. The ability to read, gain vocabulary, reason, and think are all helps to glean truth from the study of Scripture. And the world of vibrations, which we codify into music, requires cultivation so that at its highest and best, truth is revealed and expressed in terms of tone.

Musical leaders are tenders of a garden, a church music garden involving the entire assembly: children, teenagers, adults, and seniors. Anything that delays, removes, sets back, or stops musical advancement and maturation needs rectifying. Yet it is a plea that often falls on deaf ears because of insufficient knowledge or insufficient motivation. Administering musical/ spiritual discipline as is best for the congregation typically does not have a high priority. An example of this is the church's reticence to go against the grain of the widely-held practice of using background music for every conceivable purpose.

Music is ultimately effective in direct proportion to the attention given it. And background music—of whatever kind—edges people ever toward becoming sensory invalids through the catechizing effect of listener passivity. When one is forced to listen to extensive stretches of ambient musical background, a self-protection defense mechanism becomes operative in which the listener begins to pay attention to the music about as much as to walls painted a solid black. Confronted by such sound,[255] its recipients tend to shut it out, thereby unconsciously training their minds to disengage automatically from active listening when any music, muzak or not, is being sung or played. It is a kind of defense mechanism that dulls the ability to pay attention and really hear. Such is a diminishment of God's gift. Rather than enhancing musical sensitivity, such convention degrades it.

There are many ways that leaders might encourage musical growth in their congregations such as those mentioned in chapters three and four. Christian maturation encompasses the nurture of all of God's gifts to His people. And musical gifts (which all share to some degree) should not be left out. Maturation within the assembly's hereditary and contextual

---

[255] Background music such as that being played over the sound system prior to the actual beginning of the worship service, or in the foyer, or during prayer, or in the parking lot.

framework is in the plan of God for His people. It is instructive to note that believers are disciples, a word that means "student" in both Greek and Hebrew.[256] And music is one of the means a church can employ as a teaching and discipling agent.[257]

Law and Grace

Evangelicals commonly allude to the fact that they are a people under grace, not under law. There certainly is no disputing that fact, for grace forms the very foundation of the theology of the Reformers, undergirding the entire Protestant Reformation.

Yet the meaning of grace for church music ministry is often misconstrued. The common application, that since we are no longer under the law we operate free from the law, translates into limitless freedom. Such understanding morphs into the assumption that there are no constraints whatsoever concerning which music may be used in evangelical worship.

Certainly such thinking gives opportunity for indiscriminate selection of music. Without boundaries, musical inappropriateness does not exist. Any music of any sort is then possible. This belief opens the music ministry to a policy of unrestrained license. It is an invitation to cut music loose from any biblical guidelines and to embrace the prevailing cultural twists of postmodern relativism.

Beside the inferences in the Old Testament that there is a moral dimension to music,[258] Jesus brings up the subject of law and gospel in Matthew 5, a passage intended to principle all of the Christian life. He begins in verse 20 with the general subject:

---

[256] Marc Turnage, *Windows Into the Bible* (Springfield, MO: Logion Press, 2016), 412.
[257] See Calvin Johansson, *Discipling Music Ministry: Twenty-first Century Directions* (Peabody, MA: Hendrickson Publishers, 1992).
[258] Erik Routley, *Church Music and Theology* (Philadelphia: Muhlenberg Press, 1959), 16–17. Routley cites Amos 5:23–24; Isaiah 1:12–17; Isaiah 5:11–12; Jeremiah 7:1–7; Amos 6:4–6; and Ezekiel 33:32–33.

For I tell you that unless your righteousness surpasses that of the Pharisees and the teachers of the law, you will certainly not enter the kingdom of heaven (NIV).

Evidently grace has not freed us from such parameters. Continuing, Jesus then begins a step-by-step reiteration of aspects of the law and its New Testament updates:

You have heard that it was said to the people long ago, "You shall not murder, and anyone who murders will be subject to judgment." But I tell you that anyone who is angry with a brother or sister will be subject to judgment (verses 21–22).

You have heard that it was said, "You shall not commit adultery." But I tell you that anyone who looks at a woman lustfully has already committed adultery with her in his heart (verses 27–28).

Again, you have heard that it was said to the people long ago, "Do not break your oath, but keep the oaths you have made to the Lord." But I tell you, Do not swear at all…Simply let your "Yes" be "Yes" and your "No" be "No" (verses 33–34, 37).

You have heard that it was said, "Eye for eye, and tooth for tooth." But I tell you, do not resist an evil person. If anyone slaps you on the right cheek, turn to them the other cheek also. And if anyone wants to sue you and take your shirt, hand over your coat as well. If anyone forces you to go one mile, go with them two miles (verses 38–41).

You have heard that it was said, "Love your neighbor and hate your enemy." But I tell you, love your enemies and pray for those who persecute you (verses 43–44).

Be perfect, therefore, as your heavenly Father is perfect (verse 48).

It is evident in these passages that Jesus builds upon the law, redefining it by getting to the heart of the matter and applying a New Testament perspective to the various examples cited. Murder, adultery, swearing, revenge, treatment of neighbors and enemies are all turned on their heads. In each case, Jesus makes the correct behavior *more* stringent under New Testament grace than under Old Testament law. Anger becomes equivalent to murder; lust becomes adultery; a yes or a no is better than a sworn oath; turning the other cheek and loving one's enemies, counterintuitive though they may be, all illustrate the new grace-filled standard.

That standard, far from being a license for a broadly sweeping licentiousness, is a higher, more rigorous, and an even tougher mandate than that of the law. Whereas the Old Testament law is largely in the negative ("thou shalt not"), New Testament grace is predominantly positive ("thou shalt"). It is not enough to refrain from evil. Now we are to do good; replacing negative legalism with positive activity.

The transformed standard is a heart matter. Believers, acting out their Christianity in ways that witness to the veracity of the gospel in every conceivable corner of culture, are being proactive. They do so because they want to, not because they have to. The Christ life is not a matter of duty; it is a matter of opportunity. The second mile is a way of life; going beyond the minimum a loving response to the gift of Jesus, who gave His life that we might live. What higher motivation does one need for following the rigorous course indicated by our Lord? Christians belong to another realm, the realm of the Spirit. Now in a fallen world but overshadowed by the next, believers are able to live by the value system conveyed to us by our Lord. We live counterculturally.

Music ministry needs New Testament–refined, grace-dominated parameters. Admitting music without careful scrutiny leaves the assembly wide open to the values of a fallen world. Melodies, rhythms, harmonies, and instrumentation that have the comportment of penurious music, that display a musical grammar commensurate with weak creativity such as that which is characteristic of pop, entertainment, show business, rock radio, and any other aesthetic that detracts from musical wholesomeness must be avoided.

A New Testament orientation provides a positive stance in

which music is chosen that goes beyond the letter of the law. Pieces that are exemplary in their quality, that eschew the bare minimum, that are compositionally and creatively excellent, and that are composed at the level of art music[259] are the pieces that go beyond the law. This does not mean that the music of evangelicals must be complicated. Assembly songs can be simple yet compositionally exemplary. For example, the tune *Ellacombe* written in simple rounded bar form, or the straightforward eight-measure melody *Stuttgart*, or the contemporary Christmas lullaby *Martingale* are but samples of the huge array of available materials accessible to all congregations.

Open to the charge of a works-based faith, Marc Turnage reminded us that "faith is not mere belief. Faith represents action based upon one's belief. James highlights this and points to Abraham as proof: 'Was not Abraham our father justified by works, when he offered his son Isaac upon the altar? You see that faith was active along with his works, and faith was completed by works, and the scripture was fulfilled which says, "Abraham believed God, and it was reckoned to him as righteousness;" and he was called the friend of God'" (James 2:21–23, RSV).[260] James goes on to say in verse 26, "For as the body apart from the spirit is dead, so faith apart from works is dead." Faith and works are but two sides of the same coin.

No one can consistently listen to music in worship that is trite, sensational, uncreative, amusing, escapist, or entertaining without somehow forming the idea that such is a picture of the Christian gospel. Art forms are a show-and-tell of worship. The quality of our musical witness depends upon the quality of the music used.

---

[259] Often referred to as "classical music."
[260] Marc Turnage, op. cit., 261.

Mystery and Awe

Immanence

Evangelical theology emphasizes a personal relationship with God. We accept Jesus as personal savior. As one new Christian put it, "God used to be out there; now I have Him inside." This individual connection with the Almighty is one of the strengths of evangelicalism. God is not a being apart from His people. He is here with us and in us.

Such intimacy may sometimes be contorted in such a way that believers treat God as a chum, an equal, or as an agent to do our bidding. But radical immanence is a distortion of the truth. To make God a serf, unintended though that may be, is erroneous. God, the maker of heaven and earth, reduced to a vassal of human self-interest, is no God at all. Being cozy and breezy with the Almighty is not only disrespectful, it is dangerous. It puts humans in the driver's seat; mistakenly, individuals become gods.

Humans are fundamentally different from God. God is a spirit; we are material. God is uncreated; we are created. Because of the selfism residing in the human heart, Christians must take active steps to rise above the fallen nature and crucify the self. Jesus said, "If any man will come after me, let him deny himself, and take up his cross, and follow me" (Matthew 16:24 KLV).

Transcendence

As a corrective to the radical immanence so tempting to born-again believers, the knowledge of God's otherness, His unknowableness, His transcendence, is restorative. God is personal, yet cannot be fully known because He transcends us infinitely. The only things we can know about God are those that He reveals to us. This He has done through the incarnate Christ and the Word. Understanding God as both/and, the transcendent/immanent One, gives a perspective that greatly aids believers in godly prayer and praise.

We stand in awe of this God of the universe. He is beyond us absolutely and everlastingly, yet He is with us.

It is here that great artists can help us, for the fine arts have the capability of communicating the *mysterium tremendum et fascinans*[261] as no other entity can. Music, particularly adept at dealing with mystery (being the most mysterious of the arts), cannot be seen, touched, smelled, or tasted. Fleeting and abstract to a fault, great music exists in a noble plane removed at once from the earth yet simultaneously tied to it.

Worship may be enhanced by a deepened sense of wonder, mystery, and awe through the use of music that affirms and communicates something of the eternal inscrutability of God. We speak, play, and sing through a glass darkly. Music that is subtle, that suggests, whose abstractness hints at reality not seen but nevertheless existing, is a music helpful in experiencing the deeper levels of the things of God. Music that is comfy and cushy, sentimental and sweet, is not the type of music to engender awe in the listener. But music that is somewhat out of reach, stretching the mind, heart, and emotions toward the mysterious and unknown, is an experience of transcendent profundity.

Music and Truth

The category of mystery and awe hints at another imponderable reality. Music cannot be ultimate truth. But it can musically explore the vast reaches of "interstellar truth/space." That is to say, truth is so boundless, having parameters that go above our ability to fully comprehend, that it takes an art form to go beyond the facts to their truth significance. If someone

---

[261] A mystery before which man both trembles and is fascinated, is both repelled and attracted. Rudolf Otto in *The Idea of the Holy* (2nd ed., 1950) discusses at length the Creator's transcendence and immanence that simultaneously repels and attracts the created.

is perplexed at this assertion, he is on the right track. For what we are dealing in is esoteric and vague.

Human inability to know and comprehend everything shows up our limitations concerning truth. Artists help us in this regard. Poetry, literature, music, painting, architecture, and sculpture deal in the vagaries of human ineptitude, shedding rays of light from time to time as truth is caught by those touched by the warm rays of great art. C. S. Lewis found that the art of storytelling is a prime way to express truth, for truth is often best communicated inferentially, indirectly. Observe that time and time again, when discoursing on some aspect of truth, Jesus turned to an art form such as the parable, an oblique, circumlocutory method of teaching.

When Jesus was being cross-examined by Pilate, He explained that He "came into the world... to testify to the truth. Everyone on the side of truth listens to me."[262] Then Pilate asked the question that has rung down through the ages, "What is truth? (*"Quid est veritas?"*). The answer Jesus indicated is that He, Jesus, is the truth. Likewise, in answer to Thomas (John 14:6) Jesus said, "I am the way, the truth, and the life." Used about twenty-five times in the Gospel of John, our Lord indicates that truth comes from following and being faithful to His teachings.[263] It is not an insignificant point. Truth is not just something to "know;" not just intellectual assent. Truth is doing; it is active and impelling.

Postmodern society holds that truth is subjectively determined by each individual without reference to any objective source. Hence, personal taste, predilection, or disposition become the operative framework for one's own individualized fabricated "truth." But for Christians that philosophy is erroneous, even heretical, for Jesus is the truth. To accept Jesus is to accept truth as an objective reality. He is truth and all that He represents is truth.[264]

---

[262] John 18:37 (NIV).

[263] John 8:31–32, New Living Translation; Amplified Bible; Amplified Bible, Classic Edition; NIV; GNT; The Living Bible, Phillips; New Living Translation.

[264] Arthur Holmes, former philosophy professor at Wheaton College, has put it, "All Truth Is God's Truth," the title of his 1977 book published by Wm. B. Eerdmans.

Christians have cause to practice the full gospel, to hold to and obey Jesus' teachings and, in being disciples, to know the truth, the Word, the word of God Incarnate.[265] God's revelation to us in Jesus is correspondent to that of Scripture. The truth that is Jesus Christ is not different from that found in the Old Testament and New Testament. Simply, the truth as found in Scripture is fulfilled in the person of Jesus. "All Scripture is inspired by God and is useful for teaching the truth, rebuking error, correcting faults, and giving instruction for right living, so that the person who serves God may be fully qualified and equipped to do every kind of good deed."[266] The music minister and worship leader must be ready to undertake all manner of "good" (notice the adjective) musical work in the body of Christ, the church.

Ultimately then, the subject of good music is truth.[267] That is to say, when the component parts of a musical composition are at their highest and best they hint at that which is beyond the music itself. Moving fleetingly in time they sound above, below, and around the mechanistic musical material to that of the internal spirit and soul of the listener. This touching of the human spirit cannot be adequately described in words. A fruitful answer to the question, "What does music mean?" is to play the piece again; in a sense music's meaning is simply itself and remains quite untranslatable. Yet great music strikes a central core of "rightness" when the aesthetic parameters placed by God in creation are reached.

These truth principles may be summarized as: organic unity and coherence; economy of means; circumcised diversity;

---

[265] See John 8:31–32. KJV, NIV, Today's English Version, Living Bible, RSV.

[266] II Timothy 3:16–17. Today's English Version (Good News Translation [GNT]).

[267] Used in reference to music, the word "truth" is objective and knowable. It refers to music's compositional qualitative excellence and perfection as in a "tree that grows straight and true;" a "piece of wood stock that is 'flat and true;'" a piece of music that is correct, right, honest, just, perfect, whole, good, and true—qualities that are particular to composition that follows the aesthetic axioms and norms of great art as placed by God in creation and known to us via general revelation. Jesus, the truth, created all things (Colossians 1:16) and while the natural world was affected by the fall, it is possible nevertheless that general revelation reflects (to some degree) the truth, integrity, and ethos of the creator.

functional dominance of certain constituent parts of the musical texture; intrinsic worth of each contributing musical member; rhythmic flow akin to that of the natural world; a discernable formal structure; and the important gospel principle of delayed gratification. These principles are cross-cultural and timeless and form the core around which value judgments on music and art may be made. Not all music attains to what might be called truth/speech. But music skillfully and artistically constructed upon these aesthetic canons is music that reaches toward that vast cosmic unknown, the center of which is the heart and mind of the listener—a mystery indeed.

Placed by God in the created order, the aesthetic norms upon which great art depend are resident in the truth as found in general revelation. They are available to everyone, saint and sinner alike. Nevertheless, though accessible, it is common to find these compositional principles bypassed or minimized in popular culture. The resulting music is apt to be simplistic, or gaunt and hollow, perhaps just fun and entertaining. Much of it barely rises to the level of elevator music, including some that is just pleasant and of the easy-listening category. Then there are other artless musical types categorized as "functional": dance music, advertising jingles, and educational activity songs. There are also whole genres that avoid musical truth axioms, that circumvention being a component part of its style. Included here are all types of popular music such as punk rock, hip hop, rap, rock, reggae, heavy metal, honky-tonk, disco, country, and on and on. Religious music also has similar species: CCM, CWM, P&W, gospel, Christian punk. Christian R&B (rhythm & blues), hip hop, hardcore, punk, and pop style choir arrangements.

It is obvious that music that achieves the level of truthfulness is not music that is composed for entertainment, as is pop or any other type of throw-away species. Nor does functional music such as dance music, military marches, and poorly composed religious music reach the level of what we have called truth/speech. But music with high aesthetic standards—whether simple or complex—shepherds the listener toward that which is beyond the self—a truly awe-inspiring encounter, a gateway to realms of otherworldly rightness and integrity.

The abstract quality of music, its ambiguity, is its strength. In a nebulous but powerful way, its explorations of primary life conditions (such as affirmation and rejection, unity and diversity, growth and decline) exist in the vast area above, beneath, around, behind, and beyond the facts and point us toward the horizon. Great music has the ability to elicit deep emotion, grasping us in an embrace far removed from the empty-headed amusement of musical entertainment. To have the quality that enables music to explore truth, music must be artistically conceived, written, and produced.

Lost in Wonder, Love, and Praise[268]

But what about the week-after-week music-making in the average evangelical church? Is it possible for its worship to profit from a renewed appreciation of the transcendence of God, especially when leaders and people have had limited exposure to and experience with the music that engenders mystery and awe?

It is likely that within the specific distinctives of each assembly, music can be found that will fit the requirement for an increased celebration of the transcendence of God. Such music may not be specifically transferable to other congregations across the board because each set of circumstances is different. But, in general, there will be similar characteristics, individually interpreted by each congregation.

Music that is conceived to be completely and immediately knowable on the first hearing is likely to be of little lasting help to the spiritual development of the worshiper. On the other hand, that which bears repeated hearings, each time new and fresh, music that is ambiguous to the point of requiring effort on the part of the people to grasp and appreciate it, has every probability of usefulness. A cautionary note, however: if the

---

[268] The last phrase of Charles Wesley's hymn "Love Divine, All Loves Excelling."

music in question is just too difficult for the people to apprehend at all (such as 20th-century avant-garde), other material must be found.

Also, composition that is artistically inept, requiring little in the way of imagination and discipline on the part of the participant, made with simplistic twists and musical clichés, and that creates a mood of self-satisfaction and ease, is music that has no capacity to create a sense of awe and wonder. On the other hand, music that demands of the listener discipline, dedicated involvement, and emotional investment is the music that can bring the worshiper into an attitude of reverence before the one holy, awesome, and transcendent God, maker of heaven and earth.

Another aspect of choosing music is to look carefully at its texts. I have made the point previously that a song with lyrics that read "awesome God," for example, will be absolutely overridden by a music that conveys "banal God." The medium of music is far more powerful than the texts in transmitting awe and mystery. Further, words that are subjective, focusing on self rather than on God, are problematical. What is needed are objective texts set to artistically conceived and rendered music.

The conventional assumption that music "carries" words, a method of bagging up text and carting it off to the consumer, is widespread. That is lamentable, especially for church music. The essential power of the musical medium is lost sight of, thus severing its ethos from that of the text. What occurs then is a classic dichotomy. Christopher Anderson said it well, "This pernicious notion that words are delivered on the back of abstract sonority something like cargo delivered by a train, is easy to grasp...but spectacularly wrong."[269]

---

[269] Christopher Anderson, "What Do You Think You Are Doing? the Musician and Teacher 'Beyond the Page'," *The Journal of the Association of Anglican Musicians* 25, no. 5 (May/June 2016): 1.

New Testament Aesthetic Norms

Hans Rookmaaker,[270] the noted Dutch Reformed art historian, contended that the norms of great art are "basically no different from the norms for the whole of life."[271] He looked to Philippians 4:8 concerning the true, honorable, just, pure, lovely, gracious, excellent, and that which is worthy of praise (RSV) for a biblical foundation for art.[272] The characteristics enumerated here are applicable to music as follows:

Truth. This has to do with compositional rightness and craft. Composition is true when its musical structure fulfills the compositional qualities of great art. The principles upon which great art is structured are cross-cultural and timeless and are inherent in general revelation.

Honesty. A work that possesses true originality and creativity stands as honest (creativity being "that which breaks new ground with imagination and integrity").

Just. Music is considered just when its musical argument is sound and well-reasoned. Every technical element will have a qualitative goodness that builds up and strengthens the whole.

Purity. Musical composition has the ability to be constructed in a manner that is provocative and promotes fleshly desire. When created with certain melodic and rhythmic innuendoes associated with the carnality of rock music, strip clubs, and burlesque, the result is a music of bawdiness and impurity. The music of the church has no business with such sounds.

Loveliness. Coordinating the elements of music fittingly produces a harmonious whole, one of beauty, meaningful design, and purpose.

---

[270] Hans Rookmaaker, *Modern Art and the Death of a Culture* (Downer's Grove, IL: InterVarsity Press, 1970).

[271] Ibid., 236.

[272] The New English Bible renders the passage, "And now, my friends, all that is true, all that is noble, all that is just and pure, all that is lovable and gracious, whatever is excellent and admirable—fill all your thoughts with these things."

Graciousness. Understated music and that which communicates by inference rather than by rant, rage, or rave, is music that is gracious. It eschews bombast, bluster, pomposity, and exaggeration.

Excellence. This quality is concerned with skill and craftsmanship. When music is constructed well, having artistry and authentic originality, it shows the excellence characteristic of good music.

Worthy of praise. Art that is worthy because of its artistic goodness and merit is deserving of appreciation and esteem—value based on quality.

Such truths compel us to find a church music that evidences these qualities. It seems logical that music forms commensurate with the Philippians 4:8 passage prevail as the best musical vehicles through which gospel testimony can be given. To be at cross-purposes with divine revelation by programming music other than that in accord with Scripture is faith-defeating.

Gospel Tone, Timbre, Temper, and Popularity

In 1966, John Lennon of the Beatles remarked, "We're more popular than Jesus now; I don't know which will go first—rock 'n' roll or Christianity." Whatever the background that led up to this assertion, or the subtleties and inferences intended, it is clear that being popular was of some importance to Lennon. A much sought-after state of being, venerated and highly regarded, popularity is considered to be a barometer of success. If achieved, the acclaim of being popular becomes a legitimizing force dispensing abroad stature, significance, and goodwill.

Beginning at the turn of the 20th century, musical popularism evolved into a large aggregate of styles that share many of the same general traits and are all grouped under the banner of "popular music." These musical styles, though readily distinguishable from one another, all retain an underlying cast that determines their overall classification. Often termed just "pop" for short, this category of music can be found with secular or sacred words, the substantive musical style being identical for both.

Those who find music to be a neutral language, stripping music of objective frames of reference, begin and end as relativists, thus allowing style to have little or no bearing on what may be admissible in worship. This blanket acceptance of any style of music for worship (with pop as the music of choice) is the cornerstone of most current evangelical practice. Such usage whitewashes the dilemma Scripture brings to light between Christian and post-Christian thinking.

Evangelicals are in favor of the view that the new birth and its aftermath are to inform and direct all of life. Nothing is to be left out. The Christ-life affects it all. This translates into a holistic worldview in which there are no dichotomies between life categories. For the Christian, theistic worldview principles are to undergird the entirety of existence: moral, social, aesthetic, philosophical, educational, medical, vocational, spiritual, and so forth. Nothing should be omitted. The objectivity of theism has the reach and ability to disciple it all, including music.

But musical relativism, though common and thought entirely acceptable, fragments the Christian life. The unity between doctrinal belief and the material working out of that belief is destroyed. Postmodern relativism, musical or otherwise, is truly incompatible with biblical Christianity. Calling evil good is simply morally incoherent.[273] The clear objectivity of Judeo-Christian evangelical theology is irreconcilable with the subjectivity of contemporary relativism, making the words "evangelical musical relativism" a contradiction in terms. To be true to the faith, the music of the evangelical church must objectively manifest high aesthetic standards. Music shaped by biblical principles of goodness and worth is a powerful music/gospel analogue. To call music good when in fact it is aesthetically bad is not only incoherent, it is irrational and injurious to gospel witness.

---

[273] Richard John Neuhaus, "A Voice in the Relativistic Wilderness," *Crosspoint*, Summer 1994, 33.

The Gospel and Popularity

The whole tenor of the gospel is fundamentally at odds with the concept of popularity. Reading the Gospel of Matthew, especially those passages that record the teachings of Jesus, we are bound to conclude that any drive to make the Good News popular requires a diluting of Christ's message. When the integrity of the gospel is retained, easy acceptability is not one of its traits. On the contrary, our Lord says, "Enter ye in at the strait gate: for wide *is* the gate, and broad *is* the way, that leadeth to destruction, and many there be which go in thereat: because strait *is* the gate, and narrow *is* the way, which leadeth unto life, and few there be that find it."[274] The Living Bible renders the passage: "Heaven can be entered only through the narrow gate! The highway to hell is broad, and its gate is wide enough for all the multitude who choose its easy way. But the Gateway to Life is small, and the road is narrow, and only a few ever find it." There is no indication here that Christianity is designed for easy acceptance. There are definite parameters to the Christ way. It is a pilgrimage that is not easy. Faith is not costless.

The apostle John's admonition to "love not the world," underlines the distinctiveness that Christians are to maintain from the world. J.B. Phillips renders 1 John 2:15–17: "Never give your hearts to this world or to any of the things in it. A man cannot love the Father and love the world at the same time. For the whole world-system, based as it is on men's primitive desires, their greedy ambitions and the glamour of all that they think splendid, is not derived from the Father at all, but from the world itself. The world and all its passionate desires will one day disappear. But the man who is following God's will is part of the permanent and cannot die." The very idea of adopting worldly standards as the church's own is incongruous with the gospel. We are not to seek a comfortable or popular berth in the world. The gospel is quite apart from worldly values. To water down the gospel's character by attempting to express it via the

---

[274] Matthew 7:13–14 (AKJV).

pop idioms of the world is to make the gospel into a caricature of itself. Its altered form may be popular, but it is no longer true.

Dietrich Bonhoeffer's clarion call for the church to dispense costly grace rather than cheap grace has its counterpart in church music. To offer men and women grace tainted by a musical system rooted in easy acceptability changes the truth. Costly grace "...is the pearl of great price... It is the kingly rule of Christ, for whose sake a man will pluck out the eye which causes him to stumble; it is the call of Jesus Christ at which the disciple leaves his nets and follows him."[275]

Music of the church needs this more stringent, discipled, and costly way. Its notes, rhythms, and harmonies should reflect a full-gospel ascetic. The giving of salvation and the forgiveness of sins via the shed blood of the crucified Christ does not warrant a ditty. Taking up one's cross daily and following in the steps of the Master indicates a certain gravitas in living out the Christ life. The purposefully ingrained triteness that defines popular music remains far removed from the musical expression necessary for conveying the gospel truthfully. Calvin believed, "There must always be concern that the song be neither light nor frivolous but have gravity and majesty....There is a great difference between the music which one makes to entertain men at table and in their homes, and psalms which are sung in the church in the presence of God and his angels."[276]

Congruence between the underlying characteristics of popular music styles and the underlying characteristics of the Christian gospel is missing. Whereas the strongest musical gospel witness comes from music in line with gospel traits, conversely music built on pop traits weakens gospel witness. Notice some of the essential characteristics of 21st-century popular style composition:

1. It is driven by the caprice of changing taste.

---

[275] Dietrich Bonhoeffer, *The Cost of Discipleship* (New York: Macmillan, 1961), 36.

[276] D. G. Hart and John R. Muether, *With Reverence and Awe: Returning to the Basics of Reformed Worship* (Phillipsburg, NJ: P & R Publishing, 2002), 172.

2. It is transient.
3. It amuses and entertains.
4. It is crafted for mass consumption.
5. Its ease of consumption requires little travail.
6. It is composed for immediate gratification.
7. It is comfortable with pretentiousness
8. It relies heavily on novelty.
9. Its compositional quality is objectively mediocre.
10. It is profitable monetarily.

Gospel characteristics are quite the opposite. Scripture does not reveal a gospel fashioned for worldly, fleshly appeal. Note the following:

1. It is governed by unchanging principle.
2. It is permanent.
3. It accords the believer deep-seated peace and joy.
4. It requires individual acceptance.
5. It postulates a stringent, discipled commitment.
6. It dispenses delayed gratification.
7. It emphasizes meekness and humility.
8. It is profound.
9. It is qualitatively excellent.
10. It is without monetary cost.

If the features of pop music and the Christian gospel were lined up side by side, they would look like this:

Pop	Gospel
1. Driven by changing whim and taste.	1. Governed by unchanging principle.
2. Transient.	2. Permanent.
3. Amusing and entertaining.	3. Deep-seated peace and joy.

4. Made for mass consumption.	4. Made for individual acceptance.
5. Ease of consumption.	5. Stringent discipleship.
6. Immediate gratification.	6. Delayed gratification.
7. Pretentious.	7. Humble
8. Novel.	8. Profound.
9. Mediocre compositional quality.	9. Qualitatively excellent.
10. Monetarily profitable.	10. Monetarily free

The Scripture is clear about the impact of the gospel upon the stream of culture. From the Gospel of Matthew consider the following:

Blessed are the poor in spirit, for theirs is the kingdom of heaven.

Blessed are those who mourn, for they shall be comforted.

Blessed are the meek, for they shall inherit the earth.

Blessed are those who hunger and thirst for righteousness, for they shall be satisfied.

Blessed are the merciful, they shall obtain mercy.

Blessed are the pure in heart, for they shall see God.

Blessed are the peacemakers, for they shall be called sons of God.

Blessed are those who are persecuted for righteousness sake, for theirs is the kingdom of heaven.

Blessed are you when men revile you and persecute you and utter all kinds of evil against you falsely on my account. Rejoice and be glad, for your reward is great in heaven, for so men persecuted the prophets who were before you.[277]

You have heard that it was said to the men of old, "You shall not kill; and whoever kills shall be liable to judgment." But I say to you that every one who is angry with his brother shall be liable to judgment; whoever insults his brother shall be liable to the council, and whoever says, "you fool!" shall be liable to the hell of fire.[278]

You have heard that it was said, "You shall not commit adultery." But I say to you that every one who looks at a woman lustfully has already committed adultery with her in his heart. If your right eye causes you to sin, pluck it out and throw it away; it is better that you lose one of your members than that your whole body go into hell.[279]

You have heard that it was said, "An eye for an eye and a tooth for a tooth." But I say to you, Do not resist one who is evil. But if any one strikes you on the right cheek, turn to him the other also; and if any one would sue you and take your coat, let him have your cloak as well; and if any one forces you to go one mile, go with him two miles.[280]

You have heard that it was said, "You shall love your neighbor and hate your enemy." But I say to you, Love your enemies and pray for those who persecute you, so that you may be sons of your Father who is in heaven;[281]

Enter by the narrow gate; for the gate is wide and the way is easy, that leads to destruction, and those who enter by it are many. For the gate is narrow and the way is hard, that leads to life, and those who find it are few.[282]

Just these few passages alone establish the fact that the gospel was never intended or designed to be popular. It is too countercultural, too otherworldly, too antithetical to the mores

---

[277] Matthew 5:3–12 (RSV).
[278] Matthew 5:21–22 (RSV).
[279] Matthew 5:27–30 (RSV).
[280] Matthew 5:38–41 (RSV).
[281] Matthew 5:43–45 (RSV).
[282] Matthew 7:13–14 (RSV).

of the flesh to win popularity. The purpose of God's giving of His Son to redeem the world was to bring sinful humanity up to God's standard, not to bring God down to human standards.

The beatitudes given in Matthew 5 replace the law with even more stringent requirements. Hardly a move to win popular approval, verses 38–41 and 43–45 alone stand convention on its head. And in chapter 7 we have a particularly eye-opening teaching affirming that the road of redeemed life is narrow and hard. Few there be that find it. Any misconception that the gospel is to be watered down to make it acceptable to the world is hereby laid to rest. There just is no support for the view that popularity is a feature of the good news.

Popularity, on the other hand, is essential to popular music. Pop is made to be popular. To sell, the popular music industry (CCM included) provisions what listeners want to hear.[283] Pop's musical grammar (melodies, harmonies, and rhythms) is crafted in ways that will produce a widespread likeability. If people do not enjoy a song, or become disenchanted with it, it is eventually dropped. Something else will come along.

As pointed out earlier, coupling the gospel with popular music is not only misguided, it is illogical, resulting in conflicting and contradictory witness. When a pop-style medium unites with the full gospel message, that message takes on the character of the medium. Long open to the trivializing influences of popular culture,[284] the result is a different gospel, a profane gospel, a deceitful gospel. Pop cheapens and impairs the message and makes the gospel into a caricature of itself. The good news stripped of its lofty principles for those of popular culture, a culture controlled by the Adamic nature, subjects itself to the world, the flesh, and the Devil.

Peter Masters, pastor of the highly regarded Metropolitan Tabernacle in London, asserts that religious pop music "is the most powerful and determined anti-God, anti-moral,

---

[283] Anonymous, "I Am a Secretly Atheist Female Backup Singer," Reddit, February 6, 2014, www.reddit.com/r/atheism/comments/1x5yli/i_am_a_secretly_atheist_female_backup_singer_for/
[284] Hart and Muether, op. cit., 172.

anti-authority culture for centuries."[285] It is true that the degree of impairment is largely dependent upon the extent to which a song contains pop compositional traits. The more rabid the style (such as Christian punk, hardcore, metal, or hip hop) the less gospel witness is actualized. On the other hand, pop styles that may have a more temperate sound (such as praise/worship, some gospel, and CWM) do better in the damage department. But overall, CCM "does not transcend the limitations of the genre, and does not elevate the congregation's awareness to any higher purpose. Much of it is musically and lyrically trite and mediocre; and because it models the characteristics of secular pop music, it is anathema to worship."[286] The evangelical church, to be true to what it purports to believe, is better served by a message medium that displays in its very bones the character of the gospel rather than the character of the world it hopes to save.

Summary

In chapters seven and eight the assertion has been made that the music of the evangelical church is best guided by the church's ultimate authority, namely Scripture. Though one will find no direct biblical references to musical style, there are sweeping biblical principles that outline the musical parameters of an authentic and orthodox musical analogue of the gospel.

The doctrine of creation makes the claim that the first thing we are told about God other than the fact of His existence is that He is Creator. He made man in His image, which is also to say, in the creative image of the Creator. As musicians, our responsibility is to create well, composing and performing music of creative excellence and worth.

The doctrine of the incarnation considers the wide-ranging topic of relevancy. God sent His Son in the form of one to whom we could relate. Jesus, though tempted, never succumbed to the

[285] Peter Masters, *Worship in the Melting Pot* (Wakeman Trust, 2002), 34.
[286] Donn LeVie Jr., *It's All About Hymn: Essays on Reclaiming Sacred and Traditional Music for Worship* (Austin, TX: Kings Crown Publishing), 143.

temptations of the flesh. Coming to us as a servant, He taught His followers to adopt heavenly ideals, to go beyond the letter of the law, to take the high road. Believers are stewards of that which they have been given; their management is to achieve an increase for the kingdom.

Considering Jesus' teaching in Matthew 5 and 7, we learn that grace goes much beyond the law. It is a higher calling, a more stringent bidding, requirements of the heart that have no precedent. We stand in awe of this Servant Savior who is the transcendent/immanent One, the God who is holy and who has stooped to earth to lift us up. The music of the church, an analogue of the gospel, must be truthful, a quality dependent on its artistic value. The entire Christ event as recorded in Scripture shows the gospel to have an open/restrictive quality: all are invited but few come. It is not framed for popularity and has no congruence with broad-based relativism and pluralism.

To be faithful to Scripture, the evangelical church needs to practice a music ministry that does not seek a comfortable berth in this world. If it is countercultural in the gospel it preaches, it ought to be countercultural in the songs it sings. If it eschews worldly tenets in the faith it promulgates, it ought to eschew worldly tenets in the songs it promulgates. Church music fulfills its earthly mandate when it adopts heavenly ideals.

It is too facile to think that words and music are separate entities, that the kind of music one sets a text to has nothing to do with the overall message given. To mistakenly dichotomize faith and practice in this manner is to weaken the church and its ability to fulfill the Great Commission. Attempting to be relevant by adopting worldly music is a sure way to invite worldly living. In the long run it sabotages the good news.

If one embraces the belief that subjective taste is the only way to value music and its use in church, there is nothing more to say. End of discussion. Though increasingly popular, such a view is truly treasonable.

Post-Christian relativism obliterates scriptural convention. It eliminates all Judeo-Christian worldview assumptions.

Ministry founded on such presuppositions has no foundation. The dichotomy of separating belief from action is a red herring, a smoke screen—a trail that ends in the idolization of self.

A broad pastoral approach to music ministry bases church music-making on the whole theistic enterprise. Pastoral ministry fulfills best the spiritual/musical potential inherent in church music work. A theistic view takes our Lord's approach toward accommodating the gospel to culture. Accepting people where they are and as they are, without preconditions, is the beginning step. But going forward, we must teach people the purpose, meaning, and parameters of music in the church—a critical step aimed at developing discipleship and maturation. This may be done in any number of ways, from direct teaching to consistent modeling via wholesome musical usage. Spiritual adjudication of church music will assure that the aesthetics of the church music program be impacted more by divine guidance than by human caprice.

A pastoral approach to church music may be broken down into the following component parts:

1. Knowledge of the underlying Judeo-Christian worldview on which church music usage should be founded.

   All portions of the music program need to stem from one coherent, consistent, and comprehensive base. Mission and method work together best when they proceed from the same underlying theological and musical worldview fundamentals. The most logical underpinning for music ministry is the Judeo-Christian worldview. Articulated in Scripture and through the person and work of Jesus, a theistic worldview (the distinctive property of the Christian faith) has within it the stiffener needed to nourish pastoral music ministry.

2. Clearly defining a reachable goal for the music of the worshiping assembly with a time frame for each step.

While it is true that music in the church has a plurality of purposes such as enabling worship, furthering evangelism, and aiding in teaching, nevertheless church music has an all-encompassing mission to make disciples. It does this as its musical language is aesthetically appropriate to its mission and as it avoids the trite, cliché-ridden composition of immediate gratification, entertainment, and popular music. The church music's mission is to make disciples.

3. Establishing a method for effecting the goal.

Of all the things that a musician does, the most important (in our cultural milieu) is that of teaching. The teaching referred to concerns the larger theistic/ musical/philosophical issues that impact the ability of a church music program to do its work within the context of 21st-century culture. All participants in the music program, including the congregation (adults, children, and youth), should be involved. A wide-ranging teaching program is a challenge, to say the least. There are many hurdles to overcome—practical matters as well as policy matters. But long term, such teaching goes far in unifying people on this most difficult area of church life.

4. Outlining a weekly or monthly plan for implementation.

Implementing a teaching plan requires the support of clergy and other key church leaders. The problem is monumental—how to go about engaging people so that meaningful understanding and meaningful action will result. The pressure of conforming more to a worldview grounded in secular culture than in the principles of the Christian faith remains enormous and is not easily dissipated.

Each circumstance requires tailoring procedure to the particular conditions found within each congregation. Therefore, the following suggestions are not meant as the only way to design a teaching plan. Rather, it is a list of possibilities useful only as they are adapted to fit the local church. An outline of one possible approach to implementation might look something like this:

1. Formulate a foundational theological aesthetic and explain it and its impact on the following:
   A. The worship of the church.
   B. The choice of congregational song, instrumental music, choir, ensemble, and solo pieces.
   C. The wider church environment—foyers, halls, parking lot, church auditorium (pre-service), offices, and restrooms.
   D. Family life (with special attention on children and youth).
   E. The everyday workaday world.

2. Pay special attention to the staff, music participants, and church leaders (but include the congregation as well).

3. Be creative in finding times and methods for sharing the music program's working theology of music.

4. Participate in new-member orientation classes.

5. Invite questions. Respond truthfully with humility and graciousness. Be prepared to encounter hostility. Some may say, "I don't like that music," as if liking was the final word on whether or not something should be used.

6. Listen carefully, with appreciation, to concerns and observations of those in attendance. Refrain from being argumentative. Be positive and forward looking.

7. Provide a venue for those who wish to pursue further study on music in the church.

8. Utilize the church paper, bulletin, service leaflet, or website to write a series of essays on the music of the church.

9. Use music in worship commensurate with, and illustrative of, the theological/musical instruction contained in the teaching plan.

Scriptural accommodation entails having a certain openness within the parameters of Scripture toward church music. Our Lord's welcoming of people as He found them was an initiation into new covenant change. That is the critical key often missing in contemporary evangelicalism. Church music, among other things, acts as a change agent in the pursuit of Christian maturation. A music program must go beyond society's popular musical vernacular in order to fulfill a discipling role. Inherently encoded into the warp and woof of popular music is an inability to disciple believers. A mature music for a mature faith is the goal.

May the evangelical church look forward to the constructing of a music ministry commensurate with the full gospel. Not content with the status quo, let us build, like Nehemiah of old, with integrity and determination. The strengthening of music ministry is a priority we cannot put off.

Epilogue

The preceding pages contain theology, philosophy, history, aesthetics, miscellaneous facts, practics, and ideas, both old and new. They lead to the conclusion that church music, apart from text, testifies and witnesses positively or negatively concerning the integrity, authenticity, and veracity of the gospel. This is accomplished through music's compositional and stylistic makeup. Far from being neutral, music—subtly and covertly—has the power to buttress or diminish the full gospel.

Music is a cultural form. It reflects a value system within a larger worldview context. Today, certain musical genres fully absorb and emulate the attitude, standards, character, and ideals of contemporary postmodernism, a worldview far removed from biblical theism. The most prevalent style predicated upon this crowd-pleasing, fashionable, and prevailing relativistic *Weltanschauung* is popular music. With many subspecies, pop music has ingrained in its inner workings that which by definition does not reflect the values of Scripture. Its character of musical shallowness, frivolity, lightness, and drive for acceptance does not have the sober-mindedness necessary to deal with the things of God.

Adopting more mature and wholesome musical forms strengthens and revitalizes music ministry in its quest to more fully reflect biblical values. Such ministry, driven by the fire and passion of the indwelling Holy Spirit, finds its incentive in our Lord's response to the question as to which of the commandments was the greatest. Referring back to Deuteronomy 6:4–5,[287] Jesus replied, "Hear, O Israel; The Lord our God is one Lord: and

---

[287] This is the beginning of the "Shema," the principal devotion of Judaism.

223

thou shalt love the Lord thy God with all thy heart, and with all thy soul, and with all thy mind, and with all thy strength: this is the first commandment." He then went on with a second, "Thou shalt love thy neighbor as thyself. There is none other commandment greater than these."[288] Notice Jesus' emphasis on the word "all." Stated four times, nothing is to be held back, everything is to be given. Loving God and neighbor has the highest priority. Love is a powerful emotion, the most powerful motivating force known. Jesus demonstrated love's ultimate meaning by going to the cross. In the power of the Spirit, this *agape*, self-giving love provides the incentive and motivation for carrying out the will of God in music ministry.

The apostle Paul warns us that in the last days people will be lovers of themselves, lovers of pleasure, hating what is good and resisting truth.[289] Tempting though it is to rationalize the acceptance of contemporary musical values in order to evangelize, we do better to love people into the kingdom through musical righteousness, integrity, and virtue.

---

[288] Mark 12:29–31.
[289] 2 Timothy chapter 3.

Subject Index

accommodation, 136–139, 182, 211–212, 219, 222
aesthetic principles and Scripture, 161–164, 168, 170, 208-209
aesthetics, 97–98, 115, 119–122, 131–134, 158–159, 173, 205–206
amplification, 12, 28–29, 42, 52, 99, 122, 125, 130
analogue, gospel/music, 152–153, 164, 166–167, 191, 200, 210, 217–218
auditorium. *See* church auditorium
axiological schizophrenia, 162

background music (muzak), 1–2, 6, 75, 99, 101, 196
bar form, 152, 200
Bay Psalm Book, 53, 155
Berlinski, Herman, 173
biblical authority, 163–166, 204, 217
biblical musical norms, 165–166, 208–209
    truth, 208
    honesty, 208
    just, 208
    purity, 208
    loveliness, 208
    graciousness, 209
    excellence, 209

    worthy of praise, 209
biblical references to singing, 43–45, 48
blended (convergence) worship, 12, 39–40
Bonhoeffer, Dietrich, 212
Brown, Frank Burch, 142

Calvin, John, 41, 50, 73, 149, 153–155
CCM (Christian contemporary music), 3, 8–14, 39–40, 42–43, 54, 62, 125–126, 184
CCM, adoption by evangelicals, 135–139
CCM, distinguishing characteristics, 126, 129–135
character formation, musical, 145–148, 189
choir, 12, 17, 72
choir, adult, 89–96
choir, children's, 83–89, 101–102
choir, ministerial mission, 90–91
Chorister's Prayer, 88
church auditorium, 2–4, 15–17, 29, 221
church music as musical witness, 166–167, 200
church visitations, 1–8, 12–13, 15–18

congregational music-making: practical helps, 45–75
  a cappella, 50–52, 67–69
  accompaniment, 52
  altar calls and prayer time, 73–74
  applause, 74
  arranging, 57–58
  choosing songs, 53–55
  diction, 62–63
  drums, 58–60
  familiarity, 45
  fermatas, 53
  human voice, 61–62
  hymns, 69–70
  instrumentation, 60
  Is the congregation really singing? 48–49
  keys and range, 46
  lighting, 63–64
  melody, 56
  memorization of texts, 47
  more on unaccompanied singing, 67–69
  music reading, 65–67
  printed song texts, 64–65
  psalms, 71–73
  silence, 75
  sing all stanzas, 46
  song leader, 49–50
  standing, 67
  tempo, 47
  text quality, 46
  vocal quality, 61–62
congregational singing, 4, 12–13, 43–44, 52, 67–73, 92–93
conservatism, 180–181
contemporary worship, 3–6, 8–13
Cooke, Deryck, 142–143
countercultural, 115, 167, 199, 211, 215–218
creatio ex nihilo, 168

creation mandate, 170–171, 194, 217
creation, doctrine of, 168–170, 201, 217
creativity, 17, 102–103, 117, 158, 169–175, 191, 199, 208
creativity, aesthetic features, 158, 169–177
creativity, characteristics of, 171–177
  subjective phase, 171
  objective phase, 172
  compositional integrity, 172
  goal inhibiting, 172–174
  musical form, 175
  historicity, 176–177
creativity, definition, 169, 208
culture, contemporary foundation, 118–120, 164–166

decibel level, 2–3, 4–6, 52, 63, 122, 129–130, 156
delayed gratification. *See* immediate and delayed gratification
Dewey, John, 118
discipleship/discipline, 196–199, 207, 211–212, 216, 219, 222
doctrine of ethos, 146–148, 153, 156–157, 197, 207
dress, 27, 30, 50
drums, 4, 53, 58–60

ear protection, 2–3, 52
electrified bands, 8, 43
entertainment, 84, 89, 120, 131–133, 156, 189, 199, 205–206, 220
entertainment in worship, 6, 24, 189

entertainment media, 120

evangelical (narrow) core theology, 22–23

evangelical acceptance of musical postmodernism, 121–122, 139, 210

evangelical diversity, 14–15

evangelical musical style (CCM), 8, 10–11, 27, 39–40, 61–62, 129–139

evangelicalism, broad and narrow, 20–23

evangelization, 21–22, 24–25, 166, 179

faith/works, 22, 188–189, 197–200

fog and smoke, 3

form and content, 137–139, 145, 188–189

form, musical, 138, 145, 152, 175

Genevan Psalter, 73, 153–154

gospel song transition to pop, 9

gospel traits in music, 152, 191, 212–214

gospel vs. pop traits, 211–217

grace/works, 22, 200

Great Commission, 22, 34, 39, 78, 166, 170, 179, 182, 184, 218

hearing loss, 52, 129–130

hedonism, 119, 122, 128, 164

history, 176–177

holistic, musical worldview, 167, 192–210

humility/servant image, 179, 189

hymns, 13, 45–46, 54–55, 69–70, 80

imago Dei, 117, 171, 176–177, 217

immanence, 138, 201, 218

immediate and delayed gratification, 134–135, 164, 172–174, 188, 205, 213–214, 220

incarnation, 138–139, 177–178, 185, 188–190, 217–218

indirect witness, 187–189

Judeo-Christian theism, 97, 113–117, 119–121, 151, 170

Kilpatrick, William, 156

law/grace, 197–200, 218

lex orandi, lex credenda, 31

liberal progressivism, 97, 117, 180–181, 183

license, musical, 140, 197

loose-leaf song book, 66–67

Luther, Martin, 41, 53, 84–85, 149–152, 155

Marot, Clement, 154

maturation, musical, 195–196, 219, 222

medium and message, 38–39, 127–128, 137–138, 165–166, 188, 207, 216–217

metrical psalmody, 26, 72–73, 154–155

Meyer, Leonard, 134, 173–174

ministry opportunities for all ages, 76–96

academy, 82–83

children, 77–78

choir and congregational song, 92–93

choir school, 87, 101

choral activities for young singers, 83–89
Choristers Guild, 87
Christian education, 79–81
church choir, adult, 89–96
continuing education activities, 99–103
family, 76–77, 81
holistic education for children, 78
intergenerational learning, 81
musical topics for adult education, 80–81
outreach ministry topics, 82
music and text dichotomy, 38–39, 127–128, 137, 165–166, 207
music appropriate for worship, 143, 188–190
music education, general, 96–103
music reading, 65–67
music shapes worship, 160, 188–190, 206–207
music, language characteristics, 94, 141–145, 157–160
musical meaning, 142–145, 159–160, 204
musical relevancy, 178–187. *See also* relativism
musical style, 37, 39–40, 137, 157, 186, 190, 209, 217
musical witness, 152, 165–167, 191, 200, 218
muzak, 1–2, 6, 62, 99, 101, 136, 196
mysterium tremendum, 202
mystery and awe, 201–202, 206–207

nihilism, musical, 114, 141, 181
Norman, Larry, 97, 126

objective musical standards, 98, 100, 172, 190–191, 195, 210
objective truth, 38, 116, 120, 128
objectivity, 97, 210

parables, 194–195, 203
participation in worship, 4, 12–13, 41–44, 56
participation problems with CCM, 42–43
pastoral music ministry, 219–222
specific helps, 219–220, 221–222
people's music of choice, 96–99, 123–124, 135–138
performer's music (CCM and rock), 42–43, 62, 133–134
personal taste, 37, 164–165
pluralism, 126, 140, 179–180, 218
pop music, 62, 89, 99, 102, 132–135, 151, 169, 173–174, 212–217, 222
popular music, 1, 8, 16, 27, 39–40, 96, 99, 121, 123, 172, 205, 209, 212, 222
popularity, 100, 209–217
postmodern, post-Christian relativism, 77, 97, 100, 120–121, 126, 210, 218–219
postmodernism, 116–122, 140, 166–167, 197, 202
postmodernism and rock, 122–126
power of music, 144–157, 160, 189
power of music, historical references, 145–157
Augustine, 148
Basil of Caesarea, 147

Calvin, John, 73, 153–155
China, 145, 186
church fathers, 147
Churchill, Winston, 156
Egypt, 186
Ephrem, 147
Fletcher, Andrew, 148, 157
India, 146, 186
Luther, Martin, 84, 149–153
Pythagoras, 146
St. Clement, 147
pragmatism, 184–185
praise band, 3–4, 42
psalmody, 26, 53–54, 71–73
psalmody, metrical, 26, 72–73, 154–155

relativism, 97–98, 118–122, 138, 164, 167, 180, 192, 197, 210, 217–218
relevancy, 178–187, 190, 217–218
relevancy and Scripture, 185–190
relevancy, evangelical, 179–183, 188
relevancy, extreme, 183–185
rock and CCM festivals, 132
rock and roll, 11, 113–114, 209
rock, Christian, 97, 126, 138
rock music, 123–127
rock's distinguishing characteristics, 113–114, 122–126, 128–132

sacred/secular, 6, 78
satellite church technology, 5–6
schools, public and private, 77–78, 82–83
self-centeredness, 164, 201, 219
self-indulgence, 164
servanthood, 189, 199, 218
Shea, Suzanne Strempek, 7–8

Song of Moses, 45, 47
song service becomes "the worship," 28
song service leadership, 12–14
standards, church music, 39, 89, 100, 115, 205–210, 212, 217
standing, 4–5, 12, 28, 42, 67
stewardship, 192–197, 218
stewardship principles, 195
style, 19, 37–38, 42, 133, 153, 166–167, 209–210, 212–214, 217
subjective/subjectivity, 38, 97–98, 100, 119, 120, 128, 139, 166, 180, 190, 203, 210, 218
subjectivity, 97–98, 120
Sunday school, 66, 78–80, 83, 88, 99–100

Tame, David, 140
taste and preference, 8, 26–27, 30, 39, 45, 97–98, 128, 136, 164–166, 188, 195, 203
technological helps, 104–107
    metronome, 104
    miscellaneous resources, 106–107
    music notation, 105
    music readers, 104
    music theory, 105
    music writing, 104
    organizations, vocal, 106
    tuning, 104
    vocal music, 105–106
technology, 5, 28–30, 98–99
technology in worship, 3–4, 28–30
theism. See Judeo-Christian theism

theistic value system, 199–200
Top 40 popular hits, 133
transcendence, 138, 201–202,
    206, 218
truth, 38, 116, 120, 126, 128,
    135, 138, 187, 190
truth in music, 165–166, 196,
    202–206, 218, 225–226
truth principles in music,
    204–205

unaccompanied singing, 50–51,
    67–69
universal artistic principles,
    158–160

value neutrality, music, 139,
    164, 210
video screens, 3–6
vocal quality, 5, 61–62, 122, 130

Warren, Rick, 11, 137, 141, 166
Watts, Isaac, 68, 155
Wesley, Charles, 55, 206
Wesley, John, 48–49, 95
Wilkerson, David, 111–113,
    124–125, 128, 136
worldview schizophrenia, 79, 121,
    137–138
worldview, 38, 97–99, 114–117,
    138–139, 151, 153, 161–
    162, 164, 210, 218–219
worldview, basic questions asked
    of, 116
worldview, historical
    development, 116
worship, 23–27, 28, 33–44,
    162–166, 186, 202, 206,
    210, 217
worship bulletin/guide, 65–67, 96

worship service characteristics
    (evangelical), 2–15, 15–19,
    23–27, 27–32, 37–38,
    40–43, 138–139, 166–167,
    184–186
worship structure (binary), 12,
    26, 30
worship style, 37–38, 209–210
worship wars, 24, 38, 96, 138
worship, an activity, 19, 36, 51
worship, centrality of, 19
worship, heartfelt, 37

Zwingli, Huldreich, 149

Printed in the United States
By Bookmasters